CRITICAL INSIGHTS

INSIGHTS

Russia's Golden Age

CRITICAL INSIGHTS
Russia's Golden Age

Editor

Rachel Stauffer

Ferrum College, Southwestern Virginia

SALEM PRESS

A Division of EBSCO Information Services, Inc.

Ipswich, Massachusetts

GREY HOUSE PUBLISHING

Library of Congress Cataloging-in-Publication Data

Russia's golden age / editor, Rachel Stauffer, Ferrum College,
  Southwestern Virginia. -- [First edition].

  pages : illustrations ; cm. -- (Critical insights)

  Includes bibliographical references and index.
  ISBN: 978-1-61925-222-6

  1. Russian literature--19th century--History and criticism. I. Stauffer, Rachel,
editor of compilation. II. Series: Critical insights.

PG3012 .R877 2014
891.709/003

Contents

Critical Contexts

Critical Readings

Resources

About This Volume

In this volume, Golden Age [Russian: золотой век, zolotoj vek] refers to literature in nineteenth-century Russia—an unrivaled, rapidly evolving period of literary development, out of which emerged some of the most famous Russian authors in the West: Fyodor Dostoevsky, Lev Tolstoy, and Anton Chekhov. The most famous Russian poet, indeed Russia's national poet, Alexander Pushkin (1799–1837), less well known in the West, set the tone for the nineteenth century with his Romantic compositions of verse, including a novel in verse [роман в стихах, roman v stikhakh], which set the course for Russia's Golden Age of Poetry, occurring during the first half of the nineteenth century. The two terms, Golden Age and Golden Age of Poetry refer to two different, but coinciding, periods in the evolution of Russian literature from the classical, heavily European influenced literature of the eighteenth century. This volume treats the former, although the latter is certainly important within the context of the former. There are differing opinions as to when exactly Russia's Golden Age begins and ends, some believing it to have begun as early as the mid- to late eighteenth century and continued as late as the early twentieth century. For the purposes of this volume, intended as a broad overview for a general audience, we will take a more moderate view: that the Golden Age encompasses the bulk of the nineteenth century, beginning conservatively with Pushkin and continuing through Chekhov. The authors and texts that emerged in Russia's Golden Age are not only important in and of themselves, they represent a canon of works from which later Russian authors, both in the twentieth and twenty-first centuries, were and continue to be influenced. It is difficult to fully contextualize the writing of great Russian twentieth-century authors such as Mikhail Bulgakov, Vladimir Nabokov, or Aleksandr Solzhenitsyn without some acquaintance with nineteenth-century Russian literature, particularly with authors of the Golden Age. This volume seeks to provide this vital context for a general audience, while also providing an overview of Russian history and society leading up to and throughout the nineteenth century.

Four Critical Contexts pieces preface the volume's ten chapters, in order to provide much-needed insight into the historical, cultural, and societal contexts of the major texts, authors, and themes of Russia's Golden Age. In "My Country is Russian Literature," Kathleen Conti provides a much needed historical and political context of the nineteenth century that explains the surge in production of literature during the Golden Age. For the novice in nineteenth-century Russian literature, this first piece discusses the most important trends, events, and influences on Russian literary development, leaving no stone unturned. Donald Rayfield's piece on the Golden Age of Poetry is a reprint from the Routledge Companion to Russian Literature and has been included here to help the reader understand the role of poetry within the larger context of the Golden Age, providing a critical lens on Russian versification in particular, since no thematic or author-oriented chapter solely discusses this important genre. Derek Offord's chapter on nineteenth century Russian philosophy and thought provides needed comparison and contrast between relevant Russian trends and those of the West, with which many readers are likely to be more familiar. Katya Jordan's piece on critical reception offers the reader understanding of how the works discussed in the subsequent ten chapters were interpreted and critiqued in their time.

The ten chapters, of which the rest of this volume is composed, offer diverse approaches, largely based around a particular author, text, or theme of Golden Age Russian literature. The overarching topics for these chapters were selected by the volume editor, but contributors were given a great deal of space to be selective and/or creative in their approaches to their respective topics. No volume on Russia's Golden Age would be complete without attention to those authors, most of whom are well-known in Russia and in the West. Similarly, the editor wanted the volume to provide balanced representation of the two major movements of the Golden Age: Romanticism and Realism. For this reason, the volume contains chapters devoted to Romantic authors, namely Pushkin and Mikhail

Lermontov (1814–1841). Also, there are three chapters devoted to transitional authors and periods between Romanticism and Realism, including Nikolai Gogol (1809–1852) and Ivan Turgenev (1818–1883). Additionally, there are chapters devoted to a transitional period between Romanticism and Realism, known as the Natural School (1840–1855), and chapters devoted to the great Realists, Fyodor Dostoevsky (1821–1881) and Lev Tolstoy (1828–1910). One of these chapters considers the American reception to their lives and works through old newspapers.

The second-to-last chapter of the volume discusses, in detail, *The Cherry Orchard* by Anton Chekhov (1860–1904), another of Russia's many Realist authors, and the only playwright included in this volume. The last chapter by Anna Piotrowska departs from literature, presenting an intriguing look into Russian musical composition in the nineteenth century, notably by The Five, who were also known as The Mighty Handful [Могучая кучка, *Moguchaya kuchka*], and the important question of Russia's geographic identity crisis throughout the Golden Age (and persisting into the present): to be itself not quite Western or to assume more purposefully the ways of the West? The third chapter, on Pushkin and Lermontov's depictions of the Caucasus, also addresses this key question of Russian identity—a question that pervaded nineteenth century thought, literature, and discourse—analyzing Pushkin and Lermontov's depictions of Russia's neighboring south throughout its conquest of the nations and peoples north and south of the Caucasus mountain range.

Following this preface is an introduction to the volume that provides a substantial overview of the history of Russian literature up to the nineteenth century. In the greater context of Russian literature, the Golden Age stands out, in part owing to the sheer amount of writing within an otherwise short period. In comparison to other literary traditions, for example in the Greco-Roman and Arab-Islamic worlds, India, or China, Russian literature is comparatively young. Before the Christianization of Kievan Rus' in the late tenth century, there was no written Russian language. The rapidity with which the Golden Age progressed from predominantly sacred texts and heavily formularized eighteenth-century works to the production of some of the world's longest and most well-known novels (e.g., Dostoevsky's *Crime and Punishment*, Tolstoy's *Anna Karenina* and *War and Peace*), is stunning. By providing the reader with a comprehensive history of the Russian people, the Russian language, and the slow development of Russian literature from the tenth century to the dawn of the Golden Age, we hope that the unrivaled excellence and magnitude of the Golden Age will be clearly observed.

Of course it is impossible to capture the entire essence of a century in only fourteen chapters. With more space, we would certainly highlight the many poets, critics, artists, authors, and texts that are less well-known in the West, but of significance in Russia such as Vasilii Zhukovsky (1783–1852), Nikolai Nekrasov (1821–1878), Vissarion Belinsky (1811–1848), Nikolai Chernyshevsky (1828–1889), and Fyodor Tiutchev (1803–1873). An equally important inclusion, given the possibility of more chapters, would be a discussion of the few female authors in Russia's nineteenth century, such as Karolina Pavlova (1807–1893). Also valuable would be a chapter devoted to the development of Russian visual art, specifically Russian painting, which beautifully reflects the themes, perceptions, societal complexities, and movements of Russian literature and thought throughout the nineteenth century. Indeed, an entire volume could be devoted exclusively to Russian poetry of the nineteenth century or the emergent Russian émigré community, including many authors, among them Ivan Bunin (1870–1953), the first Russian to win the Nobel Prize for Literature. For those readers who wish to learn more about Russian literature in the nineteenth century, we have included two sections of resources for continued reading and research. One, "Additional Works of Russia's Golden Age," includes suggested works of literature by the authors discussed in this volume as well as a few others. The other is a general bibliography of current and canonical secondary sources commonly referenced in the field. These are excellent volumes to consult for purposes of research or for the development of deeper understanding of topics illuminated in the present volume.

This volume is intended for a general English–speaking audience. Because the Russian language presents many problems of translation and transliteration into English, we have provided titles of works in Russian, using the Cyrillic alphabet and also transliterated (written using Roman letters). Transliteration style may vary but generally follows the guidelines of the Library of Congress (http://www.loc.gov/catdir/cpso/romanization/russian.pdf) or the International Phonetic Association (IPA). Some Russian names (e.g., Dostoevsky, Tolstoy, Chekhov, Nikolai) have a more generally accepted transliterated standard that may differ from the transliteration system indicated below or the others mentioned above.

In general, the following guidelines may be used in this volume for interpreting Russian sounds using pronunciation guidelines (which are not always adequate or accurate) from American English:

Russian	English
а	a='father'
б	b='boy'
в	v='vodka'
г	g='get'
д	d='do'
е, э	je='yet', jo='yolk' or e='bet'
ж	zh='measure'
з	z='zoo'
и	i='feet'
й	j='you', and as a glide after vowels, e.g., 'boy'
к	k='coat'
л	l='light'
м	m='mom'
н	n='no'
о	o='oar'
п	p='gap'
р	r=rolled as in Spanish 'burrito'
с	s='sick'
т	t='get'

у	u='glue'
ф	f='far'
х	kh=as in Yiddish 'l'chaim
ц	v='vodka'
ч	ch='cheese'
ш	sh='fresh'
щ	shch='fresh cheese'
ы	y=high front vowel (no English equivalent)
ь	'=indicates preceding consonant is palatalized
ю	ju='you'
я	ja='yacht'

The editor of this volume wishes to express her gratitude to Grey House Publishing for acknowledging Russia's importance among literary, historical, and cultural studies meriting inclusion as a Critical Insights volume. A debt of gratitude is also owed to the contributors, who come from across the United States, as well as from Germany, Russia, and Poland. They are a fascinating group of individuals with a common interest: Russia's legacy as an artistic giant. We hope that this volume will provide an insightful and thorough introduction to Russia's nineteenth-century literary boom for those with less familiarity, although we equally hope that the volume may also be of use for those more well-acquainted with Russia and its Golden Age.

On Russia's Golden Age

Rachel Stauffer

The accomplishments of Russia's Golden Age are unmatched in any other period of Russian literature. Within a century, some of the greatest authors in Russia and in the world emerged. How was so much literature, indeed, so much great literature, produced in one country (really in two cities within that country) in only one century? Those unacquainted with the history of Russia or Russian literature might assume that Russia had a longstanding or well-established literary tradition that gradually built up to the nineteenth century, like China or India, for example, or perhaps that the important philosophies and literary accomplishments of the West heavily influenced Russia in the nineteenth century, giving way to the quality and quantity of Russian literature in the Golden Age. Neither of these assumptions would be entirely correct, although neither is entirely inaccurate either. In order to understand the Golden Age, it is also important to understand Russia's cultural history from its origins to the turn of the nineteenth century. Russia's literary history is relatively short in comparison to some of its neighbors. Georgia and Armenia, for example, have literary traditions that date back to the fourth century. Of course, the Greco-Roman world had a long-standing literary tradition predating that of the Caucasus nations. By comparison, the beginnings of Russian civilization and the establishment of its literary language occur later. Nevertheless, this late blooming nation produced some of the greatest works of fiction in the world, counting great authors such as Pushkin, Gogol, Dostoevsky, and Tolstoy among those who emerged in the nineteenth century's Golden Age.

There are different accounts and theories as to why and how the Eastern Slavs came to occupy the region of present-day Kiev, as well as why and with whom they interacted. W. Bruce Lincoln gives the most picturesque description of the Eastern Slavic settlement of Kievan Rus':

At the point where the great grass road from Inner Asia intersected with the rivers that flow between the Baltic and Byzantium, the Grand Prince of Kiev ruled a prize of even greater value than Novgorod, for at Kiev, the caravans from the Orient met the high-powered ships that made their way along the great Dnieper River highway to the Black Sea and the bazaars of Constantinople. Because its princes commanded the gateway through which much of the trade from the Near and Middle East flowed between East and West, furs, honey, wax, spices, amber, gems, rare woods, gold, silver, precious silks, and treasures wrought by the master craftsmen of the East all made their way through Kiev, and the wealth that this commerce produced soon enabled its rulers to blend great political authority with generous patronage of the arts. As the point at which the politics, commerce, and cultures of the Eurasian steppes blended with those that flowed from Europe and Constantinople, Kiev was a prize worth having, and the sovereigns who ruled Byzantium, the Holy Roman Empire, and the lands of Islam all dreamed of adding it to their domains (Lincoln 18).

The desire for access to the trade routes fueled much of the interest in Kievan Rus', which was closely tied to Novgorod, an important northern port of the waterways flowing south to Kiev and strategically positioned near northern civilizations and the Baltic Sea. The approximate date of the settlement of the Eastern Slavs is not entirely clear, although generally, we can place them in the region definitively by the eighth or ninth century. In his book *Russian Orientalism*, David Schimmelpenninck van der Oye describes the forest-dwelling tribe of Eastern Slavs transforming into a civilization allied with diverse groups, both Eastern and Western:

> The East Slavs, from whom Russians derive their ancestry, first settled Europe's wooded northeastern periphery sometime in the latter half of our era's first millennium. Precisely what enticed them to this dark, primeval land during the era of the great migrations that followed Rome's collapse remains obscure. Some of these Slavs eventually came to pay tribute to the Khazars, a more powerful nation of nomadic Inner Asian origin that controlled the region around the lower Volga River from the seventh through the ninth centuries. As

part of the Eurasian steppe's loose confederation of Turkic tribes, the Khazars profited from commerce with the great powers of the day, including the caliphate of Baghdad, Persia, and Byzantium. Culture came with coin, and their various trading partners influenced the nomads. The elite eventually adopted Judaism, while much of the general population converted to Christianity and Islam...Sometime in the eighth century this lucrative enterprise caught the attention of Scandinavia's aggressive Varangians (Vikings)...it was under their leadership that the first state eventually emerged among these Slavs (Schimmelpenninck van der Oye 12–13).

Meanwhile, in the South Slavic world (present-day Bulgaria and Macedonia), a script for the liturgical language there, Old Church Slavonic, was developed by two South Slavic missionaries, Cyril and Methodius. The script they developed was called Glagolitic:

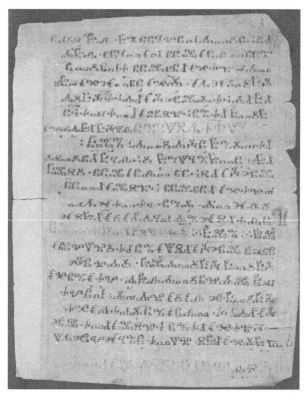

Figure 1: Glagolitic text from the latter half of tenth century [The Kiev Missal. *World Digital Library*. Library of Congress, http://www.wdl.org/en/item/7488/]

The script for Old Russian that came to be named for one of those missionaries, the Cyrillic alphabet, is believed to have been created later, as Paul Cubberley explains, summarizing a widely accepted point of view:

> Glagolitic was formed by the adaptation of cursive Greek by some Slavs […] it was formalised by Constantine, who also added letters for the non-Greek sounds; Constantine's disciplines in Bulgaria and Macedonia (in the 890s) […] perceived Glagolitic as unsuitable for Church books and made up a new Slavonic alphabet based on the 'more dignified' uncial Greek. This is the alphabet we now know as Cyrillic, formally named (much later) after St. Cyril, even though it is likely that the alphabet he created was in fact Glagolitic (Cubberley 49).

Once the written language was firmly established in Kievan Rus' in the eleventh century, the primary documents were religious, mostly translated from Greek and South Slavic sacred texts, including hagiographies, Biblical and liturgical texts, among others. This period also included the composition of the Primary Chronicle [Old Church Slavonic: Повѣсть времяньныхъ лѣтъ, Russian: Повесть временных лет, Povest' vremennykh let], allegedly an historical record of Kievan Rus', part Biblical, part folkloric, part historical, although its authenticity, as far as accurate historiography is concerned, is generally questioned. This text, for example, suggests that the adoption of Christianity occurred in Kievan Rus' in part because the adoption of Islam would have been impossible because of its prohibition on alcohol. Vladimir is quoted as saying (in two rhyming lines: Руси есть веселие пить: не можем без того быть» *Rusi jest' veselije pit': ne mozhem bez togo byt'*.): "Drinking is the joy of the Russes. We cannot exist without that pleasure" (Cross 184). There are many theories among historians about why Rus' adopted Christianity, most of which suggest that uniting with Byzantine strength and wealth was an important power play. Geographically situated precariously among a diverse network of Islamic, Judaic, and pagan tribes, with access to the Volga and Dnieper trade routes, Rus' was most likely strategic in its alliance with Byzantine military strength in order to retain some control over its domain.

The Primary Chronicle also suggests that the Scandinavian Varangians (i.e., Vikings) were invited to rule in East Slavic settlements, stating that the Eastern Slavs discovered that they were incapable of ruling themselves:

> The Slavs, the tributaries of the Varangians, drove them back beyond the sea, and, refusing them further tribute, set out to govern themselves. There was no law among them, but tribe rose against tribe. Discord thus ensued among them, and they began to war one against another. They said to themselves: 'Let us seek a prince who may rule over us, and judge us according to the law.' They accordingly went overseas to the Varangian Rus [...] The Chuds, the Slavs, and the Krivichians then said to the people of Rus: 'Our whole land is Great and rich, but there is no order in it. Come to rule and reign over us' (Zenkovsky 49–50).

Certainly, the more likely situation was that the Varangians, already demanding tribute from the Slavs and surrounding tribes of the waterways, wanted sustained access to the important rivers providing access to merchants and trade opportunities around and beyond the Black and Caspian Seas. No matter the catalyst for Varangian rule over the Slavic tribes, the result was the establishment of the Varangian Rurikid dynasty, one of only two major ruling dynasties in Russia (the other, the Romanov dynasty, began in 1613) until the twentieth century. Although the Primary Chronicle cannot be trusted as an historical document, it does provide important perspectives on Russia's origins and intersections with other civilizations. Whether or not it is a true literary text is similarly difficult to determine because by "very cleverly interweaving the actual fabric of historical material with legendary accounts and reminiscences, the annalist succeeds in creating a religious and political tradition for his newly emerged country, and points out that Russia has won a respectable status" following Christianization in 988 (Zenkovsky 12).

Therefore, the history of Russian literature technically begins around the time of Christianization in the tenth century. The liturgical and sacred text abounds, following Byzantine models, and hagiographies and sermons serve as didactic texts designed to model Orthodox Christian morals and behaviors as pre-Christian beliefs are rejected and Christian faith adopted. Outside the instructive and sacred contexts, there is one standout literary work, *The Lay of Igor's Campaign* [Слово о полку Игореве, Slovo o polku Igoreve], also known as *The Igor Tale*, which is generally considered an epic. The text is considered "the greatest, but also the most puzzling work of medieval Russian literature [...] a complex artistic response to an insignificant historical event" in 1185 (Worth, 425). It differs significantly from the chronicles, saints' lives, and liturgical texts dominating the Kievan period of literature:

> Then Prince Igor set his foot in the golden stirrup
> and rode into the open prairie.
> The sun barred his way with darkness
> and night, moaning with tempest, awoke the birds.
> The whistling of the beasts arose[...]
> Very early on the second morn
> a bloody dawn announced the day.
> Black clouds arrive from the sea
> and want to envelop the four suns.
> Blue lightning shows through the clouds.
> There is to be a mighty thundering.
> The rain of arrows will come from the great river Don
> (Zenkovsky 172–174).

The question for many is why *The Igor Tale* is so different from the majority of Kievan literature, which also has raised suspicion as to its authenticity. Without entering into this debate, we can say definitively that the *Tale* suggests a vibrant storytelling culture, which is consistent with East Slavic folkloric verbal culture, both pre-Christian, and alongside Christianity. In fact, the dual belief (dvoeverie) of the Eastern Slavs, that is, the hybridization of pre-

Christian and Christian beliefs in practice, text, and ritual, is apparent throughout the *Tale* as well as in texts of the Kievan period.

Two hundred and fifty years after the establishment of the written language, Rus' was overtaken by the Mongolian Golden Horde, led by Batu Khan, grandson of Genghis Khan. During the Mongol occupation (1247–1480), Russia's center of power shifted from Kiev to Moscow, which helped to consolidate Russia's fragmented principality-based leadership that was in need of organization and greater unity. Indeed, it was this fragmentation, in combination with the general brutality of the Mongols, of course, that made the Russian territories more susceptible to defeat. Without the influence of the Mongol occupiers, Russian culture would be significantly different in many ways. The true Russophile will complain that the Mongol occupation deprived Russia of the cultivation of its full artistic virtue, that the Russians were forced to adopt the allegedly primitive nomad culture of the Mongols, and subsequently to leave behind their comparatively more civilized ways. We really have no way of knowing what Russia would have become had the Mongol invasion not occurred. The occupation did impact Russia in many ways, both negative and positive. As historian Daniel Waugh has noted, "Mongol rule did bring with it initial destruction, the imposition of heavy financial burdens, and the loss of political independence, at the same time that it seeded political renewal in some areas and contributed selectively to economic expansion."[1] The Mongol model of imposing and collecting large tributes from the Russians led to the Russians imposing and collecting similar tributes themselves, and by the time Byzantium was taken by the Ottoman Turks in 1453, the Russians had amassed enough capital to sustain themselves, weaken the Mongol leadership, and begin to organize—this time in more unified way. As Charles Halperin has observed, "The Russians borrowed the commercial tax (tamga), the tribute (vykhod, later called the dan'), and other levies. The Russians even borrowed the Mongol term for treasury (kazna) and perhaps the institutional structure it denoted" (Halperin, 245). With new economic and political stability and a new center of power,

Russia gradually came to rule and redefine itself after the end of Mongol occupation.

Moscow came to consider itself the Third Rome, the only remaining bastion of Christianity now that Byzantium had been Islamicized. "The Tale of the White Cowl" [«Повесть о белом клобуке», Povest' o belom klobuke], written in the sixteenth century, tells how Moscow's new role was revealed to the Patriarch Philotheos many years earlier by two angels:

> The ancient city of Rome has broken away from the glory and faith of Christ because of its pride and ambition. In the new Rome, which has been the city of Constantinople, the Christian faith will also perish through the violence of the sons of Hagar. In the third Rome, which will be the land of Russia, the Grace of the Holy Spirit will be revealed. Know then, Philotheos, that all Christians will finally unite into one Russian nation because of its Orthodoxy.

> Since ancient times and by the will of Constantine, Emperor of the Earth, the imperial crown of the imperial city is predestined to be given to the Russian tsar (Zenkovsky 328).

The fall of Constantinople empowered Ivan III (Ivan the Great, ruled 1462–1505), Vasilii III (ruled 1505–1533), and Ivan IV (Ivan the Terrible, ruled 1533–1584) to pursue expansion of the Russian territory and to foster a society based around Orthodox Christian morals, rituals, and values through the development of laws and codes of conduct, in order to represent Christianity for all the world. A revitalization of Russian Orthodox Christian doctrine, morality, and behavior drove the creation of text, both sacred and secular, although perhaps not necessarily literary. For example, a household manual for keeping a good, Orthodox home, called the Domostroi, (from the roots for 'home' and 'construct') offers some insight into societal expectations under sixteenth century Russian Orthodoxy. Here, the habits of a good servant:

> People should keep servants of good character in their houses. The servants should be handy at that craft for which they are fitted and

in which they have been trained. A manservant should not ever have been a robber, carouser, gambler, petty thief, brigand, lecher, sorcerer, drunkard, or swindler. One who serves a good master should be knowledgeable, God–fearing, wise, humble, given to good deeds, far-sighted, {and well-versed in domestic management}. He should not lie, rob, or offend anyone [...] A slave should feed and clothe himself with funds awarded by his master or gained by his own efforts. He should be content with whatever his master gives him—a robe, a horse, clothes, a small field, an item to trade—and should supplement it with whatever he can acquire by his own labors (Pouncy 104–105).

And here, the rules for a happy family:

The master must himself learn and must teach his wife, children, and servants not to steal, live dissolutely, lie, slander, envy, offend, accuse falsely, quarrel with others, condemn, carouse, mock, remember evil, or be angry with anyone.

Be obedient and submissive to your superiors, loving to your equals, welcoming and kind to inferiors and the poor. Then everyone will meet your demands without delay [...] If you yourself, from carelessness and neglect, or your wife, because she lacks a husband's correction, or any of your servants—men, women, and children— because of your failure to instruct them, engage in evil deeds (such as carousing, theft, or lechery), you will suffer eternal torment together. But if you act well and live in a manner pleasing to God, you will inherit eternal life in the Heavenly Kingdom (Pouncy 103–104).

Texts of correspondence are also good examples of Russian sixteenth-century writing. Here, in a letter from Ivan the Terrible to Prince Andrew Kurbsky, "defending the Byzantine–Russian concept of autocracy, which accepted the tsar as ruler by divine right" (Zenkovsky 370), we get a sense of the Muscovite period's style and tone:

Our God, the Trinity, who has existed since eternity but now as Father, Son and Holy Ghost, has neither beginning nor end; through him we live and move about, through him kings rule and the mighty write laws…The autocracy, by God's will, had its origin in Grand Prince Vladimir, who had enlightened all Russia through the Holy Baptism…and the praiseworthy great Tsar Dmitry, who had obtained a great victory over the sons of Hagar beyond the Don, then it passed to the avenger of wrongs, our ancestor, the great Tsar Ivan, the gatherer of the Russian land from among the ancestral possessions…But we praise God for the great favor he has shown me in not permitting my right hand to become stained by the blood of my race. . . on account of a single angry word of mine, you have lost not only your own soul, but the souls of all your ancestors: for, by God's will, had they been given as servants to our grandfather, the great tsar, and they gave their souls to him and served him up to their death, and ordered you, their children, to serve the children and grandchildren of our grandfather. But you have forgotten everything and Traitorously, like a dog, you have transgressed the oath. . . (Zenkovsky 372–3).

It is important to note that even in the sixteenth century, the Russian language at this time still relied on the writing system imposed at the beginning of the eleventh century, which, by this time, bore little phonetic, morphological, grammatical, or even lexical resemblance to the spoken language. This, coupled with a general low rate of literacy, made the dissemination of moral and religious texts was challenging.

The seventeenth century was ushered in with the Time of Troubles [смутное время, smutnoe vremja, 1601–1613], which brought famine, an interregnum, and foreign wars and invaders until the establishment of the new Romanov dynasty in 1613. During the schism of the Russian Orthodox Church in the seventeenth century, which instituted Greek Church ritual in place of longstanding Russian traditions, a group known as the Old Believers, resisted these reforms. The Old Believers were punished for resisting the will of the state and the patriarch. One such dissenter was the Archpriest Avvakum, exiled to Siberia by the Patriarch and executed in 1682. Prior to his death, he told his story, creating the first Russian autobiography, *The Life of Archpriest Avvakum By Himself* [Житие протопопа Аввакума, им самим написанное,

Zhitie protopopa Avvakuma, im samim napisannoe]. This text marks a transition from the heavy, formalized liturgical language to a style that bears greater resemblance to the spoken language at the time, as Zenkovsky observes: "His narration is dynamic, and reflects the active, unbending nature of the author. Avvakum rarely used the solemn Church Slavonic literary language, but turned to colloquial Russian. He does not hesitate to use crude folk sayings that lend expressiveness to his style" (Zenkovsky 401). In some ways, Avvakum sets the stage for important developments made by Russian authors of the Golden Age such as Pushkin, who similarly revolutionized the written language to correspond with more colloquial Russian over two centuries later, and also Dostoevsky, who, like Avvakum, uses the first-person pronoun, я 'ja', as the first word of his *Notes from Underground* [Записки из подполья, Zapiski iz podpol'ja, 1864], producing his own fictionalized version of an autobiography of the Underground Man.

The eighteenth century sets the stage for the Golden Age more than any other period of Russian literature for many reasons. Beginning with the reign of Peter the Great (1689–1725) and continuing through the end of the reign of Catherine the Great (1762–1796) the fertile ground for modern Russian literature was, perhaps for the first time in Russian literary history, purposefully and thoughtfully cultivated. The eighteenth century narrowed the gap between the spoken and literary languages, introduced European thought, and increased attention to the written form as a means of artistic expression. Peter the Great, having experienced a violent childhood in the Moscow Kremlin, was eager to leave the capital. Fascinated by shipbuilding, he founded the city of St. Petersburg to be Russia's great northern port on the Baltic Sea, its window to the West, and Russia's new capital. Peter established the Russian Navy, expanded Russian territory, implemented European models and styles of conduct and clothing, eschewing archaic Orthodox practices, such as long beards, in exchange for more modern, Western European sensibilities and trends. Peter also ordered that the literary language be reformed so that the alphabet would be easier to write, to learn, and to print. The printing press had been used in Russia since the reign of Ivan the Terrible, but the simplified orthography ordered by Peter the Great made printing more streamlined:

Figure 2: Cyrillic alphabet in 1574[2]

А б В Г Д Е Ж S I К Л
М Н О П Р С Т У Ф
Х Ц Ч Ш Щ Ъ Ы Ь
Ѣ Э Ю Я Ѳ
а б в г д е ж s i к л м н о п
р с т у ф х ц ч ш щ ъ ы
ь ѣ э ю я ѳ

Figure 3: Cyrillic alphabet in 1707[3]

Peter's reign improved access to Western thought, literature, and progress, and this changed the course of literature in Russia. New sensibilities, new forms, and the increasing influx of Enlightenment-era philosophy and literature that arrived under the rule of two women, Elizabeth, Peter's daughter (ruled 1741–1762), and Catherine the Great (ruled 1762–1796), of German heritage, set Russian literature on a new path.

Several Russian thinkers contributed to the transformation of Russian literature in the eighteenth century, among them Vasilii Trediakovsky (1703–1769), Mikhail Lomonosov (1711–1765), and Alexander Sumarokov (1717–1777). Lomonosov, a philosopher, scientist, and writer is often given the credit for setting the stage for the development of Russian literature in the eighteenth century. His doctrine of the three styles established a hierarchy of formality that could be attributed to different genres of text. Texts for more formal settings, such as sermons and odes would qualify as high style, incorporating less colloquial speech and more archaic language from Church Slavonic. Low style texts were more inclusive of colloquial language and less inclusive of Church Slavonicisms. Lomonosov also observed Russian's unique capacity for syllabotonic versification in the composition of poetry. As Irina Reyfman has noted, "In his 'Letter on the Rules of Russian Versification,' Lomonosov proposed a pure, extreme form of syllabo-tonic verse, and his maximalist approach better marked the break with syllabic tradition than the more prudent approach suggested by Trediakovsky" (Reyfman 127). Aside from defining the literary forms most suited to the Russian language, authors at this time were beginning to write on Enlightenment-era philosophy. In his "Letter on the Usefulness of Glass" [«Письмо о пользе стекла», Pis'mo o pol'ze ctekla, 1752], Lomonosov marvels at the utility of glass in multiple contexts, for creating warmth, for scientific discovery, for improving eyesight and creating drinking vessels, but more importantly, he reconciles the coexistence of science and faith:

> How vast is the nature of created things! Oh how great is the Divinity who created them! Oh how great the abyss of His bounties to us

when He sent down to earth His beloved Son! He did not desist from descending to this small globe in order to save the lost through his suffering. The less we appear worthy of His bounties, the more we do marvel at His grace and charity. Through optics, Glass leads us to Him, having expelled from us the profound darkness of ignorance! The limits of refracted rays are not false in it, for they have been set by the Creator; others are impossible [...] Although nature has endowed us with sharp sight, its power does not extend very far. Despite the fact that it does not show us things at a distance and demands the rays gathered by a telescope, how many creatures it still does not reach whose small stature conceals them from us! But in our present era the Microscope has revealed to us what God created in unseeable creatures!

How delicate are their members, their systems, hearts, veins, and that which preserves animal strengths in them! A tiny worm amazes us by the complexity of its parts no less than a monstrous whale in the deep. Great is our Creator in the magnitude of Heaven! (Lomonosov 218).

Based on Lomonosov's text alone, we see that the eighteenth century makes a clean break from the staunch and overbearing texts based in Russian Orthodoxy, while still retaining aspects of faith, acknowledging scientific progress as a divinely inspired process.

Catherine the Great was also an influential figure in the latter half of the eighteenth century. In his compelling biography of Catherine, Robert Massie observes, "During her sixteen years as an isolated, embattled grand duchess, she had read many of the works of the great figures of the European Enlightenment. Of these, the writer with the greatest effect on her was [...] Voltaire[...] after fifteen months on the throne she wrote to him for the first time...Even before she first wrote to Voltaire in 1763, Catherine had reached out to [...] Denis Diderot" (Massie 330–336). Catherine's interest in French philosophy and literature strongly influenced the adaptation of Russian literature away from purely classical forms.

By the end of the eighteenth century, Russian Sentimentalism, known as chuvstvitelnost'—from the word chuvstvo 'feeling'—sought to evoke emotion from readers. Nikolai Karamzin's 1792 short story "Poor Liza" [«Бедная Лиза», Bednaja Liza] drew interest because of its wildly over-the-top emotionality, which caused the Moscow reading public to "weep buckets" (Bayley 311). This was Karamzin's and the other Sentimentalists' intention during this short-lived period, although an equally important contributing factor to this emotional response was the more colloquial style of writing in "Poor Liza". Unmatched in earlier works, Karamzin's straightforward narrative technique, like Avvakum's, utilized the language of the people, rather than the strictly proscribed eighteenth century formal standard. Although the present volume does not devote a chapter to Karamzin or to "Poor Liza" in particular, its influence on the Golden Age is important to acknowledge.

***

So why is the nineteenth century, in particular, Russia's Golden Age? Considering the erratic history of Russian literature up to the nineteenth century, the Golden Age essentially represents the first time in Russian literary history that the artistic merit and creation of literature coincided with a larger reading public and with topics of interest to that reading public. As our cultural history of Russia suggests, prior to the nineteenth century, reading and literature were reserved primarily for the elite. Additionally, the political climate of nineteenth-century Russia, beginning with the defeat of Napoleon in 1812; continuing through the conquest of the Caucasus (throughout the nineteenth century) and the Crimean War; and culminating with the increasing discontent with archaic, feudalistic social stratification, also welcomed the bold thinking of Russian and Western philosophers (e.g., Belinsky, Chernyshevsky, Marx, Hegel, Schopenhauer, Nietzsche). All of these factors set the course for significant changes in literature and thought. This tumultuous century created probably the most well-known Russian authors throughout the world, such as Dostoevsky, Tolstoy, and Chekhov, but also the most well-known within Russia, including Pushkin, Lermontov, Gogol, and Turgenev. There are certainly many other authors who should be included in this volume for their contributions to Russia's Golden Age. Similarly, Russia's Golden Age of Poetry could also fill an entire volume about the evolution of Russian verse at the beginning of the nineteenth century. The authors selected for discussion in this volume have been included because of their monumental, transformative, and unrivaled contributions to Russian literature of the nineteenth century.

Notes

1. Waugh, Daniel. "The Pax Mongolica." *Silk Road Foundation*. 2000. Web. 6 Nov. 2013. <http://www.silk-road.com/artl/paxmongolica.shtml>.

2. "Russian Language." *New World Encyclopedia*. 8 December 2008. Web. 7 Nov. 2013. <http://static.newworldencyclopedia.org/e/e5/Azbuka_1574_by_Ivan_Fyodorov.jpg>.

3. Efimov, Vladimir. "The Dramatic History of the Cyrillic Alphabet." *Project "Historical Materials." Large point civil font 1707*. 2013. Web. 7 Nov. 2013. <http://istmat.info/node/521>.

Works Cited

Bayley, John. Pushkin: *A Comparative Commentary*. Cambridge, UK: Cambridge UP, 1971.

Cross, Samuel. "The Russian Primary Chronicle." *Harvard Studies and Notes in Philology and Literature*. Cambridge, MA: Harvard UP, 1930.

Halperin, Charles. "Russia in the Mongol Empire in Comparative Perspective." *Harvard Journal of Asiatic Studies* 43.1 (June 1983): 239–61.

Lomonosov, Mikhail. "Letter on the Use of Glass." *The Literature of Eighteenth Century Russia*. Ed. Harold B. Segel. New York: E.P. Dutton & Co., 1967.

Massie, Robert. *Catherine the Great: Portrait of a Woman*. New York: Random House, 2011.

Pouncy, Carolyn Johnston. *The Domostroi*. Ithaca, NY: Cornell UP, 1994.

Reyfman, Irina. *Vasilii Trediakovsky: The Fool of the 'New' Russian Literature*. Stanford, CA: Stanford UP, 1990.

Schimmelpenninck van der Oye, David. *Russian Orientalism*. New Haven, CT: Yale UP, 2010.

Worth, Dean S. "Slovo o polku Igoreve." *Handbook of Russian Literature*. Ed. Victor Terras. New Haven, CT: Yale UP, 1985.

Zenkovsky, Serge. *Medieval Russia's Epics, Chronicles, and Tales*. New York: E.P. Dutton, 1974.

CRITICAL
CONTEXTS

"My Country Is Russian Literature": History and Literary Development in the Golden Age

Kathleen Conti

History and literature intertwine so that it is impossible to explore one without an understanding of the other. Russia's nineteenth century saw a time of unsurpassed literary genius. "Truly," literary critic Maksim Antonovich wrote in 1863, "it was the Golden Age of our literature" (Antonovich 85). From then on, this era's literature became united under the banner of the Golden Age, which saw the development of Pushkin, Gogol, Dostoevsky, and Tolstoy. Authors of this era rose to an unparalleled prominence not only for their artistic skills in crafting narratives, but because of the social and political conditions of the time. Their work created an atmosphere in which literature became a central conduit for discourse about what Russia was and what it would be. Due to the government's censorship of newspapers, it was literature that developed into an outlet for addressing the great questions facing society—even sparking social change. In this way, Russian literature became the voice of social conscience for the Russian people.

Russia's Golden Age emerged on foundations laid during the reign of Peter the Great. His thirty-year reign fundamentally changed the course of Russia over the preceding five centuries. Even today, Peter the Great remains one of the most popular figures in the Russian consciousness. Previous centuries of relative isolation from Europe meant that Russia had not substantially contributed to the great intellectual debates occurring there; many writers of the Golden Age would later subscribe to this belief of Russia's perceived backwardness in comparison to the West. Peter introduced his subjects to a broad range of Western culture and technology, which promoted a flourishing in Russia's arts, natural sciences, and philosophy. Dedicated to opening the country to Europe, Peter's efforts allowed European culture to more effectively blow into Russia through the newly-built city and port of St. Petersburg, his "window on the West," in Pushkin's phrase. Peter understood the necessity of a port city to better facilitate European connections. Despite the inhospitable terrain and weather, St. Petersburg faced the Baltic Sea and thus allowed easier access to the European continent. Peter's political, economic, and technological reforms touched all areas of life. The most influential reform was his cultural revolution, for it profoundly changed the "the architecture, the visual, and the verbal" (Cracraft 77).

A verbal revolution required more printing presses, as well as the paper to feed them. Peter oversaw the expansion of the printing industry and the construction of local paper mills so that Russia would no longer rely upon costly imports. These changes also included the standardization of the alphabet, numerals, spelling, and syntax, which had not been revised since the development of the written language more than six centuries earlier (Cracraft 97–99). Authors embraced these modifications and adapted to new styles and genres brought from Europe, including plays, satire, new prose forms, and poetry. When Catherine the Great took the throne in 1762, she expanded upon Peter's reforming legacy. Peter and Catherine's Western-oriented cultural and political reforms fueled Russia's rise to a status of global power. Catherine the Great doubled the size of the army and navy and expanded Russia's territory into such areas as present-day Poland, Lithuania, and Belarus, along with parts of present-day Ukraine, Romania, Georgia, Azerbaijan, Siberia, Alaska, and even an encampment north of San Francisco. Catherine's dedication to the arts generated many distinctive architectural landmarks that define the Petersburg landscape.

A "distinctive, if disturbed, aristocratic culture" flourished from the mid-eighteenth century to the mid-nineteenth (Billington 208). This allowed for new architectural styles and performance arts, such as theatre, opera, and ballet, in addition to the establishment in 1755 of Russia's first university by poet and scholar Mikhail Lomonosov, among others. Yet Catherine the Great also imposed strict control on works she perceived as dangerous. Alexander Radishchev's 1790 *Journey from St. Petersburg to Moscow* illuminated many of the problems facing Russian society, such as serfdom, corruption, and economic decay. In response, Catherine sentenced him to death, but eventually decided to exile him to Siberia instead (Riasanovsky, *History of Russia* 295). Similar veins of criticism did not reemerge until the later years of the Golden Age, particularly in the works of Gogol, Belinsky, Herzen, and Dostoevsky.

If writers of the nineteenth century recognized Peter's revolution as an important part of their history, they also argued that few truly outstanding Russian works of literature existed before the nineteenth century. Critic Vissarion Belinsky claimed "*we have no literature*" (Maguire 4). Others termed the eighteenth century as the "Age of Imitation," in describing Russian reception of the new art forms introduced by Peter and his successors (Rzhevsky 79). Indeed, classic Russian literature did not truly come into its own until the years following the Great Patriotic War of 1812, during the reign of Catherine's grandson Alexander I.

Tsar Alexander I ascended the throne in 1801; the Golden Age dawned during his reign. Unlike his tyrannical predecessor (and father) Paul I, Alexander I "seemed to represent the best of the Enlightenment—that humanness, progressiveness, affirmation of human dignity, and freedom, which educated Russians, one way or another, feverishly desired," (Riasanovsky, *History of Russia* 302). Russia, still a developing empire, required reforms to adapt to the rapidly changing times, such as the issues raised by the French Revolution and the growth of the industrial revolution. The question of serfdom—and how to manage it, if it should continue—gained importance, especially as much of Europe had already abolished feudal forms of social control. Pursuing reform, Alexander I reversed some of Paul's laws, such as bans on foreign books, international travel, and private publishing houses (Wachtel and Vinitsky 57). These developments, along with a dramatically expanding education system, fostered a growing literary culture. It was a paradoxical time, embodying an admiration for Western culture along with an eagerness to define and establish a distinctly Russian literary style. Within this paradox lay other contradictions, such as the generational and political struggle between Romanticism and Realism, and equal fascination with stories of traditional folk culture alongside grand military tales of modern heroes and the cult of genius surrounding figures such as Shakespeare and Goethe (Wachtel and Vinitsky 58).

While Alexander I intended to undertake great reforms, his reign was defined more by Russia's foreign relations than by domestic matters. Russia's relationship with revolutionary France had become complicated. Sometimes they allied (1807–1812), other times they were adversaries (1801–1807 and 1812–1815). Within Russia, some questioned the wisdom of absorbing French culture, particularly in light of the bloodshed in France's multiple revolutions. "Let Russians be Russian, not copies of the French," wrote Princess Dashkova, an influential intellectual and the only female president of the Russian Academy of Sciences, "Let us remain patriots and retain the character of our ancestors" (Figes 68). Nevertheless, the French models heavily influenced Russia's politics and culture, for many of Alexander's reforms often borrowed from French legislation.

Yet the French, so admired by the Russians, invaded under Napoleon's command in 1812. Napoleon hoped to introduce ideals of liberty—at bayonet point—and abolish autocratic rule in Russia. Napoleon thought he needed to swiftly defeat the Russians in order to succeed in his plans for European domination (Wachtel and Vinitsky 132). "They must be thrown back into their icy wastes," Napoleon announced to his staff in July of that year, "so that they do not meddle in the affairs of civilized Europe for the next twenty-five years at least" (Zamoyski 159). Neither swift, nor victorious, Napoleon's summer invasion did not go according to plan. Napoleon assumed his armies would crush Alexander's within three weeks, and thus they did not carry supplies to sustain them for the winter (Zamoyski 144). "When the news of the intrusion of Napoleon's countless hordes spread through Russia," Russian officer Prince N. V. Golitsyn wrote, "one can truly say that one feeling inspired every heart, a feeling of devotion to the Tsar and fatherland" (Zamoyski 200).

Patriotic fervor spread throughout Russia, rallying allegiance around Alexander I and the empire. The characterization of Alexander as a benevolent angel became more pronounced once Napoleon's troops invaded. At the insistence of his advisors, Alexander I soon left St. Petersburg for Moscow to rouse support, morale, and funds for the coming battles. His presence there became a "central episode in the myth of national sacrifice and unity woven around the events of 1812" (Wortman 109). This myth proved especially important since Napoleon stormed over the border with an army of extraordinary size, totaling over half a million men (Zamoyski 140). The Russians soon adopted a policy of strategic retreat, luring Napoleon's troops deeper into the empire's interior, where they would be further from supply lines. Meanwhile, the Russians followed a "scorched earth" policy, burning their own towns and fields to eliminate any potential supplies and fodder that the French might obtain or loot. A bloody battle at Borodino on September 7 maimed Napoleon's army but did not check its advance—Napoleon and his forces soon arrived in Moscow, only to find the city in flames. "Such terrible tactics have no precedent in the history of civilization," Napoleon wrote, "To burn one's own cities! . . . What savage determination! What a people! What a people!" (Massie 158). Napoleon's initial hope for a swift victory upon his June invasion had not materialized. He fled to Paris in October with winter rapidly approaching, leaving his men to trudge back to France. Less than one-twentieth of his men returned home, leaving the Russians victorious despite substantial losses (Milner-Gulland and Dejevsky 116).

Although 1812's main events are known, the specifics and significance of the year remained shrouded in mystery and nationalist narratives. Many accounts by British, French, and German historians significantly diminish Russia's involvement in Napoleon's downfall (Lieven 283). For Russians at the time, the war's savagery, suffering, and sacrifice remained incomprehensible and much of the literature and historical study produced in the subsequent years and decades sought to explain it (Zamoyski xv). Even today, the 1812 Napoleonic invasion resonates within Russia. Historians have studied these events more than any other moment in Russia's millennium of pre-Soviet history, and much of Russia's literature, particularly at the outset of the Golden Age, took inspiration from it (Troitskii 6).

Following the war, leading scholars and philosophers examined what it meant to be Russian. This mission to define the Russian nation carried an intrinsic threat to the Tsar and to autocratic rule. Following the defeat of Napoleon, many felt that they owed loyalty and love to the *nation*, rather than the autocratic *state*. A state is a political, governing entity—in Russia's case, the tsar and his government. A nation is a group of people who feel united by perceived commonalities, whether by language, history, religion, culture, or ethnicity. This distinction allowed writers to criticize the *state* and the Tsar's rule, while still remaining devoted to the Russian *nation*. This divide still exists between terms russkij and rossijskij (русский and российский)—where the former refers to those things that are national, purely, ethnically Russian, and the latter refers to the state, the federation, and the agents of government.

After the Great Patriotic War, many came to see that Alexander I had largely abandoned his previous course of reform. Although adored by the Russian people during the war years, Alexander's popularity later waned among the educated elites. Characterized by the division between the promise of reform and the failure to do so, Alexander I's regime set the stage for unrest. In pursuing the fleeing French after 1812, Russians had witnessed the striking contrast between Europe and their own Russia, where serfdom remained and the exchange of ideas struggled under government restrictions (Crankshaw 28). Prior to the war, Alexander I had encouraged many of these men to ponder how Russia might undergo radical and necessary reforms. Yet true to his contradictory nature, Alexander I's focus on the necessity of reforming Russia soon shifted to advocating for imposing order in the rest of Europe. Engineering the Holy Alliance of European Christian monarchs to restore conservatism, Alexander I's enthusiasm for reforms faded for Russia.

Recognizing this, political societies critical of the regime soon emerged, organizing secretly. Those who had fought in the war—specifically young officers from elite families—could not easily return to life as it had been. Although having been raised to see both peasants and serfs as morally and intellectually inferior, the officers had fought alongside the peasants and serfs, and discovered a common humanity and nation. "We had taken part in the greatest events of history," one veteran wrote, "and it was unbearable to . . .

listen to the idle chatter of old men about the so-called virtues of the past. We had to advance a hundred years" (Figes 77). These groups discussed the troubles of the times and their hopes and plans for the future. "Did we free Europe," veterans of the war asked themselves, "in order to be ourselves placed in chains?" (Riha 299). Some groups contemplated assassinating the tsar, growing increasingly agitated when he granted a constitution to Poland in 1818, but continued to deny one to Russia.

In December 1825, Alexander I unexpectedly died and left the line of succession uncertain. Taking advantage of confusion about which of his two younger brothers would and should be crowned tsar, two groups of officers, in St. Petersburg and rural Ukraine, seized the opportunity to revolt. These men, later known as the Decembrists, demanded a constitutional government and an end to serfdom. "The people have conceived a sacred truth," one later explained "that they do not exist for governments, but that governments must be organized for them" (Riha 296). Although it failed, the Decembrist "Revolution" was the first move against the autocracy and an event that resounded through Russian literature for many years thereafter.

Alexander's brother Nicholas I eventually took the throne. Personally investigating the rebellion and interrogating many of the participants, Nicholas I hoped to understand the Decembrists' grievances so as to better fortify his autocratic rule (Florinsky 754–55). He ordered the arrests of 500 Decembrists, of which over 100 were charged with treason and exiled to Siberia. Five of the ringleaders were condemned to death by hanging, despite the fact that the death penalty had been previously abolished (Figes 90). The government botched their executions and three of the five did not immediately die. "What a wretched country!" one of the still-living poignantly exclaimed. "They don't even know how to hang properly" (Figes 90).

In his manifesto of July 1826, Nicholas I painted the Decembrists as a "handful of monsters" whose ideas remained "incompatible with the ways and the character of the Russian people," arguing instead for the necessity of "gradual betterment, from above" (Florinsky 755). Yet this gradual betterment did not occur. Instead, he became known as the *Iron Tsar*. Nicholas I's reactionary beliefs, fear of chaos, and desire to preserve the autocracy proved fatal for reforms: "There is no doubt that serfdom, in its present form, is a flagrant evil which everyone realizes," Nicholas I said, "yet to attempt to remedy it now would be, of course, an evil even more disastrous" (Florinsky 755). He ordered his secret police, the Third Section, to report individuals' actions as well as their thoughts, using secret informers, in hopes of preventing anything like the Decembrists from forming again. Nicholas soon adopted Count Uvarov's ideological triad of *orthodoxy*, *autocracy*, and *nationality*. *Orthodoxy* referred to the people's religion as well as their common morality. *Autocracy* remained the only possible way of governance. *Nationality* looked back to the foundations of Russian society, largely as a conservative reaction to the threatening ideas emanating from Europe (Wachtel and Vinitsky 91).

In their attempt to preserve the autocracy, Nicholas I and his advisors froze progress in Russia for three decades (Riasanovsky, *History of Russia* 340). They believed their self-sufficient empire did not need change, proven by Russia's victory over Napoleon and its status as a great European power. To their view, rapid industrialization would fundamentally alter the Russian way of life and risk the empire's stability, so they chose to industrialize slowly. No railroad connected St. Petersburg and Moscow until 1851, lagging far behind the explosion of railroad construction in the rest of Europe (Crankshaw 67).

If Uvarov's "official nationality" claimed that history proved the centrality of autocracy and orthodoxy to Russia's survival, defining nationality or nationhood proved more difficult. The Russian Empire bestrode the European and Asian continents. Many in the Golden Age saw Russia as not fully a part of either, with consequences for Russia's historic destiny. In 1836, Peter Chaadaev published an essay that hit Russia like "a shot that rang out in a dark night; it forced all to awaken" (Riha 303). It explored the reasons for Russia's divergence from her European neighbors, claiming there was "something in our blood which repels all true progress" (Riha 306). He bemoaned that Russia constantly borrowed culture and ideas at the expense of Russian ones. "Alone of all of the peoples in the world, we have not given anything to the world, and we have not learned anything from the world. . . . We have contributed nothing to the progress of the human spirit, we have disfigured it" (Riha 306). The intensity of Chaadaev's message reverberated throughout Russia, sparking great debates and intensifying the desire for reform. In response, Nicholas I ordered that Chaadaev be declared insane.

Chaadaev's jeremiad stimulated controversy, eventually devolving into two opposing camps known as the Slavophiles and the Westernizers. Chaadaev believed that, by subscribing to Orthodoxy, Russia had rejected the historical unity embodied by the Catholic Church, divorcing itself from the shared tradition and creativity of Christian Europe. The Slavophiles bristled against Chaadaev's accusations. They argued for the merits of Russia's unique culture and Orthodox history. The Slavophiles characterized the Western influence as dangerous to Russia, believing that it would cause a "spiritual breakdown" and undermine society (Offord 25). Westernizers opposed the Slavophiles, believing them to be backward and superstitious. They instead claimed that Russia could only advance through the absorption of European culture, technology, and ideas.

Although Nicholas I's rule was increasingly repressive and stagnant, literature managed to flourish. As one writer would later explain, it became the "only outlet for their aspirations, hopes, doubts, resentments, and anger" (Terras 170). Other art forms, such as music, art, ballet, theatre, and opera, all thrived and often incorporated new written works into their productions. Yet the notion of Russian "society" is misleading in that only a very small minority lived in urban areas and 90 percent of the population were peasants. Literature did, however, become an important tool in the endeavor to incorporate the common man into national discourse, as intellectuals and veterans of the war argued that laws and literature should be written in a "language every citizen can understand," regardless of social status or education (Figes 83).

For anyone hoping to understand Russia's present, it was necessary to understand the past. N. M. Karamzin, commissioned by the Tsar as the national historian, published his twelve-volume *History of the Russian State*, selling over three thousand copies in its first month. Karamzin's work "saved Russia from an invasion of forgetting," wrote Petr Viazemsky, a relative of the war's hero, General Kutuzov. It had "called her to life, and showed us that our fatherland is truly the place many of us discovered in 1812" (Wachtel and Vinitsky 79). Karamzin's work became Russia's main historical narrative as well as a declaration of national pride. This publication greatly affected literary developments, for Karamzin's richly detailed passages motivated writers and artists to explore their country's past as inspiration for their own work.

Soon after the publication of Karamzin's history, Alexander Pushkin published his first great poem, *Ruslan and Ludmila*. At the time, a great chasm existed between spoken and written Russian. Unlike written French or English, literary Russian remained "bookish and obscure," isolated from the spoken language of high society or of the common man (Figes 50). Furthermore, since the time of Catherine the Great, the aristocracy and the elites spoke mainly in French, not in Russian. Yet in this great work, Pushkin embraced the styles and tales of Russian folklore and fashioned a poem suitable for any literate person, no matter his or her social status. Experimenting with language, subject matter, and style in his works, Pushkin shaped the modern Russian literary language. He, along with other writers of the time, endeavored to create new Russian words instead of relying on foreign imports (Figes 51).

At the same time, rising social discontent complicated the relationship between literature and the state. Many prominent authors of the Golden Age served the state in some capacity, whether as military officers or civil servants, yet this did not prevent them from questioning the social and political order in their written works. Strict government control over newspapers and other publications meant that alternative forms of literature became a vehicle for great societal debates, leading to the characterization of literature as a sort of secular saint for its ability to critique the government. As Wachtel and Vinitsky have noted, literature "did not merely reflect social and political reality, it frequently created social and political reality" (6). This new interaction among society, politics, and literature generated the circumstances for the dramatic surge in literary production during the Golden Age.

Simultaneously, an expanding educated class meant a growing literate consumer base. Now, an artist or a writer might feasibly make a living solely on his or her artistic talent—and Pushkin became one of the first to do so (Figes 79). During the 1830s, many authors published their works in "thick" journals, which printed novels in serial installments as well as shorter prose pieces and poetry (Terras 169). Considered one of the first Russian authors to incorporate realist elements into his work, Pushkin depicted life as it truly was, with all of its beauty, tragedies, humor, and difficulties (Riasanovsky, *History of Russia* 356). One of Pushkin's premier works, *Eugene Onegin* [*Евгений Онегин, Yevgeny Onegin*], was described by a literary critic as "an encyclopedia of Russian life," for the ways in which it aptly described and explored all aspects. (Falen xxii).

Pushkin, however, was not alone in his literary genius. Others, many of whom came to prominence after Pushkin's death, are discussed in greater detail in later chapters of the present volume. Their works examined contentious issues, such as the fate of serfdom, Russia's nature, its future, society, politics, and the place of women. Gogol was the first author to recognize literature's potential as a tool for social progress (Terras 191). His play *The Inspector* [*Ревизор, Revizor*], published in 1836, mocked governmental corruption in provincial Russia while his *Dead Souls* [*Мертвые души, Mortvye dushi*], first published in 1842, greatly satirized Russian life by examining its flaws. The literature of the Golden Age evolved into a forum, in which people debated the significant issues of the time. Paradoxically, the repressive and reactionary nature of Nicholas' reign allowed for such revolutionary growth in literature. Moreover, this literature repeatedly raised complicated issues facing the Russian Empire, such as serfdom. While the government considered these questions to be serious concerns, it preferred not to address them. Literature kept drawing attention to these key matters.

The legacy of Nicholas I's role in suppressing the Decembrists uprising soon played out in European affairs. Revolutions erupted across Europe in 1848, coinciding with the publication of Marx and Engels' *The Communist Manifesto.* Nicholas I, having been so victorious in squashing revolt right as he took the throne, believed he could aid European powers in also doing so (Lincoln 47). "For a long time now only two real forces have existed in Europe— revolution and Russia," author Fyodor Tyutchev penned in April 1848. "No negotiations, no treaties are possible between them; the existence of one of them means the death of the other!" (Riasanovsky, *Nicholas I* 123). Nicholas I presented Russia's robust autocracy as the only solution for containing such unrest. He even contributed funds and troops to preserve the status quo in Europe, intervening in revolutionary Hungary in 1849, for example. Nicholas I became a "compulsive meddler" in European affairs, culminating disastrously with the Crimean War (Crankshaw 119).

Nicholas I's reign saw a dramatic expansion of the Russian Empire, both in landmass and in increasing influence in the European sphere. Nicholas I believed himself to be bequeathed with the duty—and authority—to protect the Christians living in the predominately Muslim Ottoman Empire. Perceiving the Ottoman Empire to be the "sick man of Europe," Nicholas I advocated for increasing Russian influence. Yet his intentions provoked outrage by the Ottoman Turks, British, French, and Austrians, leading to war beginning in 1853 despite the fact that "all parties hoped that something would happen to inhibit the war" (Crankshaw 132). This war's consequences resonated deeply throughout the Russian Empire and Europe throughout the latter half of the nineteenth century. Russia's defeat caused it to be "seen for what it was," Marshall Poe writes, "a backward agriculture empire in the dawn of the industrial era" (Poe 74).

The Crimean War powerfully illuminated many of the fundamental flaws of the Russian Empire that writers had addressed previously, and with which they continued to struggle. Russia's loss posed a great challenge to the Iron Tsar's rule. Trounced by European nations, who had long since abandoned serfdom and embraced industrialization, Russia's rulers could no longer claim the superiority of their system, as they had after the defeat of Napoleon in 1812. "The main trouble with Nicholas I's reign," a former serf later wrote, "was that the whole thing was a mistake" (Nikitenko 190). It became apparent to all that Russia would have to industrialize and emancipate the serfs if the nation was to regain its international stature. These debates regarding serfs in Russia occurred alongside those about slaves in the United States. "Negroes on the plantations," one Russian wrote, "are happier than many of the landlords' peasants" (Dukes 125).

Nicholas I died in 1855 while the war still raged in the Crimea and his son, Alexander II, succeeded him. Although Nicholas acknowledged the evils of serfdom, his overriding fear of disorder caused by change had made substantial reforms impossible. Alexander II, whose coronation occurred on the anniversary of the Battle of Borodino, adopted a new style of rule and initiated a barrage of reforms. These changes fundamentally altered the nature of the legal codes, the military, education, and permitted the beginnings of local self-governance (Wachtel and Vinitsky 114). His most influential and sweeping reform was the emancipation of the serfs in 1861.

It remains unclear why Alexander II embarked on such extensive reforms. One of the possibilities highlights the status of Russian literature as a mechanism for change. This explanation details how Ivan Turgenev's 1852 *Notes of a Hunter* [Записки охотника, *Zapiski okhotnika*], which beautifully portrays the humanity of the serfs and the brutality of the system, affected Alexander II so deeply that he resolved to emancipate the serfs (Wachtel and Vinitsky 114). At the time, serfs and their families comprised "four-fifths of the total population": the nobility owned half, while the state or the church owned the other half (Crankshaw 168). Russia's defeat in the Crimean War painfully revealed that the previous ways of government, serfdom, and industrialization could no longer serve them. As a comparison, emancipation in the United States liberated approximately four million slaves while Russia's freed fifty-two million people; for many people, this radical transformation did not occur without substantial challenges. It was a logistical nightmare with very real consequences, often leading to "misery, despair, and anger" (Riasanovsky, *History of Russia* 372–73). Ultimately, Alexander II's reforms remained insufficient to address all of the problems facing the Empire.

The "Tsar-Liberator's" reign marked a departure from the harsher and more restrictive legislation of Nicholas I, allowing for greater freedom in publishing. The search for a national identity, arising from the 1812 war, only grew in fervor in the 1860s and 1870s. The ranks of Russia's intelligentsia—a loosely formed group of individuals that protested the state in various ways as a "critically thinking minority"—began to steadily increase in both size and influence (Offord 45). Yet the advent of some reforms fueled the people's desire for further reforms. The number and intensity of peasant revolts grew, as did the prevalence of revolutionary groups. A string of suspicious fires burned in St. Petersburg and other nearby areas and soon Poland, a part of the Russian Empire, rebelled in 1863 (Riasanovsky, *History of Russia* 379). It was in this decade of revolutionary ferment and increasing demands for change that truly great works of literature were published, such as Turgenev's *Fathers and Sons* [*Отцы и дети, Otsy i deti*, 1862], Dostoevsky's *Crime and Punishment* [*Преступление и наказание, Prestuplenie i nakazanie,* 1866], and Tolstoy's *War and Peace* [*Война и мир, Vojna i mir*, 1869]. Nikolai Chernyshevsky wrote his novel, *What Is To Be Done?* [*Что делать? Chto delat'?*, 1863] from prison, proposing female emancipation and a provocative blueprint for Russia's future.

Turgenev's novel illustrated the generational split between the "fathers" of the 1840s and their "sons" of the 1860s. These sons became characterized as "nihilists." A bit of a misnomer, the nihilists did not believe in nothing, as traditionally associated with this term, but rather "placed great faith in science as the key to the world and a panacea for its problems" (Offord 61). Nihilists strongly believed in personal freedom, whereas an alternate movement, populism, found solace in the unity of the Russian people. The populists, who became an important force in the 1870s, believed that by "going to the people," they would discover Russia's true national identity in the virtues of the peasants and their communal society—and that these particular qualities would serve as a model to change the rest of society (Riasanovsky, *History of Russia* 382).

During this time, the pendulum between reform and reactionary measures frequently swung back and forth as society grappled with major changes in a very short period of time. Intense debates about Russia's future continued in literature, particularly because the emancipation, while a great boon for human rights, had tremendous economic and societal implications. The year 1877 marked the beginning of Russia's tenth war against Turkey since 1676 (Crankshaw 241). This war, grim and expensive, ended with a victorious Russia, yielding the acquisition of territory in the Caucasus, in addition to greater expansion of the empire into Central Asia and the Far East unrelated to the war (Riasanovsky, *History of Russia* 387–90). Revolutionary activity in Russia escalated, primarily embodied by the Populist Land and Freedom Movement and its revolutionary rival, the People's Will [народная воля, *narodnaja volja*]. After at least seven unsuccessful attempts, the People's Will assassinated Alexander II on March 13, 1881 (Dukes 154). His son, Alexander III, succeeded him. Understandably, the assassination of his father was a great personal loss to Alexander III, and he came to believe that the people had thanked his father, the Tsar-Liberator, for his reforms by killing him. In return, Alexander III staunchly advocated strong monarchical power, rejecting the efforts to accommodate educated society that had begun in his father's reign. Shortly after taking the throne in 1881, he declared, "Constitution? Is the tsar of Russia supposed to take an oath to a bunch of cattle?" (Chernukha 364). Later, he proclaimed, in a letter to his brother, that he would "never permit limitations on autocratic rule" (Chernukha 357). Dissatisfaction with the nature of Alexander III's rule became increasingly widespread in elite society. Two famines and a cholera epidemic occurred under Alexander III's rule, challenging the authority of a regime claiming to make Russia a respected and powerful presence in the modern world. "From 1891 on," historian Richard Robbins writes, "the Tsar's government faced a crescendo of criticism and opposition which would culminate first in the revolution of 1905 and then in the total collapse of 1917" (Robbins 176).

In the face of a political regime that purposefully complicated change and advancement, literature again became the primary medium for discussing the nation's fate. "Literature," as one Russian critic wrote, ". . . is a reflection of society," exposing its flaws and provoking conversation (Antonovich 90). It is in this way that a writer's work might influence the direction of a nation, helping to define it and reveal how it might navigate the future. The Golden Age stands out for its unparalleled surge of literary production in response to politics, thus creating a literary canon that still resonates for people today, both within and beyond Russia's borders. "My country is not Russia," one man wrote at the end of the Golden Age. "My country is Russian literature" (Crankshaw 94).

Works Cited

Antonovich, M. A. "Literaturnyj krizis." *Sovermennik* 94:2 (February 1863): 81-110. *Google Book Search.* Web. 14 Oct. 2013.

Billington, James H. *The Icon and the Axe: An Interpretive History of Russian Culture.* 2nd ed. New York: Knopf, 1967.

Chernukha, V. G. "Emperor Alexander III, 1881–1894." *Emperors and Empresses of Russia: Rediscovering the Romanovs.* Ed. Donald J. Raleigh and Akhmed Akhmedovich Iskenderov. Armonk, NY: M.E. Sharpe, 1996. 334–368.

Cracraft, James. *The Revolution of Peter the Great.* Cambridge, MA.: Harvard UP, 2003.

Crankshaw, Edward. *The Shadow of the Winter Palace: Russia's Drift to Revolution, 1825–1917.* 1976. Reprint. New York: De Capo Press, 2000.

Dukes, Paul. *A History of Russia c. 882–1996.* 3rd ed. Durham, NC: Duke UP, 1998.

Falen, James E. Introduction. *Eugene Onegin: A Novel in Verse.* By Alexander Pushkin. Trans. James E. Falen. Oxford, UK: Oxford UP, 1995. *Google Book Search.* Web. 4 Oct. 2013.

Figes, Orlando. *Natasha's Dance: A Cultural History of Russia.* New York: Metropolitan Books, 2002.

Florinsky, Michael T. *Russia: A History and an Interpretation.* 1953. New York: Macmillan, 1965.

Lieven, Dominic. "Russia and the Defeat of Napoleon (1812–14)." *Kritika: Explorations in Russian and Eurasian History* 7.2 (Spring 2006): 283–308. *Project Muse.* Web. 10 Jan. 2012.

Maguire, Robert. Introduction. *Gogol from the Twentieth Century: Eleven Essays.* Princeton, NJ: Princeton UP, 1974. *Google Book Search.* Web. 15 Oct. 2013.

Massie, Suzanne. *Land of the Firebird: The Beauty of Old Russia.* 1980. Reprint. New York: Simon and Schuster, 2004.

Milner-Gulland, Robin and Nikolai Dejevsky. *Cultural Atlas of Russia and the Soviet Union.* 2nd ed. New York: Facts On File Publications, 1998.

Nikitenko, Aleksandr. *The Diary of a Russian Censor.* Trans. Helen Saltz Jacobson. Amherst, MA: U of Massachusetts P, 1975.

Offord, Derek. *Nineteenth-Century Russia: Opposition to Autocracy.* New York: Pearson Education, 1999.

Poe, Marshall. *The Russian Moment in World History.* Princeton, NJ: Princeton UP, 2003.

Riasanovsky, Nicholas V. *A History of Russia.* 4th ed. New York: Oxford UP, 1984.

Riasanovsky, Nicholas V. *Nicholas I and Official Nationality in Russia, 1825–55.* Berkley, CA: U of California P, 1859. *Google Book Search.* Web. 1 Oct. 2013.

Riha, Thomas. *Readings in Russian Civilization, Volume II: Imperial Russia, 1700–1917.* Chicago: U of Chicago P, 1964.

Robbins, Richard G. *Famine in Russia: 1891–1892: The Imperial Government Responds to A Crisis.* New York: Columbia UP, 1975.

Rzhevsky, Nicholas. *An Anthology of Russian Literature from Earliest Writings to Modern Fiction: Introduction to a Culture.* Armonk, NY: M.E. Sharpe, 1996.

Terras, Victor. *A History of Russian Literature.* New Haven: Yale UP, 1991.

Troitskii, Nikolai Alekseevich. "The Great Patriotic War of 1812: A History of the Subject." *Russian Studies in History* 32.1 (Summer 1993): 6–7. *Metapress M.E. Sharpe Inc.* Web. 24 Sept. 2013.

Wachtel, Andrew and Ilya Vinitsky. *Russian Literature.* Cambridge, MA: Polity, 2009.

Wortman, Richard. *Scenarios of Power: Myth and Ceremony in Russian Monarchy.* Princeton, NJ: Princeton UP, 2006.

How a Canon Is Made: A Critical Response to Russia's Golden Age Literature _____

Katya Jordan

The concept of Russia's Golden Age is retrospective in its essence, for it is only when we look back at the period in question that we can truly determine its significance in the development of Russian literature. The authors, whose contributions will be discussed in this chapter, were familiar with Russia's literary past and built on it, but aside from their own literary tastes and creative inclinations, they had to be aware of the response that their writing inspired in their contemporaries. Whether the authors took that response to heart or chose to disregard it, literary criticism was an integral part of cultural life in nineteenth-century Russia. Furthermore, the criticism that was published after the end of the nineteenth century continued to shape the Russian literary canon. What is offered in this chapter is a collection of some of the most influential or otherwise informative statements made by professional critics and writers regarding what is now known as the Golden Age of Russian Literature.

Pushkin

In 1815, while still a student at The Imperial Lyceum, Pushkin drew the attention of Gavrila Derzhavin, Russia's greatest poet of the eighteenth century who, already quite aged at that time, recognized in the young Alexander a talented poet and proclaimed, "I am not dead! This is who will replace me!" Pushkin was continuously praised for the lucidity of his style and for the liveliness of his verse. Although he wrote increasingly more prose towards the end of his life, he is nonetheless best known and loved for his poetry.

In 1837, immediately after Pushkin's tragic death, the critic Vissarion Belinsky confessed that he couldn't articulate his full understanding of the magnitude of Pushkin's talent; however, in 1849, he wrote that Pushkin "expressed and exhausted by himself the entire depth of Russian life, and into his wounds we can insert our fingers in order to feel the pain of our own wounds and to heal them. His poetry is our redemption" (qtd. in Mashinskii 351).

By contrast, roughly a decade later, another critic, Nikolay Dobroliubov, accused Pushkin of lacking the popular spirit and of being unfamiliar with the life of the Russian people. In Dobroliubov's opinion, Pushkin was a true aristocrat who stood above the interests of the ordinary folk. Another progressive critic, Dmitry Pisarev, believed that Pushkin's novel in verse *Evgenii Onegin* (1823–1831) was "nothing but a brilliant and sparkling apotheosis of a most joyless and senseless *status quo*" ("Pushkin and Belinsky" 55). Pisarev asked, "what human suffering did Pushkin manage to observe and consider necessary to carol?" (55). He answered his own question: "First of all, boredom or melancholy; secondly unrequited love; and thirdly ... and thirdly ... nothing at all. Apparently no other forms of suffering existed in Russian society in the 1820s" (55).

Pushkin's fellow writers, regardless of their own literary styles and concerns, almost unanimously praised Pushkin's work. Nikolay Gogol called Pushkin "an extraordinary phenomenon," "a Russian national poet," in whom "can be found, as if in a lexicon, all the rich diversity, strength and sensibility of [the Russian] language" (1). In Ivan Turgenev's opinion, "Pushkin's independent genius ... quickly freed itself both from the imitation of European examples and from the temptation to hide under a purely Russian form" ("Pushkin" 65). And Fyodor Dostoevsky noted that this poet appeared exactly at the time when the Russians "were beginning to achieve a sense of self-awareness ... which was born a whole century after the reforms of Peter the Great" and that Pushkin's appearance "helped to cast a bright and guiding light on to the dark road before [them]. In this sense, Pushkin is both a prophet and a guiding star" ("Pushkin" 73).

Later, Soviet critics, for the most part, sided with Belinsky and praised Pushkin for the innovative way of depicting the Cossacks, the Russian peasants, and the Caucasians. But perhaps the most succinct description of Pushkin's controversial talent has been articulated by A.D.P. Briggs, who described Pushkin as "a series of paradoxes," "a chatterbox with serious things to say, a simpleman of great complexity, a delightful entertainer who not infrequently touches on tragedy (xix). Pushkin's work "will provide the light-minded reader with quick entertainment, the scholar with niceties of style, and the committed amateur of good literature with an endearing and dependable source of cultural enrichment" (xix). Thus, Pushkin still enjoys the status of Russia's national poet and has retained his place at the very center of the Golden Age of Russian Literature.

Lermontov

Mikhail Lermontov was Pushkin's younger contemporary and remained a prominent poet despite the fact that, after Pushkin's death, the Russian literature of the nineteenth century made a gradual shift towards prose. Belinsky wrote in 1839:

> A new powerful talent has appeared in Rus' – Lermontov … Such imagery! – you see everything in front of you, and having seen once, you will never forget it! A marvelous picture – everything shimmers with all the brightness of oriental colors! Such vividness, musicality, power and strength in every individual verse. (qtd. in Gillelson 300)

In the late 1850s, Alexander Gertsen noted the personal quality that imbued all of Lermontov's writing: "His works are always a truthful expression of what was experienced deeply and felt fully, always an internal necessity, brought about by some situation, some special impulse" (qtd. in Gillelson 136).

Lermontov's most notable prose work was his 1840 novel *A Hero of Our Time*. Its initial publication was poorly received. The novel's protagonist, an officer Pechorin, inspired much controversy. His apparent egotism and insensitivity lead some critics to view him as a sick creation of the writer's mind and others as Lermontov's self-portrait. Following a personal conversation with the author, Belinsky observed that Lermontov was a marvelous person, "Pechorin himself," with a cool and embittered view on life and people, yet possessing seeds of deep faith in the nobility of both (Gillelson 310).

Vladimir Nabokov thus summarized the essence of the debates regarding Lermontov's literary contribution:

What matters is that this very young, arrogant, not overeducated man, mixing with people who did not care a fig for literature, somehow managed, during the short period granted him by the typically perverse destiny which haunts geniuses, to produce verse and prose of such virility, beauty, and tenderness that the following generation placed him higher than Pushkin. ("The Lermontov Mirage" 31)

Boris Eikhenbaum insisted that, in order to accurately evaluate Lermontov's work, critics must look at it historically. Eikhenbaum argued that Lermontov's task was to discover a certain poetic style that was needed specifically in the 1820s in order to "provide a way out of the poetic impasse" that became palpable at that time (*Lermontov* 13). Although he did not create anything new, Lermontov provided a "reconciliation and summation of results [of] the struggle between the various poetic tendencies" (13).

The Romantic quality of Lermontov's fiction appealed to Soviet critics in the twentieth century, who saw in it an attempt to balance the pathos of strife with the reality of life, and a lack of faith in humanity with a thirst for human interaction (Golovanova 4). In the 1930s, Lermontov's verses about the Caucasus became a source of inspiration for contemporary poets, and during the Great Patriotic War, Lermontov's "Borodino," a poem about the defeat of Napoleon, was especially valued (5).

Gogol

Nikolay Gogol's first work, the 1829 narrative poem *Hans Kuechelgarten*, caused critics to wonder what possessed a publisher to ever make it available to the reading public. Following the initial failure, Gogol wisely switched his attention to prose. Over time, three main approaches to his work have emerged: the realist, the religious, and the aesthetic (de Jonge 70). Belinsky spearheaded the realist approach. He praised Gogol for celebrating the lowly and the downtrodden while condemning the wealthy and the idle representatives of Russian society; however, Belinsky was disappointed when, in the late 1840s, Gogol turned away from denouncing the authoritarian regime and began writing works that seemed to support it, such as an 1847 collection of essays titled

Selected Passages from Correspondence with Friends. The same year that the collection was published, Belinsky wrote an open letter to Gogol in which he called him "a preacher of the knout, an apostle of ignorance, a champion of obscurantism" ("Pis'mo Gogoliu" 501).

Dmitry Merezhkovsky formulated the religious approach. Gogol himself once wrote in a private letter that his "sole concern has long been that after [his] work people should have a good hearty laugh at the Devil" (qtd. in Merezhkovsky, "Gogol and the Devil" 57). This desire, combined with the nineteenth-century Russian intelligentsia's interest in spiritualism, lead Merezhkovsky to conclude that:

> [i]n Gogol's religious outlook, the Devil is a mystical essence and a real being, in which eternal evil, a denial of God, has been concentrated. Gogol the artist investigates the nature of the mystical essence in the light of laughter; Gogol the man contends with this real being using laughter as a weapon: Gogol's laughter is man's struggle with the Devil. (57)

The third approach, the aesthetic, was formulated in the twentieth century by Andrey Bely, and later elaborated on by the Formalists. Boris Eikhenbaum observed that the structure of Gogol's fictional text "is not determined by plot at all, but only some comic situation … serving, as it were, merely as an impetus or pretext for the elaboration of comic devices" ("How Gogol's Overcoat is Made" 270). A special place within the fictional text is allotted to *skaz*, a first-person narration full of colloquial expressions that conveys a particular character's persona.

Early Soviet critics believed that Gogol's tragedy was due to the fact that he was "both a Romantic and a Realist" (Strong 530). In the 1950s, however, a stronger statement was produced by the critic Ermilov, who wrote: "Gogol is our great ally in the struggle to oppose with ruthless satire all the forces of darkness and hatred, all the forces hostile to peace on earth" (528).

Vladimir Nabokov, by contrast, saw in Gogol primarily a great narrator of invented stories. Of Gogol's novel *Dead Souls*, Nabokov said that "Gogol's heroes merely happen to be Russian squires and officials" and that their prototypes "underwent such a thorough permutation and reconstruction in the laboratory of Gogol's peculiar genius" that one cannot tell what they used to be and where they used to live originally (*Lectures* 15).

Dostoevsky

From the very beginning of his writing career, Dostoevsky was hailed as a genius. Having read Dostoevsky's first work, the short novel *Poor Folk* of 1846, Belinsky exclaimed: "Honor and glory to the young poet whose Muse loves people in garrets and basements and tells the inhabitants of gilded palaces: 'look, they are also men, they are also your brethren'" (qtd. in Wellek 1). Yet only two weeks later, Belinsky was disappointed when he read Dostoevsky's short novel *The Double*, since it was excessively fantastic for the critic's taste.

Towards the end of the nineteenth century, two interpretations of Dostoevsky's writing emerged. The philosopher Vladimir Solovyov considered Dostoevsky to be a seer and a prophet for the Russian people. This approach was elaborated a number of years later when, also focusing on the spiritual power of Dostoevsky's writing, Dmitry Merezhkovsky and Lev Shestov saw in it a prediction of apocalypse and an attempt to establish a new, antirationalist religion (Wellek 4).

On the contrary, the liberal critic Nikolay Mikhailovsky saw in Dostoevsky a sadist and an expounder of the human vice. Mikhailovsky agreed that "the broader the artist, the more precious" he is to the reading public, yet he was convinced that "one ought not to demand that a poet should depict with equal force and truth the sensations of a wolf devouring a sheep and of the sheep being devoured by the wolf" (186).

Maxim Gorky later helped to formulate a third approach. A few years before the Russian Revolution, Gorky admitted that Dostoevsky "is a genius, but an evil genius of ours." In 1934, he reiterated: "[T]he genius of Dostoevsky is unquestionable. His talent of artistic portrayal is perhaps equal to that of Shakespeare. But as far as his personality is concerned, as a 'judge of the world and the people,' one can very easily see him in the role of a middle-age inquisitor" (qtd. in Shneidman 524). In the 1950s, another prominent Soviet critic, A.V. Lunacharsky, conceded that it is only proper to familiarize oneself with Dostoevsky's works, "but it would be very shameful, and ... socially unbecoming, to fall under his influence" (qtd. in Shneidman 525). Although Mikhail Bakhtin offered a Formalist interpretation of Dostoevsky's works, according to which each voice in the narrative is independent and does not represent the author's ideological position (what he called "literary polyphony"), the official doctrine of Socialist Realism was incompatible with Dostoevsky's propensity to expose human psychology and to decry nihilism. Thus, although the reading of Dostoevsky was not forbidden in the Soviet Union, his humanitarian ideas were separated from and preferred to his thoughts on religion and spirituality.

Tolstoy

When comparing the two Russian literary giants, Daniil Granin observed that whereas "Dostoevsky helps us to grasp the impossibility of ever knowing man [and] shows us how unfathomable man is ... how much there is in him that is contradictory and beyond understanding," Lev Tolstoy, on the other hand, "helps us to understand man; he shows us the impulses in his nature, the sources his thoughts spring from. He guides us into the depths of his soul" (54). Indications of this deep insight were present already in Tolstoy's first work to be published, the novel *Childhood* of 1852. Upon reading it, Nikolay Nekrasov wrote to Tolstoy that its author "has talent" and that "the author's direction, simplicity and vigor of the content" are advantageous attributes of this work (551). Three years later, when Tolstoy's war story "Sevastopol in December" was published, Ivan Turgenev also stated that this work was a "marvel" and that he "wept while reading it and cried 'Hurrah!'" (*Letters* 92).

Not all response was positive, however. Some accused Tolstoy of failing to reconcile form and content, of using analysis to excess, of introducing irrelevant details, and of lacking ideas and direction (Sorokin 40). Nikolay Chernyshevsky, perhaps the most prominent radical literary critic of the day, called Tolstoy's 1957 novel *Youth* "a rotten product of the pure art school," but he entertained a hope that once Tolstoy began to focus more on social issues, his writing would improve (41). Chernyshevsky later conceded that the novelty of Tolstoy's style was largely due to the writer's ability to convey the stream of consciousness and to break down each feeling into its composite parts.

The Slavophiles and the *pochvenniki* were more tolerant of Tolstoy's ideas, especially when the writer turned his attention towards peasants. Still, Tolstoy's greatest novels—*War and Peace* (1869) and *Anna Karenina* (1873)—were problematic, and the writer's attempts to reveal the hidden parts of human nature left them unimpressed. N.N. Strakhov, for example, characterized *Anna Karenina* as a high-quality work on an inconsequential theme.

The aesthetics criticized Tolstoy for creating works that fit none of the already developed forms. Some of the Russian Symbolists, who came on the literary scene a little later, saw value in Tolstoy's powerful descriptions. Others, like Merezhkovsky, noted that Tolstoy's pursuit of greatness harmed the artistic quality of his prose: he was too explicit, and his descriptions drew too much attention to themselves (*L. Tolstoy i Dostoevskii* 137–8). It is these descriptions, however, that inspired Viktor Shklovsky to point out Tolstoy's use of *ostranenie*—the literary device that allowed the writer to present familiar things as something new and strange.

Mikhailovsky, a critic from the *narodniki* camp, quickly dispensed with Tolstoy's search for spiritual truths and focused on the social message of his writing. Tolstoy's deep interest in peasants somewhat redeemed him in the eyes of the radicals and the revolutionaries. In 1908, Vladimir Lenin even went as far as to call Lev Tolstoy "a mirror of the Russian Revolution." Maxim Gorky, who also subscribed to the Marxist approach to literature, recognized Tolstoy as a faithful chronicler of Russian life, if one is willing to ignore the religious digressions.

In the next few decades, after the revolutionary fervor had passed, critics began to adopt a more holistic approach to Tolstoy. As Sergey Bocharov noted, speaking of Tolstoy's writing, "psychological precision for an artist is not an end in itself" (7), but neither is a narrow and exclusive focus on social forces at work.

Turgenev

Ivan Turgenev began his literary career in 1847 with the publication of stories in Nekrasov's journal *Sovremennik*. In 1852, these stories came out as a collection titled *A Sportsman's Sketches* (1852) and immediately advanced Turgenev to the forefront of Russian literary life. As Dmitry Mirsky noted in 1926, Turgenev's "consistent presentation of the serf as a being, not only human, but superior in humanity to his masters, made the book a loud protest against the system of serfdom" (195). By some accounts, the *Sketches* helped to prepare both Tsar Alexander II and the public in general for the abolition of serfdom.

To some extent, Turgenev's popularity is explained by the fact that his art appealed to various tastes: "It painted life as it was, and chose for its subjects the most burning problems of the day. It was full of truth and, at the same time, of poetry and beauty. It satisfied Left and Right" (195). Yet the appeal of Turgenev's later works was not universal. Regarding the novel *Fathers and Children* (1862), Pisarev wrote that, although artistically the novel is quite satisfactory, it had neither a turning point nor a denouement, but only character types and scenes through which the author's personal sentiment can be seen ("Bazarov" 153). The novel's defect, therefore, was in the fact that it conveyed the vision of the fathers and failed to show the worldview of the children.

European critics were favorably impressed by Turgenev's work. In his last article, titled "Ivan Turgenev" of 1868, Prosper Mérimée observed that "[t]he name of Ivan Turgenev in our days is very popular in France … Turgenev is called one of the leaders of the Realistic school" (Qtd. in Grigor'ev, 41). Also writing from abroad, Vladimir Nabokov observed that *Fathers and Sons* specifically "is not only the best of Turgenev's novels, it is one of the most brilliant novels of the nineteenth century"; however, Nabokov noted, "there was a common debility about Turgenev's nature and art: he was incapable of making his masculine characters triumph within the existence he invents for them" (*Lectures* 71).

Soviet critics also noticed the lack of resolve in Turgenev's characters, and although the writer was recognized as a classic, readers had to be aware of the fundamental ideological insufficiency in Turgenev's works. Lunacharsky called Turgenev "a penitent nobleman," affirming that the rule of the Soviet reading public was "not to disregard any of the gifts from the past" and that what Turgenev's art had to offer was "sometimes useful for a more nuanced understanding of the past and of the disappeared classes, dying varieties of culture that with various threads, negative and positive, are connected with our 'today' and our 'tomorrow'" (132).

Today, Turgenev is viewed as a classical Russian writer whose descriptions of nature remain unsurpassed and in whose works lyricism and realism blend seamlessly to convey a portrait of declining Russian gentry.

Chekhov

Anton Chekhov once expressed his own attitude towards criticism in a letter to his brother: "Solitude in creativity is a painful thing. Bad criticism is better than none..." (*PSS* 19:95). He was still a medical student at Moscow University when he started to publish his works. The first collection of his stories, *Melpomene's Tales* of 1884, was successful, and his second book, *Variegated Stories* of 1886, made Chekhov quite popular, albeit controversial (Kuzicheva 271).

Yet some of Chekhov's readers had trouble identifying the genre of his stories and dismissed them as rubbish. Others saw the promise of talent in this new writer. The third group was cautiously curious. The most perceptive readers, mostly artists, writers, composers, and art connoisseurs, recognized that Chekhov gave them a new, active role in the reading process— they were given the task of deciphering the motivation of the characters' actions, the author's worldview, the conflict, and its resolution (273).

Chekhov's initial experiments in drama were unsuccessful. Two of his short stories were transformed into one-act plays in 1887–1889, but Chekhov was dissatisfied with the results. In 1896,

Chekhov's play *The Seagull* was staged in St. Petersburg. This production was a failure, unappreciated either by the audience or the critics. The play was restaged two years later in the Moscow Art Theater, where Chekhov's quest for a new form was realized by the vision of Konstantin Stanislavsky and Vladimir Nemirovich-Danchenko. The three plays that followed were also well received and are staged to this day.

Yet reactions to Chekhov's works continued to be controversial. In 1905, Innokentii Annenskii confessed that he did not like Chekhov's works because "there is no soul" in them and because Chekhov's "is a dry mind, and he wanted to kill Dostoevsky in us" (460). Lev Tolstoy, despite his own dislike for Chekhov's liberal views, admired Chekhov's stories for their deep insight. And Vladimir Posse, a journalist and a revolutionary activist, having read Chekhov's story "In the Ravine" (1900), commented: "What a pitiless, what an ominous truthfulness! There is not the slightest searching for effects yet the impression is tremendous, penetrating the soul and continuing to grow gradually even after one has finished reading" (*PSS*, 26:271). The Marxists accused Chekhov of aimlessness and a lack of commitment to socialist ideology. Over the years, however, the Russian critics began to agree that Chekhov, just like Tolstoy, sought to depict the truth "without omissions or reservations, evasiveness or timidity" (Lakshin 149).

Works Cited

Annenskii, Innokentii. *Knigi otrazhenii*. Eds. B. F. Egorov and A. V. Fedorov. Moskva: Nauka, 1979.

Belinskii, V.G. "Pis'mo Aksakovu K.S." 14 iiunia 1840. *N.V. Gogol v vospominaniiakh sovremennikov*. Ed. S.I. Mashinkii. Moskva: Khudozhestvennaia literatura, 1952.

Bocharov, S. *Roman L. Tolstogo "Voina i mir."* Moskva: Khudozhestvennaia literatura, 1987.

Briggs, A D. P. *Alexander Pushkin: A Celebration of Russia's Best-Loved Writer*. London: Hazar, 1999.

Chekhov, Anton Pavlovich. *Polnoe sobranie sochinenii v tridtsati tomakh*. Vols. 19 and 26. Moskva: Nauka, 1974.

Chernyshevskii, N.G. "Rasskazy grafa L.N. Tolstogo." *L.N. Tolstoi v russkoi kritike*. Ed. S.P. Bychkov. Moskva: Khudozhestvennaia literatura, 1952. 105–112.

Gogol, N.V. "A Few Words on Pushkin." *Russian Views of Pushkin*. Eds. D.J. Richards and Roger Cockrell. Oxford, UK: W.A. Meeuws, 1976. 1–6.

Dostoevsky, F.M. "Pushkin." *Russian Views of Pushkin*. Eds. D.J. Richards and Roger Cockrell. Oxford, UK: W.A. Meeuws, 1976. 73–88.

Eikhenbaum, B. "How Gogol's 'Overcoat' is Made." *Gogol from the Twentieth Century: Eleven Essays*. Ed. Robert A. Maguire. Princeton, NJ: Princeton UP, 1974. 269–291.

Eikhenbaum, B. *Lermontov: A Study in Literary-Historical Evaluation*. Ann Arbor, MI: Ardis, 1981.

Gillelson, M.I. and O.V. Miller, eds. *M.Iu. Lermontov v vospominaniiaskh sovremennikov*. Moskva: Khudozhestvennaia literatura, 1989.

Golovanova, T. P. *Nasledie Lermontova v sovetskoĭ poezii*. Leningrad: Nauka, 1978.

Granin, Daniil. "The Russian Perspective —100 Years Later." *Readings on Crime and Punishment*. Ed. Derek C. Maus. San Diego: Greenhaven Press, 2000. 53–8.

Grigor'ev, A.L. *Russkaia literatura v zarubezhnom literaturovedenii*. Leningrad: Nauka, 1977.

Jonge, A. de. "Gogol." *Nineteenth-Century Russian Literature: Studies of Ten Russian Writers*. Ed. John Lister Illingworth Fennell. Berkeley: U of California P, 1973. 69–129.

Kuzicheva, Alevtina. "'Breaking the Rules': Chekhov and His Contemporaries." *Chekhov Then and Now: The Reception of Chekhov in World Culture*. Ed. J.D. Clayton. New York: Peter Lang, 1997. 269–284.

Lakshin, V. *Tolstoy i Chekhov*. Moskva: Sovetskii pisatel', 1975.

Lunacharskii, A.V. *Stat'i o literature*. Moskva: Khudozhestvennaia literatura, 1988.

Mashinskii, Semen I. *Gogol' v vospominaniiakh sovremennikov*. Moskva: Khudozhestvennaia literatura, 1952.

Merezhkovsky, Dmitry S. and E A. Andrushchenko. *L. Tolstoi i Dostoevskii*. Moskva: Nauka, 2000.

Merezhkovsky, Dmitry. "Gogol and the Devil." *Gogol from the Twentieth Century: Eleven Essays*. Ed. Robert A. Maguire. Princeton, NJ: Princeton UP, 1974. 55–102.

Merezhkovskii, D.S. *L. Tolstoi i Dostoevskii. Vechnye sputniki*. Moskva: Respublika, 1995.

Mikhailovskii, N.K. "Zhestokii talant." *Polnoe sobrannie sochinenii F.M. Dostoevskogo*. Vols. II and III. Sankt-Peterburg: Tipografiia brat'ev Panteleevykh. 1889. 180–263.

Mirsky, D.S. *A History of Russian Literature*. New York: Vintage Russian Library, 1958.

Nabokov, Vladimir. "The Lermontov." *Russian Review* 1.1 (1941): 31–39.

Nabokov, Vladimir V. and Fredson Bowers. *Lectures on Russian Literature*. New York: Harcourt Brace Jovanovich/Bruccoli Clark, 1981.

Nekrasov N.A. "Pis'mo Tolstomy L.N." Seredina avgusta 1852. *L.N. Tolstoi russkoi kritike*. Ed. S.P. Bychkov. Moskva: Khudozhestvennaia literatura, 1952.

Pisarev, D.I. "Bazarov." *Izbrannye literaturno-kriticheskie stati*. Ed. L. A. Saveleva. Magadan: Magadanskoe knizhnoe izdael'stvo, 1973. 153–207.

Pisarev, D.I. "Pushkin and Belinsky." *Russian Views of Pushkin*. Eds. D.J. Richards and Roger Cockrell. Oxford, UK: W.A. Meeuws, 1976. 56–61.

Shneidman, N.N. "Soviet Theory of Literature and the Struggle Around Dostoevsky in Recent Soviet Scholarship." *Slavic Review* 34.3 (1975): 523–538.

Sorokin, Boris. *Tolstoy in Prerevolutionary Russian Criticism*. Columbus, OH: Ohio State UP for Miami University, 1979.

Turgenev, Ivan Sergeevich and David Allan Lowe. *Letters in Two Volumes*. Ann Arbor, MI: Ardis. 1983.

Turgenev. "Pushkin." *Russian Views of Pushkin*. Eds. D.J. Richards and Roger Cockrell. Oxford: W.A. Meeuws, 1976. 63–72.

Wellek, René. *Dostoevsky: A Collection of Critical Essays*. Englewood Cliffs, NJ: Prentice-Hall, 1962.

The Golden Age of Russian Poetry _____

Donald Rayfield

'Golden Ages' are recognized only in hindsight: not until the 1880s, when Russian poetry and prose seemed to be in the doldrums, did it become usual to refer to the age of Pushkin, and particularly to its poetry, as a Golden Age. When Russian poetry revived in the 1900s to create a Silver Age, the term implied the emulation of a Golden Age a century before. For our purposes, the Golden Age begins in 1813, with the surge of creative optimism that followed on Russia's defeat of Napoleon, reaches its climax in 1825 at the end of Alexander I's reign and persists until about 1845, when Nicholas I's censorship, the emergence of a wider readership and the triumph of prose gemes over verse marks the Age's demise. The Golden Age, inevitably, is studied as though it were a planetary system of poets revolving around Pushkin the Sun and, although the Golden Age marks the appearance of the first truly great works of prose fiction and verse comedy in Russian literature, we shall nevertheless here survey the age as primarily one of poetry, when lyric poets incorporated into an already established Russian verse canon all that European Neoclassicism and Romanticism could give, and gave poetry not just a proliferation of originality and musicality but a public importance that it would take many decades to regain.

The Golden Age built on the achievements of the eighteenth century in arriving at a literary language that could bridge the colloquial speech of educated Russians and the official Church Slavonic patois that had been cobbled together as the language of administration and commerce. Technical questions of poetic form, metre, rhyme had been solved by the middle of the eighteenth century. In its choice of geme (elegy, ode, fable and so on), however, the eighteenth century had been motivated primarily by the fact that poetry's main function was to be a response to patronage, its role as a court entertainment. The Golden Age moved away from gemes subservient to the state and the patron, such as the ode, and thus from the ruler as patron. As educated circles broadened, poets could find readers among their peers, even if the Russian reading public was still too small to make a poet, or any journal he or she published in, financially independent. The confidence of a poet that he was an autonomous being, even the romantic pretension to being an unacknowledged legislator of the world, was a precondition of the Golden Age.

The generation of young officers returning from the Napoleonic wars included two key poets in the first years of the Golden Age: Konstantin Batiushkov and Vasilii Zhukovsky. Those who sojourned in Paris and London brought with them not just the fruits of Romanticism, the verse of André Chénier, Walter Scott and Friedrich Schiller: they brought back the concept of a poet's independence. Those who did not fight but were educated in St Petersburg and Moscow did not lag behind. The *lycée* at Tsarskoe Selo, where so many poets were schooled, was staffed by many a survivor of the French Revolution or refugee from Napoleon, who gave their pupils a sense of history and an intellectual's role in shaping it. Moscow University numbered among its teachers such refugees as Baron Stein, future Foreign Minister of Prussia. The education of poets to come - who, by some enigmatic demographic wave, were born in unprecedented numbers in the late 1790s and early 1800s - was thus not just infused by printed examples of Romanticism and its beliefs in the primacy of nature, folk poetry, the rights of man and the power of art: it was stimulated by a living generation of revolutionaries, royalists and renegades. The one element of Romanticism that is strikingly absent in the poetry of Russia's Golden Age is the renewed Christianity that infuses so much English and French Romantic poetry. In this respect the Neoclassical and Voltairean eighteenth-century spirit remained undimmed.

The poetry of Konstantin Batiushkov (1787-1855) was the main bridge from the eighteenth century to the Golden Age. Batiushkov could write satire in the same mode as eighteenth-century radicals such as Radishchev; but his Neoclassicism went further, with his elegies which mourned not just the loss of life but the loss of love and of inspiration. First an officer in the Napoleonic wars, then a diplomatic official in Italy, Batiushkov saw in western Europe an Arcadia, from which he was very soon expelled. In his earlier verse he took plasticity of syntax and melodiousness of phonetic line further, emulating the virtues of the two main works of the unjustly neglected French hedonist and free-thinker Evariste Parny: *La Guerre des dieux* and *Les Déguisements de Vénus*. Without incorporating any new system of beliefs into his work, Batiushkov's extraordinary gift for cadences gives his work a deep melancholy which approximates it to Romantic 'spleen'. As disasters struck him - he was dismissed from the service, jilted by his fiancée, prone to more and more persistent bouts of clinical depression, Batiushkov's elegiac mood deepens: his poem of 1815, *The Shade of a Friend (Ten 'druga),* in which the ghost of a warrior companion appears during a journey at sea, has the Romantic conviction in the reality of the otherworldly which is to infuse the best of the Golden Age. Like his successors, however, Batiushkov was to discover that no Romantic beliefs in the numinous could overcome the tragic Hellenic outlook that Russian poets had inherited from their eighteenth-century predecessors. Batiushkov's light touch with the sounds of Russian, miraculously approximating it to Italian, was emulated by Pushkin. But by the time Pushkin had matured, Batiushkov was in an asylum, and the example of his melancholy was to act as a *memento mori* for the next decade of the Golden Age. Batiushkov's only partly demented *Imitations of the Ancients (Podrazhanie drevnim)* shows a remarkable synthesis of Hellenic pessimism and Romantic aspirations which is typical of the Golden Age: numbers 4 and 6 of the elegies run:

When the maiden departs in suffering and the livid corpse grows cold, - vainly love pours ambergris and flings a cover of flowers over it. She is pale as a lily in the corn-flowers' azure, as a wax cast; limp ringers take no joy in flowers, and fragrance is vain...

Do you want honey, son? then fear not the sting; a crown of victory? - boldly to battle! You long for pearls? - then go down to the bottom where the crocodile gapes under the water, do not be afraid! God will decide. He is a father only to the bold: only the bold win pearls, honey or perdition . . . or a crown.

Batiushkov had mined deeper the French (and Italian) vein which permeates the Golden Age; Vasilii Andreevich Zhukovsky (1783-1852), another returning officer, turned Russian poetry in a direction that was primarily German and secondarily British. Zhukovsky's work was mostly translation or adaptation, but was nonetheless influential for that, however much his imitation provoked his contemporaries to parody and even mockery. Germanic maidens borne off to the other world by their dead lovers are given their Russian equivalents by Zhukovsky:

> And Minvana is no more . . . When mists rise from the currents, hills and fields, and the moon shines without rays, as through smoke - two shades can be seen: merging, they fly to the shelter they know . . . and the oak moves and the strings sound.

But these popular Romantic ballads of ghostly love are only part of the baggage that Zhukovsky had brought back from the West. He also presented Russia's poets with a new role, as a demiurge, as a mouthpiece for the people. As well as pursuing melodiousness, Zhukovsky widened the genres available with pseudo-folk ballads and songs, with the concept of effusion and fragment to replace the symmetrical ordered classical poem. If Zhukovsky, appointed by Nicholas I to sift through Pushkin's heritage, to compose a national anthem and even a ceremony for carrying out capital punishment, and to tutor the heir to the throne, seemed in the 1830s to betray the role of the free spirit, then we must remember those other Romantics who failed to die young: Wordsworth with his *Sonnets on the Death Penalty* or Lamartine with his candidacy for the Presidency. Zhukovsky for most of his life set the younger poets of the Golden Age an example of idealism: 'Blessed is he who amid life's destructive disturbance has . . . scorned and forgotten the vileness of the real'.

From 1815 to 1818 Batiushkov and Zhukovsky, together with Pushkin's uncle Vasilii, became closely linked with their successors, especially Pushkin, when they became founder-members of the Arzamas circle: the society was founded in the name of a tavern in the provincial town of Arzamas, known for its fat geese, and was meant to satirise the 'Conversation of Lovers of the Russian Word' ('Beseda liubitelei russkogo slova'), a conservative, chauvinist group of writers surrounding the now forgotten Admiral Shishkov. These innovative and disrespectful poets were known by nicknames: Batiushkov was called 'Achilles', Zhukovsky was known as 'Svetlana', Petr Viazemsky was 'Asmodeus', the adolescent Pushkin was 'Cricket'. In its short existence (which ended when Shishkov's group melted away), Arzamas became a centre not just for burlesque mockery of the establishment but for the propagation of Romantic ideas and Romantic genres. It brought together many St Petersburg poets of the Golden Age - notably, Petr Viazemsky - and its mockconspiratorial aura led many members into the more ominous secret societies that fomented the Decembrist revolt of 1825.

If Batiushkov and Zhukovsky widened poets' horizons, out of the Napoleonic wars came a new confidence in the intellectual's ability to see further than the statesman. The poetry of the Golden Age is inseparable from the *Lettres philosophiques* circulated by Petr Chaadaev, Russia's first original political thinker (until he, too, like Batiushkov was overcome by depression - in his case a selffulfilling diagnosis of madness made by an indignant Tsar). Chaadaev's mission was to infuse Pushkin and his circle with a belief in the flame of history, in Providence: a cornerstone of Romanticism being its conviction that history was not a series of senseless recurrences, but the unfolding of Providence, a journey from the fall to paradise. The prospects of western Europe, spiritually free even in political turmoil, were articulated so well by Chaadaev that almost all the poets of the Golden Age became, at least for a while, convinced of man's ability and duty not just to understand but to change the world with the word.

If the officers returning from the Napoleonic wars were responsible for the import of new ideas and modes of poetry, a new model of the poet-rebel and poet-innovator came a decade later, when many of the poets of the Golden Age were scattered over Russia. Byron's reputation (largely because of the common sympathies of Russian and British poets for the Greeks' struggle to win independence) spread all over Russia, as it had over Europe in the 1820s, a reputation that became godlike when Byron died of fever at Missolonghi. When we consider that Pushkin and the other 'Golden Age poets who were influenced by Byron read him not in English, but in a mediocre French prose version by Pichot, the extent to which Byron influenced Russian poetry is astounding. Byron showed how to develop intuitively, almost cinematically constructed narrative poems, and gave Russian poets, if only for a few years, new themes: doomed love that transcended the boundaries of Christian and Moslem; the poet as an unrepentant Faust, Don Juan and Don Quixote all rolled into one.

If the Golden Age is a solar system, then we should begin by examining the work of the poets who were closest to the sun - those who were educated in close proximity to Pushkin and whose work is often a dialogue with him: the poetry of Del'vig, Iazykov and (although he is almost a decade older) Viazemsky.

Anton Antonovich Del'vig (1798-1831), Pushkin's closest friend, has been somewhat underestimated: a short and slothful life left a slender *oeuvre:* one volume of verse published two years before his death, a narrow range of vocabulary and images have led critics to consign him to the rank of a minor poet. His theme, however, was the end of a private and poetic idyll, the death of Arcadia, and was best expressed in a poem *The End of the Golden Age (Konets zolotogo veka)* - written, ironically, at the very climax of what was to be known as Russia's Golden Age. Del'vig seems to have welded Shakespearean tragedy into the Neoclassical games of Daphnis and Chloe: in Del'vig's Arcadia, the nymph drowns as she sings, like Ophelia:

> Amarylla was borne by the current, singing her song, not feeling perdition close, as if born to be in water by her ancient father Ocean, without finishing her sad song, she drowned.

The death of an abandoned heroine was a theme inherited by the Golden Age from Karamzin's sentimental prose tale *Poor Liza*

(Bednaia Liza), but Del'vig raised it to a far greater significance, which we find echoed in Pushkin's narrative poems - *The Prisoner of the Caucasus (Kavkazskiiplennik), The Fountain of Bakhchisarai (Bakhchisaraiskii fontan).* Del'vig's last elegies, inviting death to dinner and to bed, foreshadow the elegies of Pushkin's last period: Del'vig's death affected Pushkin perhaps more deeply than that of any of his circle. In one aspect Del'vig went further than even Pushkin: he was the first Russian poet to master sonnet form, and his sonnet *Inspiration (Vdokhnovenie)* is not only a perfect example of a form which succeeds relatively rarely in Russian but quintessentially Del'vigian in its stress on a private morality in an amoral world, for Del'vig places the poet even higher than his fellow Golden Age poets:

> Wandering alone under the skies, He speaks with ages yet to come; He puts honour above all other parts, His fame takes vengeance on slander And he shares immortality with the gods.

Del'vig's techniques and themes were a century later to exert an influence on Mandel'shtam. Even better than avowedly folk poets, such as Kol'tsov, Del'vig was able to catch the tone and subtly displaced rhythms of folk poetry in a number of pastiches; he was also one of the most successful poets of his day in providing texts for the Russian equivalent of *Lieder:* a number of his poems are now best known as *romansy* set to music by Glinka.

Petr Andreevich Viazemsky (1792-1878) appears to be the opposite of Del'vig, and not only in longevity. He was more heavily influenced by his cosmopolitan background. Irish-Swedish on his mother's side, he was influenced by a Voltairefrancophile father. Although seven years older than Pushkin and (like Batiushkov and Zhukovsky) a veteran of the Napoleonic wars, Viazemsky mixed with Pushkin and his fellow lycéens on equal terms. Viazemsky was (with Baratynsky and Iazykov) one of the Golden Age poets who for reasons not entirely of his own choice moved to Moscow - a move which seemed to almost all Russian poets, in the 1920s even more than in the 1820s, to be an exile from Europe and order into Asia and chaos. Unlike the depressive Del'vig, Viazemsky was combative, dissident to the point of physical discordance. In Gogol's essay of 1846 'What is Actually the Essence of Russian Poetry . . .', the first thorough appreciation of the Golden Age's achievement, Viazemsky comes in for harsh criticism; Gogol's main point still stands:

> next to a verse which is stronger and firmer than any other poet's, we find another sort, quite unlike the first; at one moment he will show the pain of living flesh ripped from the heart, at another he will repel with a sound that is almost alien to the heart, which is quite out of tune with the subject; you can feel his lack of inner consistency, a life which is not filled with strength.

Pushkin, as a close friend, was bold enough to tell Viazemsky in 1826: 'Your verse is too clever. Poetry, God forgive me, has to be a bit stupid.' To this criticism might be added Viazemsky's refusal to make concessions to melodiousness: he is perhaps the only poet of the Golden Age whose texts no composer was able or willing to set to music.

Like Fedor Tiutchev, Viazemsky was the only poet of the Golden Age to live his full three score and ten; unlike Tiutchev, he was not restored to the canon by the critical re-evaluations of the early twentieth century. His life-long disgruntled and uncompromising stance made him unattractive: to write on Russia *(The Russian God [Russkii bog],* 1828) as he did, as unpatriotically as Turgenev in the novel *Smoke (Dym)* was not to court popularity:

> Full of grace to the stupid, mercilessly strict to the clever, God of everything inappropriate, that is him, the Russian God. God of everything that is outlandish, unseemly, out of place, God of mustard after supper, that is him, the Russian God.

The death of Pushkin (not to speak of five of his own children) led Viazemsky into a pessimism bleaker than even Pushkin's darkest moments. Though he was to know Europe and modern times better than any other survivor of the Golden Age, progress only deepened Viazemsky's gloom. A train journey from Prague to Vienna left his convictions unaltered:

Man has been armed with a bold and rebellious force; he is burning forever with an insatiable, uncontrollable passion. The battle of elements, of contradictions, the discord of conflicting forces has all been trampled down by the human mind and subordinated to calculation. Thus plugging through the universe, because of his passions and plans the master of limited days arrogantly forgets himself. But if the slightest mishap occurs and our mighty giant goes off the tracks, if only by a hair's breadth, Then all the calculation, all the wisdom of the age is just zero, and the same zero and nonentity of man will fly off its stilts into dust and ashes.

Viazemsky, unlike the other rebellious spirits of the Golden Age, consistently saw life as an old dressing-gown, a comforting membrane that could never be discarded. His *Farewell to the Dressing-Gown (Proshchanie s khalatom)* of 1817 is echoed in 1877 with the lines: 'Our life in old age is a worn-out dressing-gown . . . The two of us have long since grown together like brothers; We can't be repaired or renovated.'

If Viazemsky represented the irredentist intellect, then Pushkin's friend Nikolai Mikhailovich Iazykov (1803-46) was all instinct and impressionable emotion. Although he knew Del'vig and Zhukovsky from his student days and mixed with Pushkin's friends and relatives during his university years at Dorpat (Tartu), he did not actually meet Pushkin until the Golden Age had endured its great crisis, the retribution exacted in 1826 by Nicholas I on real and suspected Decembrists. At Trigorskoe, next to Pushkin's estate Mikhailovskoe, the two poets met and in his poem *Trigorskoe* Iazykov celebrated one of the most productive encounters in Russian poetry: Iazykov expresses Pushkin's feelings at having escaped exile to the south or, worse, to Siberia with an effusiveness that Pushkin's reserve would not have allowed:

How sweet for the young prisoner, leaving the darkness and weight of chains, to look at daylight, at the shine of the rippling water, to walk along the meadow shore, to sate himself on the fields' air. How comforting for the poet to escape the world of cold vanity, where numerous hopes and dreams run to the Lethe, where in a heart beloved of the muse, sometimes, like a stream of flame extinguished by thick smoke, because of the unbearable roar of passions, the life forces weaken, - to take refuge, a free man, in the beautiful world, in nature's gardens and suddenly and proudly forget his lost years.

Iazykov's poetic fire was dampened very soon after this climax. His elegies on love are full of erotic fire, and his poetry from his years of travelling Europe's spas being treated for syphilis produces some memorable scenic poetry in a Byronic genre. But Iazykov's burning radicalism, despite the execution of friends such as Ryleev, cooled and he even began to deplore Pushkin's free-thinking and narrative fecundity.

Those poets who took an active role in the revolt of December 1825 ran on an orbit more distant from Pushkin's closest circles. Nevertheless, two of them, Kondratii Fedorovich Ryleev(1795-1826) and ViPgePm Karlovich Kiukhel'beker (1797-1846) were poets of note, if not of genius. Ryleev was one of the youngest veterans of the Napoleonic wars, but what he had learnt and wished to propagate was more political than literary. Patriotism and civic courage were ideals blazed by the heroes of his narrative poems, and of modern poets only Byron influenced him, more as a fighter than a poetic innovator. Before his fatal involvement with revolution, however, Ryleev and a co-conspirator founded an annual almanac, *Poliarnaia zvezda (The Polar Star)* which was to be the model for Russia's 'thick' periodicals which, from the 1830s to this day have been - even more than book publishing - the mainstay of all imaginative literature in Russia and can be regarded, together with the monthly *Sovremennik (The Contemporary)* that Pushkin subsequently founded, as the most durable of the Golden Age's bequests to posterity. Ryleev's political views, like most of the Decembrists', were eclectic and contradictory; his high regard for the constitution of the United States of America was at odds with both the aristocratic constitutionalism of the 'northern' rebels and the totalitarian dictatorial views of the 'southerners' - views which were, unfortunately, to prevail among Russia's opposition thinkers.

Although Kiukhel'beker fired a pistol at a Grand Duke and was sentenced to beheading, he paid for his involvement with the Decembrists not with his neck but with his liberty and, eventually, his eyesight. More naive and independent than Ryleev, he was the more original and productive poet. Although his family was German-speaking and he was heavily influenced by Goethe's mythopceia, he was (perhaps in compensation for his Germanic surname) an ardent Slavist, adhering more to the archaicists in his determination to write a purely 'Slavonic' Russian. He was a fellow-pupil of Pushkin's and his traits were copied to create the naïve poet Lensky in *Evgenii Onegin.* It might be said that he was Pushkin's polar opposite, as Lensky was Onegin's, and his departure for hard labour and exile in Siberia affected Pushkin as deeply as Lensky's death is described as affecting Onegin. Classical Hellenic values, as much as Byronic romanticism, underlie Kiukhel'beker's radical stance. Like many Russian intellectuals of the Golden Age he saw no contradiction between his defense of Greek national self-determination and his valiant military service in the Caucasus in the early 1820s, waging under General Ermolov a genocidal war against Chechens and Dagestanis.

In solitary confinement Kiukhel'beker was allowed to continue writing. Arguably, his best poetry came from reflection. Of all the Golden Age poets he was the most ambitious: his long verse work *Izhorsky* is a mystery play that appears to emulate Goethe's *Faust Part II* and he produced two very long historical verse epics. In his lyric verse, however, Kiukhel'beker remains close to the best of the Golden Age. He remained convinced of ultimate justice and, in a poem *To a Slanderer (Klevetniku)* attacking the officers in charge of his fate, warned:

> Believe me, there is Nemesis in the world, and she notes any offence and enters it in a book, and silently a mysterious maiden reads this book day and night and chooses victims and punishes them without wrath, but without pity too. Lies and slander will eventually be paid for with the same slander, and the murderous arrow of evil lies will penetrate your heart too . . .

His poem on *The Fate of Russian Poets (Uchast 'russkikh poetov)* remains a harsh but well-judged model for later poets' self-induction:

> Bitter is the fate of poets of all races; fate punishes Russia worst of all. . . God gave their hearts fire, their minds light, yes, their feelings were inspired and ardent – What then? They are hurled into dark prisons, killed by the freezing cold of hopeless exile . . . Either disease brings night and fog to the eyes of the far-sighted and inspired; or the hand of despicable favourites puts a bullet in their sacred brows; Or else rebellion rouses the deaf rabble, and the rabble tears to bits him whose flight, dazzling us with thunderbolts, would have flooded his native land with radiance.

Many Russian poets were to be threatened with execution and punished with exile; when, a hundred years later, Stalin made it the normal fate for almost any poet worth his salt, none was so eloquent in his self-defence as Kiukhel'beker had been.

The Golden Age's greatest poets, it might be argued, are those who escaped Pushkin's orbit and became luminaries in their own right. Those who lived and wrote in Moscow escaped the Pushkinian influences that were particularly overpowering after 1827, the year of Pushkin's return from exile. Of all Pushkin's cohort Evgenii Abramovich Baratynsky (1800-14) was most clearly an equal. He too began his literary career writing melodious elegies under the influence of Batiushkov and Parny; he too was exiled (but to Finland rather than the South). Like Pushkin, Baratynsky developed the narrative poem, with a Finnish rather than a Crimean or Caucasian setting, as his main genre. But Baratynsky's often touching narrative poems are no longer widely read, even though Pushkin praised them; his early elegies - despite the fact that some, for example 'Do not tempt me with the return of your affection', are still treasured as the texts for the most affecting Russian *Lieder* - have been superseded in critical esteem by his later work. Baratynsky was alienated first from Moscow life and then from life in general. His increasing discontent led him to a language which is more and more austere and precise and to a conviction that art was the only salvation:

Chisel, organ, brush - happy is he who is drawn to them as to sensual things, not stepping across their boundary. He has intoxication at the world's feast-day. But before you, as before a naked sword, o word, bright ray, earth's life goes pale.

Particularly after Pushkin's death, Baratynsky became a poet very modern for his times: the poems of his 1842 collection, *Twilight (Sumerki)* compare with Theophile Gautier's *Émaux et camées* in their pursuit of pure form in art and thought, and his conviction in the power of death to divest all experience of any meaning anticipates the world-view of the Symbolist and Decadent. Like Gautier, Baratynsky symbolized the destruction of poetry by technology by the image of a steamboat crushing water nymphs. Baratynsky was the first to foresee the nineteenth century ousting the aesthetic from life. In his poem *The Last Poet (Posledniipoet)* he declares: 'The age marches along its iron path, acquisitiveness is in hearts, and the common dream is every hour more obviously and shamelessly about the everyday and the useful.' His economy of language echoes his idealization of the sculptor as the ideal artist, adding and making nothing, merely removing surplus material. Baratynsky achieved greatness towards the end of his life and that of the Golden Age: it was left to the Symbolists, on the centenary of his birth, to recognize his extraordinary importance. The frequent and vibrant echoes of Baratynsky in Mandel'shtam's work suggest that of all Golden Age poets Baratynsky has most to communicate to the twentieth century.

Those Golden Age poets for whom Moscow was home, rather than exile from St Petersburg, lived in an atmosphere imbued with German Romantic mysticism rather than French Classical rationalism: Schelling meant more to them than Voltaire. They were relatively immune to radical political ideas or to the Byronic model, and out of their ranks would come the Orthodox theology and Pan-Slavist political ideals of the Slavophiles. The most charismatic of these poets was Dmitrii Vladimirovich Venevitinov (1805-27) whose short life, terminated by tuberculosis and pneumonia, has led readers to infer from the handful of poems he left a potential genius. For a brief time, surrounded by a circle of friends to whom his poems were addressed, Venevitinov played the same solar role in Moscow as Pushkin did in St Petersburg, but the impassioned rhetoric of his valedictory verse is valuable mostly as a harbinger of unrealized greatness.

Far more significant was Venevitinov's fellow Muscovite, a lowly poet, the illegitimate son of a merchant, Aleksandr Ivanovich Polezhaev (1804-37). Because of his bawdy masterpiece *Sashka* (which has never been published in full), Polezhaev was both famed and destroyed. A pastiche of Chapter One of Pushkin's *Evgenii Onegin,* its hero Sashka is likewise a roue dependent on his uncle; Polezhaev's witty verse evokes the debauchery of Moscow's students and whores. Polezhaev shows all the talent for graphic burlesque of the eighteenth-century erotic poet Ivan Barkov and of Pushkin's uncle Vasilii. The poem's notoriety led to an interview with Nicholas I and the Minister of Education. Polezhaev was forced to recite the poem in full, after which he was sentenced to serve as a rank and file soldier in the Caucasus. Although Polezhaev fought bravely, his plebeian status deprived him of protection. Floggings and military prison wrecked his health and before he died of tuberculosis his achievement was limited to little more than one fine narrative poem, *Chir-Yurt,* on the vicious war of attrition against Chechens and Circassians - a poem which anticipates Lev Tolstoy's sketches of the Caucasian wars - and a valedictory poem entitled *Consumption (Chakhotka):* its portrayal of a doomed poet anticipates Apollon Grigor'ev's record of self-destruction thirty years later and the despair of the Symbolists:

> Fateful consumption stares me in the eyes and, distorting its pale face, I can hear, it hoarsely says: 'My dear friend, you have long invited me to come with the ringing of bottles. Thus I appear with a bow - give your slave a comer to live in. We shan't live a boring life, believe me: you will cough and groan, and I shall always, inseparably, be ready to console you.'

The Golden Age was not ready for Polezhaev, and like Pushkin's and Lermontov's bawdy verse, his work was consigned to the foreign or private press and to manuscript circulation.

If Polezhaev was a Moscow parodist of Pushkin, Russia's greatest metaphysical poet, Fedor Ivanovich Tiutchev (1803-73), took as his point of departure Pushkin's lyrics on the otherworldly nature of inspiration, on the indifference of nature to man and on the fatal, unrequitable nature of love. In the 1830s some of Tiutchev's lyrics were published by Pushkin in *Sovremennik*. Tiutchev's work, however, followed other directions; his Moscow education and his diplomatic career took him into a Germanic orbit. In Munich he met Heinrich Heine and an improbable mutual respect sprang up between the left-wing German Jew and the right-wing Russian aristocrat, a respect founded on their common pessimism about the outcome of their poetic and political struggle. In 1833 Tiutchev, an intensely self-critical poet, whose surviving lyrical poetry (if we exclude political and translated verse) barely amounts to a hundred poems, destroyed a large amount of what he had written. Publication in 1836 attracted little attention - a subsequent edition in 1854 passed almost unnoticed. Tiutchev may belong to Pushkin's generation, but his poetry, so scandalously ignored in his lifetime, is not really part of the Golden Age: its dawn came posthumously and his poetry, based on a systematic opposition of light and dark, order and chaos, male and female, belatedly found its place in the twentieth century's Symbolist and Acmeist schools. In his metaphysical poetry, Tiutchev did not scorn the dissonant sounds and displaced rhythms of the eighteenth century's first experimenters; in his later love poetry, chronicling the distress and death of his mistress, Tiutchev found a simple tone, breathtakingly dangerous in its closeness to banality, a tone which is not to recur in Russian poetry until Pasternak's last lyrics. Tiutchev thus does not belong to the Golden Age - he is too much a timeless poet even to belong to the nineteenth century.

The Golden Age's last generation was born in the mid-1810s: writers such as Turgenev were soon to abandon verse for prose fiction and belong to the so-called Realist school of the 1850s and 1860s. The only major poet of this generation is

Mikhail Iur'evich Lermontov (1814-41). Lermontov is linked to Pushkin primarily by his obsessively (however much denied) Byronic poetic persona and by his insistence on hiding his deepest feelings, outside the parameters of his verse, behind the mask of an officer and gentleman. His permanent adolescence meant that Lermontov's thought, a refusal to accept a world governed by a hostile God and despicable humanity, developed little; his outlook was never matured by observation or experience, even though at the end of his life he was able to produce a novel *A Hero of Our Time (Geroi nashego vremeni)* which is one of the most original pieces of psychological prose ever written and stands, together with *Evgenii Onegin,* as the Golden Age's main achievements in the novel. Conversely, Lermontov's verse became more and more plastic in the last four years of his life, reaching its extraordinary combination of evocative musicality and hypnotic narrative in his two poems of the Caucasus, *The Demon (Demon)* and *The Novice Monk (Mtsyri).* Lermontov and Pushkin, alone of the Golden Age poets, raised the narrative poem to parity with the lyric.

The Golden Age did not die a sudden death. From the mid-1840s poetry began to recede from public esteem. The only estimable woman poet of the Golden Age, Karolina Pavlova, emigrated to Germany. By a strange demographic response, nature seemed to have dried up the supply of poets. The late 1810s-1820s gave birth only to Afanasii Fet, Nekrasov and Aleksei Konstantinovich Tolstoy. Afanasii Fet, like Tiutchev, was to be largely ignored, even mocked, in his own century, and his daring love lyrics, sometimes verbless, sometimes shaped vertically as if a translation from the Chinese, had to wait until the twentieth century to make their impact. Nikolai Nekrasov, on the other hand, was to be idolized from the middle of the century to his death in 1877, but only as a honorary prose writer, because of his laudable democratic sentiments and his choice of subject matter among the impoverished peasantry and urban poor. His poetic genius, which at its best was extraordinarily innovative in rhythm, passed with little comment. Aleksei Tolstoy was one of the few poets of the nineteenth century to articulate Christianity – both Orthodox in his recreation of the hymns of St John Damascene, and evangelistic in his cruel *Ballad of Delarue (Ballada o Delariu)* about the gruesome fate of the altruist. Alone, he revived the eighteenth-century genre of historical verse drama. Like Fet, Aleksei Tolstoy was to be valued only posthumously.

In the forty years after 1825, even fewer poets were born: only six major poets, compared with, say, two dozen in the preceding forty. True, 'junk' poetry (by poets now largely forgotten, such as Maikov, Benediktov, and Mei), not to mention a still overrated pseudo-folk poetry by the Voronezh poets Kol'tsov and Nikitin, commanded a somewhat Philistine following, in the same way as the neo-Romantics of the late nineteenth century in England, France and Germany provided a diluted bourgeois version of the true Romanticism of the Napoleonic era.

The heritage of the Golden Age is a dual one. The Russian novel took from poets many of the themes first explored by poets: Pushkin's Onegin and Lermontov's Pechorin are models for superfluous heroes in Turgenev and Tolstoy; the intuitions of Tiutchev's love poetry are the underlying force behind the tragic fate of *Anna Karenina*. Baratynsky and Iazykov in Italy outline the reactions to be found in Russian novelists' peripatetic heroes. The less immediate heritage came into force with the birth of the Silver Age. Without the rediscovery of Batiushkov, Tiutchev and Baratynsky at the beginning of the twentieth century, the development of Aleksandr Blok or Osip Mandel'shtam would have been unthinkable; and, at a broader level, Russian poets would have not been able to foresee and cope with their ephemeral role, had they not had before them the example of their forefathers a century earlier.

The Routledge Companion to Russian Literature, 1971-1953, Fitzroy Dearborn, Edited by Neil Cornwell, Copyright © 2001, Routledge. Reproduced by permission of Taylor & Francis Books UK.

Further Reading

Austin, Paul M. *The Exotic Prisoner in Russian Romanticism,* New York: Peter Lang, 1997.

Beaudoin, Luc J. *Resetting the Margins: Russian Romantic Verse Tales and the Idealized Woman,* New York: Peter Lang, 1997.

Brown, William Edward. *A History of Russian Literature of the Romantic Period,* 4 vols., Ann Arbor: Ardis, 1986.

Greenleaf, Monika and Stephen Moeller-Sally (eds) *Russian Subjects: Empire, Nation, and the Culture of the Golden Age,* Evanston, Illinois: Northwestern University Press, 1998.

Offord, Derek (ed.) *The Golden Age of Russian Literature and Thought,* London: Macmillan; New York: St Martin's Press, 1992.

Rayfield, Donald, Hicks, Jeremy, Makarova, Olga and Pilkington, Anna (eds and trans.) *The Garnett Book of Russian Verse,* London: Gamett Press, 2000.

Nineteenth-Century Russian Thought and Literature

Derek Offord

In the rich corpus of nineteenth-century Russian belles-lettres it is hard always to establish a clear boundary between essays in thought (within which further boundaries between the aesthetic, moral, religious, social, political and other spheres may also be blurred) and works of fiction. Such writings as Herzen's cycles of *Letters from France and Italy (Pis ma iz Frantsii i Italii,* first published in book form in 1855) and *From the Other Shore (S togo berega,* first published in German in 1850) or Dostoevsky's *Winter Notes on Summer Impressions (Zimnie zametki o letnikh vpechatleniiakh,* 1863) function on one level as essays in social or political thought or reflections on cultural identity and national destiny. And yet they are themselves literary artefacts, exemplars of the genre of the travel sketch. Similarly, in *My Past and Thoughts (Byloe i dumy,* 1861-7) Herzen leaves both an intellectual history of his generation and a carefully crafted example of the personal memoir. At the same time the classical Russian novel, although a supremely polished art form, may operate as a sort of intellectual history too. For example, Turgenev's novels - as distinct from his novellas, according to Turgenev's own definition of the two genres - may be seen as providing a history of the development of the consciousness of the educated Russian during the middle decades of the century from idealistic but ineffectual 'superfluous man' *(lishnii chelovek)* to disaffected rationalist and revolutionary. The novel could also function as a polemical contribution to contemporary intellectual life. Thus in the reign of Alexander II (ruled 1855-81), there developed as distinct sub-groups of the novelistic genre both works extolling the militant younger generation, such as Sleptsov's *Hard Times (Trudnoe vremia,* 1865), and the so-called antinihilist novel, in which certain writers (for instance, Pisemsky and Leskov) took issue with contemporary radical thought.

In any case the two bodies of work, thought and fiction, were interdependent and mutually enriching. Literary critics, such as

Belinsky and Dobroliubov, or religious, social and political thinkers, such as Chaadaev and Chernyshevsky, exercised profound influence on the views of their contemporaries, including writers of fiction, and often conveyed their ideas through discussion of works of fiction. Conversely, when thinkers failed to exercise influence it was sometimes because their purview seemed too narrowly literary. This was the case with Druzhinin, a talented critic of the middle decades of the century, who insisted on treating a work of art as a thing in itself with no broader, extra-aesthetic implications that interested him. The novelists, for their part, often took up and developed themes addressed by contemporary thinkers, as did Dostoevsky in *Crime and Punishment* (*Prestuplenie i nakazanie,* 1866), which carries certain contemporary radical ideas to what Dostoevsky sees as their logical conclusion. Writers who ignored the demand for topical content of civic import and subscribed to the doctrine of art for art's sake, like the poet Fet, risked marginalization. Often the examination of a subject by a thinker complements one or more literary studies of the same subject. Chaadaev's *Philosophical Letter* (first published in French in 1836 as *Lettre philosophique)* and Pushkin's *Eugene Onegin* (*Evgenii Onegin,* written in the period 1823-31) illustrate the point. Thinkers themselves resorted at times to overtly fictional genres in order to convey their ideas, as did Ivan Kireevsky in a fragmentary work of Utopian literature, *Island* (*Ostrov,* 1838), Herzen in *Who is to blame?* (*Kto vinovat?,* 1845-6), and Chernyshevsky in *What is to be Done?* (*Chtodelat'?,* 1863).

It is not surprising, in view of this interdependence, that the rhythms of thought and fiction were often in harmony. For example, the flowering of classical literature in the 1830s and 40s coincided with the unfolding of debate about the nation's destiny. On the other hand the period 1848-55, known as the 'dismal seven years', when governmental fear that the revolutionary disturbances of 1848 in western Europe would spread to Russia provoked particularly severe official repression, was notable by contrast for the dearth of both major works of imaginative literature and thought. In the period immediately following the Crimean War (1853-6) and the accession of the more liberal Alexander II to the throne, work in both fields was again profuse and rich.

It is the fluid boundary between nineteenth-century Russian thought and imaginative literature, the bearing which the thought has on that literature, and the interplay between them, that this chapter will survey.

It may be rewarding as a first step to consider briefly the oneness of Russian thought and imaginative literature in the eighteenth century, at the very beginning of the modern period of Russian culture, when writers were already starting to address topical issues. The earliest Russian users of western literary genres tended to see their writings as part of a general civic service or endeavour. From the Petrine epoch on, many Russian writers - Prokopovich, Kantemir, Fonvizin, Derzhavin, Radishchev and, to a lesser extent, Lomonosov and Sumarokov - held government office or were close to court or sought to influence state policy or the heir to the throne or even the succession. It was therefore natural that they should take a keen interest in social and political matters and directly address or at least obliquely touch upon a large number of interrelated subjects of topical significance: the immensity of Russia and her natural wealth; military prowess and imperial conquest; the reception of western culture and values; education and upbringing; relations between husbands and wives and between parents and children; the rights and obligations of the nobility; the lot of the peasantry and the domestic serf; the outlook and conduct of the clergy; life and conduct at court; the abuse of power by the *vel 'mozha* or grandee; official corruption; and - perhaps most daringly – the nature of tyrants and the qualities of the virtuous ruler.

The tradition of engagement with topical issues that had been begun in the eighteenth century was continued by the nineteenth-century intelligentsia, particularly after 1825 when government no longer commanded the respect of the embryonic public opinion articulated by the small - and at that time mainly noble - educated class. The corpus of thought which that intelligentsia produced, and which was to inform the literature of the classical period, may be divided into a number of interrelated fields and paid particular attention to certain quite clearly definable questions. It contained a wealth of literary criticism, which examined among other things the nature of beauty and inspiration, the relation of art to reality, the function of art, and the mission of the writer and critic. Writings on social questions, often seen through the prism of imaginative literature, literary criticism and literary history, explored the role of the intelligentsia itself, the nature of the common people or *narod,* and the relationship between the intelligentsia and the *narod.* Examination of political questions tended to be less explicit but often, insofar as censorship allowed, touched upon serfdom and urban poverty and on the nature of autocracy and its perniciousness or suitability in Russian conditions. Essays in what might be best described as moral philosophy included evaluations of Russian and Western mores and enquiries on the themes of egoism and altruism, duty, service and self-sacrifice. There were discussions of a theological nature into the relationship between rational knowledge and faith and the differences between Orthodoxy and the western forms of Christianity, and at the same time speculation on the extent of the jurisdiction of scientific method, its implications for religious faith, and the similarities and dissimilarities between science and history. In the field of history itself thinkers reflected on the principles that might underlie historical development, on the existence or lack of pattern in history, on chance and necessity, the role of Providence and great individuals, and the role of the state in Russian history. Almost invariably Russian thinkers were also - perhaps above all - preoccupied with the problem of the historical destiny of individual nations, the relationships between nations, and in particular the relationship of 'Russia' to 'the West' (though these two concepts, it should be noted, reached beyond geopolitical entities).

Turning from these broad, general considerations to a chronological account of the way in which the concerns of Russian thinkers impinge upon and find expression in classical Russian literature, we should perhaps dwell first on Chaadaev's *Philosophical Letter,* written in 1829. This letter was the first of a series of eight but the only one published in Chaadaev's lifetime. Chaadaev, who had imbibed the ideas of French Catholic thinkers of the early nineteenth century during a prolonged stay in western Europe in the 1820s, believes nations and societies derive their character from the religious ideas that prevail in them. He shares the Romantic view of the Middle Ages as a period when the notions of duty, justice, law and order that give unity and continuity to Western civilization were established and when the individual personality began to assert itself. It is Russia's profound misfortune, Chaadaev argues, that she remained outside the religious, moral and social development of the Renaissance, with the result that educated Russians find themselves without history, stable values or moral foundations for their existence. In a spiritual sense the educated Russian is a rootless traveller, more nomadic than the shifting tribesmen who inhabit Russia's Asiatic borderlands. This problem of individual identity, role and purpose also exists on a national scale, for nations 'are just as much moral beings as individuals are'. Russia herself, an immense geographical space between the Bering Straits and the Oder, seems to Chaadaev to be suspended as a civilization between Asia and Europe. The fact that Chaadaev chose to write his letter in French not only reminds us of the curious fact that a foreign language was freely chosen as a vehicle for social intercourse among the Russian nobility in the late eighteenth and early nineteenth centuries but also, at a deeper level, serves to illustrate Chaadaev's thesis about the lack of a substantial native culture in Russia.

Chaadaev's *Letter* expresses the loss of purpose experienced by the patriotic Russian nobleman, with his residual sense of a duty to serve, in the increasingly bureaucratic Russian state. It also reflects the nobleman's despondency at the lack of opportunity for concrete political change in the aftermath of the Decembrist Revolt of 1825. It will also readily be seen that the malaise Chaadaev describes is essentially the same as that which afflicts the itinerant 'superfluous man' who features so prominently in classical Russian literature from the 1820s and who is represented, in that decade, by Onegin in Pushkin's novel in verse and, at a later date, by Pechorin in Lermontov's *A Hero of Our Time (Geroi nashego vremeni,* 1840). Mutually acquainted, Chaadaev and Pushkin both portray a man who lacks guiding principle and moral compass, is out of harmony with his society and cannot settle or find a satisfying mission in it.

In the course of the 1830s, Russians increasingly imbibed German philosophy and literature, studied in German universities and, as Turgenev put it when writing about his own youth, plunged into the 'German sea'. Inspired in particular by the young nobleman Stankevich, they avidly devoured the works of Schelling and, especially, Hegel until, as Herzen recalled, the overused tomes disintegrated. The intoxication with German Romantic culture - which is foreshadowed in the poetic references to separation, sorrow, *'a certain something* and *a misty faraway'* by Onegin's friend and victim, Lensky, who has studied in Gottingen – provided solace from the harshness of Russian social and political reality. It gave rise to opaque abstractions on the transcendental nature of art and the Absolute Idea, admiration of the Schillerian 'noble soul' *{die schone Seele),* and a cult of chivalrous friendship. This unpractical otherworldly idealism, with its exaltation of heart over mind, is embodied in a further incarnation of the 'superfluous man', the eponymous hero of Turgenev's first novel *Rudin,* set in the late 1830s or early 1840s though written in 1855-6 at a time of change when the character of the Nicolaevan age seemed in retrospect more clearly definable. Although Onegin's world-weariness and cynicism are supplanted in Rudin by ardent attachment to apparently altruistic ideals, nevertheless Rudin, like Pushkin's protagonist, is at heart egoistic and incapable of lasting attachments or dedication to a practical cause. He is conceived by Turgenev and perceived by Turgenev's contemporaries as typifying the form which the rootless educated Russian has assumed a decade after Onegin's time.

The enthusiasm for western culture among the Russian educated class naturally precipitated debate about the relationship of that culture to Russian culture and the degree to which western culture could or should be accommodated in Russia. Consideration of these questions was in any case encouraged by the growth of interest within Western thought and literature in national distinctiveness and in the relative contribution of different peoples to the development of human civilization. This interest, which emanated from Germany in the late eighteenth century, found expression in the early nineteenth century among many European peoples in a curiosity in their language, history, literature, music and customs, everything that gives a people its specific cultural identity. Thus the question broached by Chaadaev in 1829 unfolds into a broad debate that continues to colour intellectual life for the rest of the century - and arguably still colours Russian intellectual life today - as to the actual national identity of Russia and the attitude it should adopt in relation to other nations. The Slavophiles and Westernizers, as the opposing camps in this debate came to be known (the appellations were rather jocular, gibes invented by their opponents), were broad churches within which there were various shades of belief. Both groups, particularly the Westernizers, tended to define themselves in relation to their adversaries.

The Slavophiles - notably Khomiakov, Ivan Kireevsky, Konstantin Aksakov - believed Russia possessed a distinct national identity which was not only worth preserving but provided a defence against the rationalism, materialism, individualism and collapse of faith that they believed were undermining the West. They abhorred Peter the Great as the ruler who had supposedly set Russia on a western path and looked back nostalgically to an imagined pre-Petrine golden age. They favoured Moscow - the ancient capital, associated from the fourteenth century with the development of a new Russian Orthodox state as the Tartar yoke was thrown off - over St Petersburg, Russia's window on to the pernicious West: the capital founded by Peter in 1703 and built in response to imperial diktat by western architects in an alien style on inhospitable marshland where no township had previously stood. Khomiakov argued that Russian civilization was informed by a different principle (a principle of inner freedom, which he termed 'Iranian') from that which informed Western societies (the 'Kushite' principle, a principle of compulsion). This inner freedom supposedly found expression in the Orthodox Church, which unlike the Catholic Church had not been tainted by the secular world of learning and politics and which cultivated an all-inclusive *sobornost* \ or conciliarism, and resisted organization into a hierarchy like that dominated by the Pope. As for the Russian common people, the *narod,* they remained uncorrupted by the westernization that had infected the nobility. Indifferent to worldly goods and private property, the *narod* manifested a truly Christian leaning towards the life of the spirit. Uninterested in practical secular matters, they willingly conceded political authority to the autocrat. Their capacity for brotherly love was exhibited in the institution of the commune, the *mir* or *obshchina,* which periodically partitioned the land at the disposal of the peasant community according to the changing needs of the families within it. The Slavophiles' interest in the distinctiveness of their own culture found expression in some philological research of dubious scholarly value by Konstantin Aksakov, in the same man's habit - a source of some amusement to his contemporaries - of attiring himself in national costume, and in the collection of Russian folk songs by Petr Kireevsky, brother of Ivan.

The opposing westernist camp included the historian Granovsky, who held a chair at Moscow University in the 1840s; Annenkov, author of travel notes on France and Italy and of valuable literary memoirs as well as of less distinguished literary criticism; Botkin, a wealthy merchant, another ardent traveller, author of a notable travelogue on Spain in the late 1840s; and Turgenev, whose literary career began in the mid-40s. Perhaps Westernism's most brilliant representative was Herzen, who in his essays of the 1840s on science and nature tried to reconcile Hegelian philosophy and French socialism. In 1847 Herzen emigrated to the West with his family and in further cycles of letters on life in western Europe shortly before, during and after the revolutions of 1848 he defended individual liberty in the face of all coercive systems, both political and ideological. However, more influential than any of these men on the intellectual life of his age was the literary critic Belinsky, 'furious Vissarion' as he was known on account of his fierce engagement with moral and social issues as well as literary ones. In the course of his journalistic career, which lasted from 1834 to his death in 1848 at the age of thirty-seven, Belinsky succumbed to numerous intellectual enthusiasms, or more accurately passions: from Schellingian transcendental idealism and a 'reconciliation with reality' in all its grimness, inspired by Hegel, to fanatical espousal of Utopian socialism and even a measure of respect for the bourgeoisie. What remained constant in Belinsky's writing, though, was a passionate concern for the state of Russian literature and a view of it as a civilizing force, in the absence of other outlets for free expression.

Although individual Westernizers were personally close to Slavophiles in the early 1840s and certainly shared the Slavophiles' deep love of Russia, it was their antipathy to Slavophilism that united them more than anything else. The Westernizers viewed Slavophilism as a defence of an antiquated way of life and medieval superstition. They equated it with repudiation of the scientific and social benefits which western European countries, for all their inequalities and social problems, had brought about and with stubborn resistance to progress, which Belinsky discussed in a review of the state of Russian literature in 1847. With their extensive knowledge of the German states, France, England, Italy and other countries, derived both from their reading and from the travels that several of them had made, the Westernizers believed that Russia needed to learn and borrow - judiciously - from the more advanced members of that same European family of nations to which she herself belonged.

The stirrings of debate about the national destiny are evident in the famous final passage of Part I of GogoP's *Dead Souls (Mertvye dushi,* 1842), where the nefarious Chichikov's *troika,* speeding away from the provincial town from which Chichikov has to flee, is transformed into an image of Russia, hurtling towards an enigmatic destiny as other nations stand aside. Gogol' himself, although championed by Westernizers as a writer who revealed the social and moral squalor of Russian reality with great power, was personally closer to the conservative nationalist camp and was eventually berated by Belinsky, in the latter's famous *Letter to Gogol* (1847, seen by contemporaries as the testament of the dying critic), for the reactionary views he had expressed in his *Selected Passages from Correspondence with Friends (Vybrannye mesta izperepiski s druz'iami,* 1847). The debate about national identity finds an echo in Turgenev's second novel, *A Nest of Gentry (Dvorianskoe gnezdo,* published in 1859 but set in the early 1840s), where the hero Lavretsky struggles to reconcile the disparate parts of his upbringing and in which Turgenev offers a portrait of a superficial Westernizing official in the Ministry of the Interior in the character of Panshin. The debate also informs the literature of the 1840s and 1850s in an implicit way, inasmuch as concerns widely expressed in that literature - for example, compassion for the poor and oppressed in both town and country; respect for the individual personality and a sense of the dignity of the individual; interest in the life and culture of western societies, as expressed in a rich travel literature - reflect civilized values of western provenance which shine brightly in the gloom of Nicolaevan Russia.

Within the Westernizers' camp differences that were eventually to become significant began to develop at an early stage. Already in the 1840s some Westernizers took up more or less extreme positions. Belinsky, in 1841, declared himself prepared to countenance revolutionary violence in order to achieve social justice, defending the wave of terror unleashed by the French Jacobins in 1793-4. Herzen, impressed by the work of the German left-wing Hegelian Feuerbach, whose *Essence of Christianity* (1841) had a major impact in Russia in the 1840s, embraced a materialist outlook. Moreover, as soon as he arrived in western Europe in 1847 as a political refugee, Herzen set about indicting the bourgeoisie, the regnant class in the France and England to which he came, as egoistic, oppressive and morally bankrupt. At the same time he began to preach a Russian socialism which envisaged the Russian peasant, whose collective spirit was manifested in the commune, as the bearer of values that would underpin a new civilization as the 'old world' destroyed itself. A further member of the westernist circles of the early 1840s, Bakunin, embarked on a life of political rebellion that led him to various European barricades in 1848 and subsequently, after imprisonment in the Peter and Paul Fortress in St Petersburg and exile to and escape from Siberia, to renewed emigration in England, Italy and Switzerland, where in the 1860s and 70s he was to play a leading role in the international anarchist movement. On the other hand, more moderate men among the Westernizers (Granovsky, Botkin, Annenkov) resisted complete rejection of religious belief, maintained that the bourgeoisie, for all its faults, had proved a partly positive social force in the West, and in general counselled moderation. They argued for evolution, that is to say gradual change that would not destroy what was valuable in the existing society along with what they deplored, rather than revolution which would sweep away everything.

The cracks apparent in the westernist camp in the 1840s developed into a major fissure in the period after the Crimean War and the death of Nicholas I (1855), when the new tsar, Alexander II, encouraged discussion of the emancipation of the serfs and oversaw the reform itself in 1861. Censorship was relaxed and journalism and literature again flourished. The more radical variant of Westernism was now articulated by militant younger men of lower social origin than the so-called 'men of the 40s'. These 'men of the 60s', led by Chernyshevsky and Dobroliubov (both sons of the lower 'white', or non-monastic, clergy), venerated natural science and invoked its authority. They prized it both as a practical tool for the material improvement of society and as the source of a method - entailing observation, measurement, experimentation, deduction, formulation of laws - that could be applied to human problems in such fields as sociology, psychology, criminology and even ethics and aesthetics as well as to natural phenomena within such disciplines as physics, chemistry and biology. Armed with this tool they launched a wide-ranging attack on what they saw as prevailing values. In aesthetics they rejected the view of art as capable of transcending reality and assigned to it the more menial role of reproducing reality. They argued that art should not be viewed as an end in itself but as a means to an end, which in their own place and time was civic or social. They preached a rigid determinism, according to which one's path in life and even one's everyday actions were dictated not by free will but by physiological or environmental factors. Seen in this light, crime was a product of adverse social conditions and would be almost entirely eliminated when causes such as hunger and poverty were removed. The 'men of the 60s' subscribed to a utilitarian ethics, according to which humans pursued pleasure and sought to avoid pain and were motivated solely by self-interest. Their belief that humans did not really exhibit altruism or compassion was consistent with their atheism, which was based on the thought of Feuerbach and the so-called 'vulgar materialists' Buchner, Moleschott and Vogt. That is to say, they denied the existence of spirit and held that matter is the only substance. Their egoism they reconciled with socialism by arguing that since humans were rational as well as selfish it was possible to persuade them that their own best interest lay in co-operation with their fellows. The interests of the individual were overridden in their minds by those of the larger group or social class - thus in Russia, the peasantry had priority over the nobility - or by the interests of the nation as a whole.

The rebellion initiated in the 1850s by Chernyshevsky and Dobroliubov was continued after Dobroliubov's death in 1861 and Chernyshevsky's arrest in 1862 by Pisarev, who himself died at the age of only twenty-seven in 1868. Pisarev echoed Chernyshevsky's philosophical materialism and shared his reverence for science. He also pressed Chernyshevsky's rejection of art as an end in itself and his demand for utility in art to the limit: for example, he avowed that he would rather be a shoemaker than a Raphael and wrote an article on the 'destruction of aesthetics'. He 'went further' than Chernyshevsky and Dobroliubov, as Dostoevsky once put it, both by virtue of the vehemence of his iconoclasm and by exalting the individual liberated from the constraints of convention and tradition. He did not flinch from the conclusion that that individual, recognizing no authority outside himself, spiritual or political, enjoyed extraordinary power and the freedom to exercise it as he chose, for ends that might be socially destructive or even criminal as well as for socially useful purposes or in the service of charity. It is Pisarev, more than any other Russian thinker, who is associated with 'nihilism', the term coined by Turgenev to denote the moral rebellion of the radical intelligentsia.

Numerous issues examined in Russian literature in the age of Alexander II – for example, tension between the generations; class conflict; attitudes to art and science; the fate of the superfluous man and the emergence of a new positive type of hero; the role of the common people in Russian history; the role of women in Russian society - have their roots in, or are entangled with, the debates agitating Russian thinkers in the post-Crimean period.

The classic fictional exposition of the debate between the older moderate Westernizers and the younger militant ones is Turgenev's masterpiece *Fathers and Children* (or 'Sons': *Ottsy i deti,* 1862), with its portrait of the 'nihilist' Bazarov (whom Pisarev, in two famous essays, took as an example of the 'realist' to be emulated). Bazarov and Arkadii Kirsanov, who is at first his disciple, reject art as a vehicle for pursuit of beauty, a pursuit which they see as a dangerous form of self-indulgence. Accordingly they plan to introduce Arkadii's gentle father, Nikolai, to Büchner's *Force and Matter* (1855) as an alternative to Pushkin's poetry, which they notice him reading. Nature, beloved by the older generation as a beautiful object of contemplation and mysteriously entwined with their emotional lives, is for Bazarov 'not a temple but a workshop' in which the scientist - such as himself, a medical student - can conduct experiments that have practical utility. People Bazarov regards - in the first half of the novel, at any rate - not as individualized beings with a legitimate inner world of their own but as representatives of a type: he compares them to trees in a wood which interest a botanist not on account of their idiosyncrasies but only insofar as they offer material on which to base generalizations. In endowing Bazarov with a capacity for the inexplicable romantic feeling whose existence his ideology seems to preclude, Turgenev transmutes contemporary polemic into a timeless artistic comment on the human condition. Nevertheless it is the stuff of contemporary polemic from which the novel is fabricated. Moreover, with its underlying antagonism between the nobility, represented by the two generations of the Kirsanov family, and the *raznochintsy,* represented by Bazarov, it lays bare the element of class conflict in the struggle between the 'men of the 40s' and the 'men of the 60s'.

Turgenev's novel touches upon a further question that again reverberates between thought and literature in the post-Crimean period, namely the study of the nature of the typical educated Russian of the epoch. All of Turgenev's first four novels reflect a movement, or an aspiration, over the period 1840-60, away from the ineffectual 'superfluous man' of noble origin and towards the more practical 'positive hero' of lower social origin, the *raznochinets,* who is capable of achieving the goals he sets himself. The comparison of these two types, the 'superfluous man' and the 'positive hero', was one to which Turgenev himself gave much thought. In his essay *Hamlet and Don Quixote* (1860) he addressed it with reference to Shakespeare's and Cervantes' characters on an axis running from egoism to altruism. Hamlet is an attractive but ultimately ineffectual hero dogged by introspection ('reflection' as the Russians put it). Since he lives only for himself, he is unable ever fully to give himself to anyone or any cause. Don Quixote, on the other hand, lives entirely for something outside himself and is therefore capable of self-sacrifice. The subject has political implications, which are taken up by Dobroliubov in his famous essays of 1859-60 on Goncharov's *Oblomov* (1859) and Turgenev's *On the Eve* (*Nakanune,* published 1860 but set in 1853-4), in which the radical critic associates the 'superfluous man' with the ineffectual liberal, full of fine phrases but disinclined to disturb the status quo. These implications are further developed by Chernyshevsky in his novel *What is to be Done?* Chernyshevsky offers a cast of positive heroes, the 'new people', led by the proto-revolutionary Rakhmetov, the 'salt of the salt of the earth', who applies a clinical rationalism to all problems and strengthens himself mentally and physically for the coming battles by depriving himself of luxuries - except cigars - and lying from time to time on a bed of nails.

The extent to which the conception of the 'positive hero' represents a description of what actually obtained in contemporary reality, on the one hand, or a prescription as to what thinkers and writers thought it desirable to find, on the other, is problematical, as is the more general question as to the extent to which literature was shaped by or itself helped to shape reality. The fact that Insarov, the hero of Turgenev's third novel, *On the Eve,* is not a Russian but a Bulgarian preparing to help to liberate his country from Turkish rule is suggestive of the unavailability as yet of this type in Russian reality. Moreover, Bazarov in *Fathers and Children,* it will be noted, not only dies before fulfilling any ambition but was also conceived by Turgenev, as he once put it, as standing only 'on the threshold of the future'.

Alongside ideological tension, conflict of generations and classes, and eager anticipation of the appearance of the 'positive hero', thinkers in the post-Crimean period show growing interest in the nature and welfare of the popular masses. This interest combines with the new aesthetics propounded by Chernyshevsky and others, with its demand for an art faithfully reproducing reality and serving the cause of social justice, to stimulate many works of literature (by, for instance, Nikolai Uspensky, Levitov and Sleptsov in the 1860s and Zasodimsky and Zlatovratsky in the next decade) in which the common people were depicted, generally in a sympathetic light. Thinkers also champion the emancipation of women, advocating their emergence as complete social equals of men with the same rights to education, with freedom of choice in marriage and with similar opportunities for socially useful activity. The most energetic and single-minded spokesman for this cause in the immediate post-Crimean period is perhaps M.L. (or M.I.) Mikhailov. However, again it is Chernyshevsky who most famously argued the case, in his novel *What is to be Done?*. Chernyshevsky's heroine Vera Pavlovna escapes with the help of Lopukhov from the tyranny of her family, chooses a new partner, Lopukhov's friend Kirsanov, and establishes a Utopian social unit, a successful female co-operative of seamstresses.

The moral rebellion of the 1860s, and the revolutionary ferment of the late 60s and the 1870s to which it gave rise, found expression in the writing of Dostoevsky. Indeed nowhere is the boundary between thought and art more difficult to define than in Dostoevsky's work and it is doubtful whether Dostoevsky himself conceived of a distinction of this sort. For one thing Dostoevsky, as *de facto* editor of the journals *Vremia (Time, lS6l-3)mdEpokha (Epoch,* 1864-5), participated directly in the polemical journalism of the early 1860s and then again, intermittently, through his *Diary of a Writer (Dnevnik pisatelia)* in the period 1873-81. Together with Grigor'ev, an exponent of 'organic criticism' who saw artists as an expression of the inner life of their people, Dostoevsky was a leading representative of *pochvennichestvo* or 'native-soil conservatism', a variant of romantic conservative nationalism close to Slavophilism. The *pochvenniki* dreamed of reconciliation between the westernized educated class, who had been steered away from national roots by the 'Petrine reform', and the Russian common people, who preserved their Orthodox faith. Both Grigor'ev and Dostoevsky formulated a dichotomy, which pervades Dostoevsky's fiction, between predatory and meek types, whom we might identify within these thinkers' schemes of things with western peoples and Russians respectively.

It is true that Dostoevsky's novels, as multifaceted works of art, stand above any single ideological position and in any event they often state a powerful case for a position which Dostoevsky is unlikely personally to have endorsed. And yet the questions agitating the Russian intelligentsia - aesthetic, ethical, spiritual, social and political, and ultimately the question of national identity and mission - are assimilated in his fiction. For example, his *Notes from Underground (Zapiski iz podpoVia,* 1864) takes an irrationalist standpoint to ridicule the blithe Chernyshevskian view of humans as reasonable beings capable of devising a perfect society and to challenge the Victorian notion of progress. In *Crime and Punishment* Chernyshevsky's rational egoism and Pisarev's legitimization of the superman, Utopian schemes, the contemporary loss of faith and denial of altruism are all subjected to withering scrutiny. Again, in Dostoevsky's third major novel, *The Devils (Besy,* 1871-2), both the liberal Westernism of the 1840s and early Russian socialism as represented by Nechaev, with its cynical Machiavellian tactics, are presented as portending, indeed liable to precipitate, an apocalypse. In *The Brothers Karamazov (Brat Ha Karamazovy,* 1880) - set, it should be noted, in the 1860s, the age of moral and incipient political revolt - the murder of old Fedor Karamazov and the enquiry into the legal and moral responsibility for it of his sons unfolds into the broadest disquisition on the disintegration of the Russian family, the relationship between the spiritual and secular domains represented by Church and state respectively, the distinctions between Orthodox Russia and the West, and overarching questions about faith and justice, human and divine. What for Dostoevsky was no less important than these questions, or even separable from them, the novels also passionately uphold the integrity of art and speak of a person's spiritual need for the beauty it embodies against the prevailing utilitarianism of the radical intelligentsia.

Tolstoy's major novels, *War and Peace (Voinaimir,* 1865-9) and *Anna Karenina* (1875-7), are less closely related to the topical concerns of the Russian intelligentsia of the time when they were written than are any of Dostoevsky's novels. Towards the end of the 1870s, however, Tolstoy himself underwent a spiritual crisis that made him repudiate his former way of life and the art he had hitherto produced. This crisis found expression in his *Confession (Ispoved',* 1879-81) and gave rise to various tracts in which he himself made a contribution to Russian political thought, or rather apolitical thought inasmuch as the doctrine Tolstoy puts forward is a form of anarchism. His last novel, *Resurrection (Voskresenie,* 1899), clearly discloses the many objects of Tolstoy's condemnation in this period: the coercive apparatus of the state, that is to say its army, its penal system and judicial practices and institutions, which are not at all concerned with human justice but uphold existing inequalities and sanction abuses; the rituals and hypocrisies of the Church, which has departed radically from the simple and holy teachings of Christ, exemplified by the Sermon on the Mount; the institution of private property, the greed of the privileged classes and the plight of the underprivileged and the oppressed. No longer, in this case, is the Russian novelist fashioning the reality around him, including the polemics that swirl within that reality, into a work of art that incorporates topical ideas within a plausible living world of timeless appeal. Rather Tolstoy has crossed the boundary into mere advocacy of his single viewpoint, or at least he teeters on that boundary.

With the assassination of Alexander II by terrorists of the party The People's Will in 1881 the optimism and millenarian expectations of the Russian intelligentsia gave way to pessimism and acceptance of' small deeds', that is to say concentration on fulfillment of modest ambitions. Chekhov's stories and plays reflect the despondent mood of the *fin de siecle*. In any case the golden age of Russian culture came naturally to an end with the death of Dostoevsky in 1881 and Turgenev in 1883 and with Tolstoy's spiritual crisis. Russian thought now became more sharply polarized. At the radical end of the political spectrum, Populists and Marxists - represented by Plekhanov and, later, Lenin - engaged in debate on the history of and prospects for capitalism in Russia. At the conservative end of the spectrum several thinkers, such as Danilevsky, Pobedonostsev and Leont'ev, who continued to stress the distinctiveness of Russia's civilization and the importance of protecting it from contemporary western influences, expressed reactionary views more boldly than their romantic conservative predecessors had done. At the same time the bond that had existed between literature and thought throughout the classical period was somewhat weakened. Admittedly, thinkers continued in the late nineteenth and early twentieth centuries to address literary questions and writers continued to touch upon issues of social, political or broad national significance. Thus Plekhanov discussed aesthetics from the Marxist standpoint and applied Marxism as a tool for the examination of literature, whilst Gor'ky evinced pity for the lower classes and wrote in a way that appealed to the swelling revolutionary ranks. And yet the greatest creative writer of the turn of the century, Chekhov, eschewed political involvement and did not directly engage in his stories and plays with the issues agitating contemporary political thinkers. As for the poetic movements of the last years of the nineteenth century and the early years of the twentieth, they tended to give precedence to metaphysical and religious concerns over social and political ones. Perhaps it was not until the Soviet period that imaginative literature again engaged with social and political issues as intensely as it had in the period 1825-81. Then, from the 1920s, topicality once more became overt in works conforming to the dictates of the official doctrine of socialist realism, while even writers who sought to evade the party's injunctions, such as Zamiatin, Bulgakov, Pasternak and Solzhenitsyn, raised questions which in the totalitarian state inevitably assumed political significance.

Further Reading

Berlin, Isaiah. *Russian Thinkers,* London: Hogarth Press, 1978.

Dowler, Wayne. *Dostoevsky, Grigor'ev and Native-Soil Conservatism,* Toronto and London: Toronto University Press, 1982.

Edie, James M., Scanlan, James P. and Zeldin, Mary-Barbara (eds) *Russian Philosophy,* 3 vols., Chicago: Quadrangle Books, 1965.

Kelly, Aileen M. *Toward Another Shore: Russian Thinkers between Necessity and Chance,* New Haven and London: Yale University Press, 1998.

Lampert, Eugene. *Sons against Fathers: Studies in Russian Radicalism and Revolution,* Oxford: Clarendon Press, 1965.

Studies in Rebellion, London: Routledge and Kegan Paul, 1957.

Leatherbarrow, W.J. and Offord, Derek (eds and trans.) *A Documentary History of Russian Thought: From the Enlightenment to Marxism,* Ann Arbor: Ardis, 1987.

Martinsen, Deborah (ed.) *Literary Journals in Imperial Russia,* Cambridge: Cambridge University Press, 1997.

Moser, Charles A. *Antinihilism in the Russian Novel of the 1860's,* The Hague: Mouton, 1964.

Esthetics as Nightmare: Russian Literary Theory, 1855-1870, Princeton: Princeton University Press, 1989.

Offord, Derek. *Portraits of Early Russian Liberals: A Study of the Thought of T N. Granovsky, V. P. Botkin, P. V. Annenkov, A. V. Druzhinin and K. D. Kavelin,* Cambridge: Cambridge University Press, 1985.

Schapiro, Leonard. *Rationalism and Nationalism in Russian Nineteenth-Century Political Thought,* New Haven and London: Yale University Press, 1967.

Terras, Victor. *Belinskij and Russian Literary Criticism: The Heritage of Organic Aesthetics,* Madison: University of Wisconsin Press, 1974.

Walicki, Andrzej. *A History of Russian Thought from the Enlightenment to Marxism,* trans. Hilda Andrews-Rusiecka, Oxford: Clarendon Press, 1980.

The Slavophile Controversy: History of a Conservative Utopia in Nineteenth-Century *Russian Thought,* Oxford: Clarendon Press, 1975

CRITICAL
READINGS

Pushkin: A Monument to Poetry

Mary Helen Kashuba

For most speakers of English, the great Russian authors are Tolstoy, Dostoevsky, and more recently, Pasternak. For a Russian, another name comes to mind first, Aleksandr Sergeevich Pushkin. He is the beloved poet whose verses they memorize, the author whose home at Mikhailovskoye they visit even in the dead of winter, the celebrated genius whose works come alive at poetry readings and celebrations. Although they may not be able to analyze the literary qualities of his work, to them, he represents the Russian soul and nation. Others have succeeded him and refined his work, but they have not eclipsed his influence.

Aleksandr Sergeevich Pushkin (1799–1837) was born into a family of impoverished nobility. Pushkin and his family were justifiably proud of their ancestry. The poet himself vaunted his Abyssinian, or Cameroon, (Binyon 4) forebear, Ibrahim Hannibal. A favorite of Peter the Great, Hannibal inspired Pushkin's unfinished prose work, *The Blackamoor of Peter the Great.* Pushkin's appearance gave strong evidence of his ancestry, in which he took pride. At home, his parents paid little attention to him, and his childhood memories revert rather to his nurse, Arina Rodionovna, whom he immortalized in his verse and whose folk tales inspired his later work.

Pushkin lived in a time of change for Russia, when the first rumblings of revolt in 1825 set the stage for the eventual and infamous 1917 Revolution. Few recognized the unrest, however, and Pushkin himself grew up in an atmosphere, which hardly encouraged political dissidence. He owed his education to the liberality of Emperor Alexander I, who opened the Imperial Lyceum in 1811 in the town of Tsarskoye Selo, which the Soviets later renamed Pushkin. Here, the most promising young men were trained to become leaders in the civil administrative service, a bureaucratic system of ranks that contributed to one's status in society. Pushkin was among the thirty members of the first graduating class. Not a model student, he nevertheless made his mark as a promising writer.

During Pushkin's formative years, Russia entered combat with Napoleon I of France, Alexander I's former friend and ally. Even as a student, Pushkin lauded Russian heroism in this ultimately victorious conflict, nonetheless a tumultuous time for Russia. As a result of these wars, Alexander abandoned his earlier liberal views and became suspicious of any political movements. This, in turn, precipitated Pushkin's exile from the capital in 1820, when he was ordered to the Caucasus, Crimea, Kishinev, and Odessa. His liberal verses had aroused suspicion, in particular his "Ode to Liberty." The official letter of transfer states, "the latter poem (Ode to Liberty) displays dangerous principles acquired in the school of the day, or. . . in that system of anarchy which bad faith calls the system of human rights and the freedom and independence of peoples" (Troyat 136).

Pushkin remained away from the capital until pardoned by Nicholas I in 1826. Thus he escaped the fateful Decembrist Uprising of 1825. Members of several secret groups, led by officers of the military, took advantage of the interregnum between the death of Alexander I and the accession of Nicholas I to agitate for a constitutional monarchy and other reforms, including the abolition of serfdom. Poorly organized, the protest witnessed the death of many during the revolt and the subsequent execution of five leaders, along with the exile to Siberia of hundreds of others. Pushkin's sympathies with the rebels leave no doubt, and in his private interview with Nicholas, he admitted that he would have been among them had he been in Petersburg. He signed a statement promising to refrain from membership in any secret society and to avoid anti-government publications. Yet in 1827, he handed his "Message to Siberia" to one of the Decembrists' wives leaving to join her husband. This short poem is a message of hope to all who fight for freedom and an obvious political statement:

> In the depths of your Siberian mines
> Preserve your courage, patience, pride;
> Your toil, your burden's not in vain,
> Your noble vision shall not fail. (lines 1-4)

Pushkin loved the balls and high society of his day, as evidenced in the lines of *The Bronze Horseman*, in which he evokes the noise and chattering of Petersburg balls. His ten short years back in Moscow and St. Petersburg returned him to the temptations of his youth, namely, women and gambling, and led him to marriage with a beauty of the day, Natalia Nikolaevna Goncharova. An ill-fated match with a woman whose tastes did not correspond to her husband's literary genius, it ended in a duel with a rival for her affections and in the poet's death on January 29, 1837. Immediately, the intellectual world knew that it had lost a great writer.

Pushkin began to write with few Russian literary models. He had read widely in his youth, but in a desultory way, without supervision and not always understanding what he read. He read mostly in French, the language of culture at that time, and was especially fascinated by Voltaire, along with the great classical writers of the seventeenth century: Corneille, Racine, and Molière. From them, he inherited a strict economy of words typical of French classicism and a taste for the universal. Later, he came to know Byron, the English romantic admired by many continental writers. He added a dash of romanticism to his classical bent, resulting in a brand of literature heretofore unknown in Russia.

Russian literature before the nineteenth century was heavy with classical themes and meters, totally unsuited to the language. Some of the great predecessors of Pushkin include Ivan Krylov (1769–1844), Nikolai Karamzin (1766–1826), and Vasilii Zhukovsky (1783–1852). Krylov's fables, while revealing the Russian spirit, are mainly based on foreign models, notably La Fontaine. Karamzin's prose reflects the tradition of sentimentalism rather than true romanticism, and his verse echoes classical and French models. Vasilii Zhukovksy, friend and contemporary of Pushkin, considered the father of Russian poetry, began the emancipation from traditional norms, yet his poetry is known today only among scholars.

One of Pushkin's noted predecessors, Gavrila Derzhavin (1743–1816), attended the qualifying examination at Tsarskoye Selo in 1815, where Pushkin recited his poem entitled *Recollections of Tsarskoye Selo*. The nodding Derzhavin suddenly took notice of the young poet and recognized his successor. In the same fashion, Zhukovsky, in 1820, dedicated a portrait of himself to Pushkin with the inscription "To the victorious pupil from his vanquished master." This was on the occasion of Pushkin's first successful publication, *Ruslan and Ludmila,* a mock-epic in the tradition of Russian folklore. It tells of the abduction of Ruslan's bride by the magician Chernomor, and Ruslan's adventures in reclaiming her. The prologue evokes images of the learned cat on the green oak tree, who tells the witty tale. This publication by the twenty-year old Pushkin, heading off to exile, unleashed a storm of criticism, from Belinsky's praise to conservative criticism. Where Belinsky saw "fine lines, intelligence, and common sense," others noted "vulgar comparisons, obnoxious enchantments, voluptuous images" (Troyat 142). Yet the work remains popular, and among other influences, inspired Mikhail Glinka's light-hearted 1842 opera of the same name.

Pushkin's southern exile inspired him with a love of nature and interest in the exotic. Like many of his contemporaries, he envisioned himself as a Byronic hero, disillusioned, in conflict with a society to which he is superior, the victim of fate. In the spirit of Chateaubriand's *René,* he nursed a melancholy disposition, hid himself in nature, and yearned for the freedom of the autumn leaves. These sentiments come into play in the three short poems, *Prisoner of the Caucasus, The Fountain of Bakhchisaray,* and *The Gypsies* (1820–1824). *The Gypsies* is considered the best of the three, both from its stylistic use of language and the virtual disappearance of the typical Byronic hero. In the spirit of Chateaubriand, it illustrates the impossibility of a return to the untamed pre-civilization world, here exemplified in the European Aleko's futile attempt to integrate himself into a Gypsy community. He kills his bride Zemfira for her unfaithfulness to him. The wise Gypsy elder tells him:

> Leave us, you proud, disdainful man!
> We are savage, and we do not have laws,
> But we do not torture, and we do not kill.
> We have no need of blood or groans

But to live with a murderer we have no wish.
Your lot was not cast to be born with the free,
And freedom you wish for only selfishly.
Your voice forever would be ghastly to us,
We are gentle and our natures are kind,
You are brazen and evil, and you must leave us.
Farewell, and peace live in your mind". (lines 510–520)

As interpreted by Vickery, "*The Gypsies* is not a demonstration of the superiority of the primitive to the civilized. It is, rather, the awareness of the fragility of human happiness and destiny" (44). Pushkin's poem inspired Sergei Rachmaninov's ballet *Aleko* of 1893 and has strong echoes in Prosper Mérimée's *Carmen* and Bizet's opera of the same name.

In 1824, Pushkin was officially dismissed from government service, both for his indiscrete relationships and his suspected authorship of the witty but blasphemous poem *Gavriiliada*. He returned to Mikhailovskoye, where he remained in exile until 1826. Here, he led a solitary existence, broken mainly by the company his nurse, Arina Rodionovna, and visits to his neighbors at Trigorskoye. During this period, he composed a number of lyric poems, a large portion of *Evgenii Onegin,* and completed *Boris Godunov,* a historical tragedy in the Shakespearean tradition.

Written in 1825, *Boris Godunov* was not published until 1831 and not approved by the censors until 1866. It has been called "the first modern Russian historical drama" (Brody 857), understandably so, since Russia had a limited dramatic tradition. It recaptures the "Time of Troubles" (1598–1613), when the throne passed by devious means from one contriver to the next and has become a symbol for political disturbances and dissensions. Critics have noted many flaws, such as the lack of unity of theme and place, the absence of the main character in most of the scenes and his unexplained death. The play however does present a strong psychological focus, emphasizing Godunov's guilt in the murder of Dmitri, the heir to the throne. It is a drama of character, as noted by Mirsky (99). The first performance of the play took place only in 1870, and most attempts at staging proved mediocre. Mussorgsky's opera of 1874 has had better success in the theater. However, Pushkin forged a play, which resurrects a crucial period in Russian history and thus has succeeded in creating the atmosphere of historic realism. Vickery comments, "This is, first and foremost, a play about power, about the evil and futility of ambition, about a man wracked by his guilty conscience" (68).

Pushkin continued his dramatic works in his "little tragedies," namely, *The Covetous Knight, Mozart and Salieri, The Stone Guest,* and *The Feast During the Plague.* Mirsky, among other critics, rates them higher than *Boris Godunov,* placing them among Pushkin's greatest works (99–100). His idea came from a little-known English author, Barry Cornwall (1781–1814). The tragedies are brief, from 200–500 lines, and are difficult to stage. However, they remain lyrical masterpieces marked by economy of words and excellent literary style. *The Feast During the Plague* is basically a translation from the English of John Wilson, which Mirsky sees as superior to the original (99). *Mozart and Salieri* explores the probable murder of Mozart by a jealous Salieri and consists of only two scenes. While too short for the stage, it nevertheless contains a complex message. Like *The Covetous Knight,* it explores the theme of envy, complicated by the sympathy the reader feels for Salieri.

The best of all four remains *The Stone Guest,* derived from the Don Juan legends, mainly through Molière, Mozart, and Tirco de Molina. Pushkin completed it in 1830, but it was published only posthumously. While many of the traditional plots are farcical in nature, Pushkin has created a romantic tragedy. The reader observes a certain sincerity of emotion in Don Juan, absent in most stories. His rendezvous with Doña Anna, in the shadow of the monument to her husband whom Don Juan has murdered, ends in his tragic hand-shake with the statue, the "Stone Guest," just as he anticipates her acceptance of his advances. Critics, notably Roman Jacobson, have analyzed Pushkin's fascination with statues, and the role of art in his works (Herman 3 ff.).

Pushkin's exile, while frustrating to him, continued to be fruitful for the literary world. *Eugene (Evgenii) Onegin,* Pushkin's masterpiece and his only novel in verse, dates back to 1823. Pushkin published it in serial form between 1825 and 1832. The complete edition appeared in 1833, with a definitive version in 1837. He composed an original "Onegin stanza" of iambic tetrameter, with a complex rime scheme. The novel consists of eight chapters, or cantos, as Pushkin called them informally. The hero, Evgenii, or Eugene, illustrates the "superfluous person," typical of the Russian aristocracy of Pushkin's age. He is an intellectual, but aimless and indolent, more interested in his appearance than in a meaningful life. An inheritance brings him from Petersburg to the country, where he establishes a vague friendship with Lensky, a mediocre poet. In an idle quarrel over Olga, a neighbor whom Lensky is courting, Onegin and Lensky engage in a duel, resulting in Lensky's death. Tatiana, Olga's sister, falls madly in love with Onegin, and declares her love in a famous letter. Onegin rebuffs her, and continues his aimless wanderings. When he returns, more mature, he seeks Tatiana's hand. She is now married, and although she would prefer Onegin, she remains faithful to her husband and bids Onegin farewell.

While the plot is simple, the novel itself is more complex. It addresses the questions important to the early nineteenth-century Russian society, such as the wasteful aristocracy, social life in the cities, or the boredom of country existence. Maxim Gorky expresses the Soviet viewpoint of class struggle when he states:

> Without doubt, Pushkin was an aristocrat—he himself on occasion flaunted the fact; but it is important for us to know that he sensed in his youth the narrowness and stuffiness of aristocratic traditions, realized the intellectual poverty of his class, its cultural impotence, and pictured the life of the aristocracy, all its vices and weaknesses, with unequivocal veracity. ("Pushkin: An Appraisal")

The novel also involves moral questions pertinent to all times: artificiality or authenticity, truth or falsehood, integrity or compromise. Russians of Pushkin's time identified with the heroes and their surroundings as truly resonating with their spirit. Not only does Pushkin tell a story; he paints the picture of an age and of a place. His nature descriptions, especially those of the Russian winter, are among the most exquisite in Russian literature. His verses on the seasons evoke the inevitable passage of time. His characters live on in the Russian memory, and children memorize the verses. Tatiana has long remained the ideal of the Russian woman, although her decision may not resonate universally. More than a moral victory, Tatiana's refusal of Onegin represents a world without second chances, and the novel ends on a fateful note (Vickery 129). Tchaikovsky has captured Pushkin's spirit in his 1878 opera of the same name.

With *Eugene Onegin,* Russia entered into the age of the realistic novel, to be developed later by Gogol, Tolstoy, and their successors. While Pushkin's work did not have the sophistication of the later authors, or that of Balzac and Dickens, he laid the groundwork for the development of the novel as the art form destined to dominate the nineteenth century and even the beginning of the twentieth.

A shorter work, but no less a masterpiece, is Pushkin's enigmatic poem, *The Bronze Horseman*, completed in 1833. He based his poem on a historic event, the Petersburg flood of 1824, and once again on a statue, the Falconet monument to Peter the Great erected by Catherine the Great in Petersburg in 1782. The poem consists of only 481 lines in two parts and an introduction. Pushkin begins by recapping Peter's foundation of his city on a marshy swamp in the early eighteenth century. A hundred years have passed, and now the city shines bright on land and sea, equal to its western counterparts. By contrast, the devastating flood has destroyed the future of a young clerk, Evgeny, who loses his fiancée Parasha to the storm. He goes mad, as he imagines that the statue is pursuing him. Strangers later find him dead on a desolate island.

Naturally, the question arises: was Peter's dream of glory worth the loss of lives that it entailed? Pushkin leaves the question unanswered, but critics have not hesitated to speculate on the significance of the poem. On the one hand, Pushkin praises Peter:

Now, city of Peter, stand thou fast
Foursquare, like Russia, vaunt thy splendor!

The very element shall surrender
And make her peace with thee at last.
Their ancient bondage and their rancors
The Finnish waves shall bury deep
Nor vex with idle spite that cankers
Our Peter's everlasting sleep! (lines 84-91)

On the other hand, he sympathizes with "my, poor, poor Evgeny," as he continues:

There was a dreadful time, we keep
Still freshly on our memories painted;
And you, my friends, shall be acquainted
By me, with all that history:
A grievous record it will be. (lines 92-96)

Soviet critics see the poem as a glorification of the state over the individual, while others view it as a response to the Polish poet Adam Miskiewicz, and a defense of Russia. On the other hand, Pushkin has the merit of creating in Evgeny one of the first of many "little people," the lowly and forgotten, the downtrodden and the desperate, who are the victims of bureaucracy. Gogol's Akakii Akakievich, for example, is a direct descendant of Evgeny. These people struggle to survive, and their number increases as contemporary society becomes more complex. Pushkin has created a figure who unfortunately will endure far beyond his *Bronze Horseman*.

Around the same time, Pushkin composed his "skazki," or tales taken from Russian folklore. They include *The Tale of the Tsar Saltan* of 1831, *Tale of the Fisherman and the Fish* of 1833, *The Tale of the Dead Princess and the Seven Heroes* of 1833, and *The Tale of the Golden Cockerel* of 1834. While Pushkin was indebted to his nurse, Arina Rodionovna, for the initial inspiration, he did not hesitate to use other sources, such as the Brothers Grimm, or his own imagination to develop the tales. Some stories are familiar to western readers, especially *Snow White* as the dead princess, and the three wishes in the *Tale of the Fisherman*. The Golden Cockerel, a lesser-known story, is a lesson in broken promises. *The Tale of the Tsar Saltan,* considered the best, is a complex tale of jealousy and intrigue, from which truth eventually triumphs. The great merit of these tales lies in their evocation of the Russian spirit, or "narodnost." Pushkin achieves this not only through his material, but also through his style: his choice of words, taken from the language of the people, and his rimes and rhythms, which capture the folk tradition, all defy translation and ring true only in the original.

Pushkin instinctively recognized the triumph of prose over poetry in the nineteenth century, only too evident in the twenty-first, as noted by Bethea (*Metaphors* 1). Thus in the 1830s, Pushkin created a number of prose works. Among the most important are *The Tales of Belkin* (1830), *The Queen of Spades* (1834), and *The Captain's Daughter* (1836). Debreczeny maintains that Pushkin turned to prose not because of its marketability, but rather his sense of its necessity to express ideas where poetry failed (12). He also notes the influence of Sir Walter Scott on Pushkin's use of the imaginary and often omniscient narrator (63). This is especially evident in *The Tales of Belkin.* The volume consists of five tales, each one short, sparse in words and simple in syntax, and easily accessible in Russian even to beginning students. Each story has a twist, and often a parody on existing conventions. Vickery notes, for example, *The Stationmaster* as "a rebuttal of the Sentimentalist fallacy that poor girls are by nature innocent, and that the results of their seduction are bound to be catastrophic" (154). In fact, in this story, the young girl leads a comfortable life, while her father pines away and dies. The same twist occurs in *The Shot,* where the winner of a duel eventually pardons his opponent because he sees true emotion in him.

The Queen of Spades is a tale of obsession, this time with gambling, a passion which devoured Pushkin as it did Hermann, the tragic hero, who, like Evgeny in *The Bronze Horseman*, goes mad at the end. It has its somber side, fraught with risks as Hermann must find his way into the room of the elderly Countess at night to learn her secret. He obtains it, and it might have worked, had he not mistaken the ace for the queen of spades. It is an excellent short story, and Pushkin has woven a tale of suspense through literary simplicity and sparseness of detail. However, in his analysis of the symbolism inherent in the story, Debreczeny has shown that it is close to poetry (212–228). The tale has exerted wide influence. Gogol's *Diary of a Madman* tells a similar story of the descent into lunacy. Dostoevsky borrowed heavily from it in such works as *The Gambler, Crime and Punishment,* and *The Adolescent,* as noted by Debreczeny (186). Finally, Tchaikovsky's 1890 opera recreated Pushkin's story, with great success.

In *The Captain's Daughter* Pushkin relates a fictitious account of the Pugachev Rebellion of 1773–1774. His *History of Pugachev* (1834) was an extensive two-volume work, the second volume being totally composed of notes, intended for the Tsar alone. Pushkin had spent many months researching this important revolt under Catherine the Great, using the archives in Moscow, Petersburg, and Orenburg. While the finished work has contributed greatly to scholarship of the rebellion, the popularized fictitious version remains more accessible to the general reader. *The Captain's Daughter* is not only a historical novel in the manner of *Boris Godunov;* it is also a family story, like *War and Peace,* and explored as such by O'Bell (48). Pushkin has attempted to give an authentic historical note to his fictional account. While the adventures of the young Pyotr Andreevich Grinyev grip the reader, Pushkin has introduced a number of incongruities into his account, as noted by Debreczeny (261-269). Among them are Pyotr's chance meeting with Pugachev and the thwarted attempts at Pyotr's execution. Debreczeny also observes that, despite the excellence of Pushkin's prose works, he attains his highest potential when using the techniques that served him best in poetry, namely allusions, symbols, and juxtapositions (299).

Finally, Pushkin's art remains essentially poetic. This is his genius, probably most evident in his lyrical works. Short, yet filled with meaning, they span his entire career, almost his entire life, since he began writing poetry while still in the Lyceum. His first-known poem goes back to age thirteen (Binyon 32). Yet the verbal economy and melodic resonance of his verse defy translation. The idea is so tightly fused with the language that it is literally "lost in translation." The very simplicity of his poetry renders all but experiencing it impossible. He treats simple subjects. They range from love to nature, from nostalgia to protest, from despair to hope. They are visual: a carefree bird in a tree, knowing no anxiety or cares; a troika racing through the snowy woods on a winter's night; a passing vision of a beautiful woman. They are auditory: the howling storm on a winter's evening:

> The storm covers skies in darkness,
> Spinning snowy whirlwinds tight,
> Now it wails like a beast wildest,
> Now it cries like a week child,
> Now suddenly it rustles
> The old roof's dry thatching mass,
> Now, a traveler, late and gusty,
> It knocks at our window's glass. (lines 1-8)

They are tender:

> I loved you: and, it may be, from my soul
> The former love has never gone away,
> But let it not recall to you my dole;
> I wish not to sadden you in any way.
>
> I loved you silently, without hope, fully,
> In diffidence, in jealousy, in pain;
> I loved you so tenderly and truly,
> As let you else be loved by any man. (entire poem)

They are playful, toying with the familiar and formal terms of address in Russian:

> She substituted, by a chance,
> For empty *"you"* — the gentle *"thou"*;
> And all my happy dreams, at once,
> In loving heart again resound.
> In bliss and silence do I stay,
> Unable to maintain my role:

"Oh, how sweet you are!" I say --
"How I love thee!" says my soul. (entire poem)

And his verses are prophetic. In the words, which echo the Roman poet Horace, he writes, ironically in 1836, six months before his death:

I've raised a monument no human hands could build. . .

Not all of me shall die: in verses shall my soul
Outlive my mortal dust and shall escape decay—
And I shall be renowned so long as on this earth
One single poet is alive. (lines 1, 5-8)

Pushkin rightly predicted his immortality. Russian literary criticism has focused on him from his first publication in 1820, *Ruslan and Ludmila.* Vissarion Belinsky (1811–1848), literary critic and philosopher, was among the first to publicize Pushkin's talent. He wrote articles on Pushkin and acclaimed him as a national poet, emphasizing the aesthetic quality of Pushkin's work. Belinsky became the basis for nineteenth-century literary criticism. However, Binyon notes that Pushkin's popularity began to diminish in the years before his death and did not recover until the 1880s (xvi). Bethea names a number of biographers in the second half of the nineteenth and early twentieth century who provided archival material on Pushkin's life and its association with his works (*Handbook* xviii). Others, following the tradition of Vladimir Soloviev, posited a messianic and prophetic message to Pushkin's work.

Belinsky's views remained popular among the Marxist-Leninist writers, who developed them into "socialist realism." Lunacharsky notes a social evolution in Pushkin, away from the aristocracy to the bourgeoisie, and his subsequent appraisal of changing economic realities. Gorky sees in Pushkin a person for whom the nation was greater than his own class. Marxists praised Pushkin for his *narodnost',* or sense of the people. While Bethea deplores the use of Pushkin for Soviet purposes, he lauds the compilation of Pushkin's works with textual histories, which they undertook, and notes especially the work of B.V. Tomashevkii (xxi). While the first part of the twentieth century follows the positivist tradition, the second half is dominated by formalism, especially in the work of I.A. Lotman and Roman Jacobson. Other authors undertook comparative studies of Pushkin with writers in other countries, such as Voltaire, Shakespeare, and Byron.

Among the more popular editions available in English is Henri Troyat's *Pushkin,* originally published in France in 1946. It emphasizes Pushkin's biography foremost, as well as his works. Paul Debreczeny's *The Other Pushkin* studies Pushkin's prose fiction, as do numerous articles by the same author. T. J. Binyon published a biography of Pushkin in 2002. In it, he aims to separate the real Pushkin from the "heroic simplicity of Pushkin the myth," (xxix) concentrating mainly on his life rather than his works. Among twenty-first century works on Pushkin, a number have begun to concentrate on Pushkin's African ancestry, among them Black Canadian Studies (Barnstead 367) and conferences, such as that held at Harvard University in April of 2008: "Aleksandr Pushkin: An Historic Symposium at Harvard. Exploring the Dual Heritage of Russia's Greatest Poet, Father of Modern Russian Literature, and the Black Russians of the 20th Century" (Frazier 189).

As he himself foresaw, Pushkin has erected a deathless monument. He developed the realistic novel, the historical drama, and lyric poetry. He spoke for freedom and a new era:

> In my cruel age I sang blessed freedom's praise
> And for the fallen mercy begged. ("I raised a monument," lines 15-16)

In his short life, he brought Russian poetry into the modern world. He gave it a distinctively Russian touch, developing the language to a high potential, fusing folk elements with refinement, combining sound with meaning. He treats ordinary themes and touches topics common to everyone: love, anger, jealousy. Pushkin is a poet of this world, who knew its pleasures and its problems and who knew how to express them in exquisite language. Bethea states that, like Shakespeare, Pushkin "is beyond good and evil. He is the world discovering itself, becoming self-aware" (*Realizing Metaphors* 7). Russians revere him, and the many translations of his work make him more and more accessible to speakers of other languages, who can thus become familiar with one of the world's great authors.

Works Cited

Barnstead, John A., "Black Canadian Studies as the Cutting Edge of Change: Revisioning Pushkin, Rethinking Pushkinology." *Journal of Black Studies* 38.3 (Jan. 2008): 367–373.

Bethea, David M. ed. *The Pushkin Handbook.* Madison, WI: U of Wisconsin P, 2005.

_____. *Realizing Metaphors: Alexander Pushkin and the Life of the Poet.* U of Wisconsin P, 1998.

Binyon T. J. *Pushkin, A Biography.* New York: Vintage Books, 2004.

Brody Ervin C. "Pushkin's *Boris Godunov*: The First Modern Russian Historical Drama." *The Modern Language Review* 72.4 (Oct. 1977): 857–875.

Debreczeny, Paul. *The Other Pushkin.* Stanford CA: Stanford UP, 1983.

Frazier, Melissa. "Pushkin and Blackness on the Web." *The Pushkin Review* 11(2008): 189–191.

Gorky, Maxim. "Pushkin: An Appraisal." *Pushkin: Homage by Marxist Critics.* 1937. Ed. Irving D. W. Talmudge. Marxist Internet Archive, Jan. 2001. Web. 12 Dec. 2013. <http://www.marxists.org/archive/gorky-maxim/misc/pushkin.htm >.

Herman, David, "Don Juan and Don Alejandro: The Seductions of Art in Pushkin's Stone Guest." *Comparative Literature* 51.1 (Winter 1999): 3–23.

Mirsky, D.S. *A History of Russian Literature.* New York: Vintage Books, 1958.

O'Bell, Leslie. "Pushkin's Novel *The Captain's Daughter* as Fictional Family Memoir." *Pushkin Review* 10 (2007): 47–57.

Pushkin, Alexander. *The Works of Alexander Pushkin. Lyrics, Narrative Poems, Folk Tales, Plays, Prose.* Ed. Avrahm Yarmolinsky. New York: Random House, 1936.

_____. *The Complete Prose Tales of Alexandr Sergeyevitch Pushkin.* Trans. Gillon R. Aitken. New York: W. W. Norton, 1966.

Troyat, Henri. *Pushkin.* New York: Doubleday and Co., 1970.

Vickery, Walter N. *Alexander Pushkin.* New York: Twayne Publishers, 1970.

Unseen Beauty, Shadows of Liminal Space, and the Caustic Passions of Exile: The Life and Writings of M. Yu. Lermontov

Michael Marsh-Soloway

Do not forsake me, all powerful God, and I pray do not punish me, because I love the gloomy darkness of the earth with all her sufferings; because the streams of your living spirits rarely enter my soul; because my intellect casts me into error far away from you; because the lava of inspiration thrashes inside my chest; because wild waves obscure the glass panes of my eyes; because for me the earthly world is too constricting. (M. Yu. Lermontov, "Prayer" ["*Molitva*"], 1830)[1]

To be so dependent on Pushkin, so totally, so completely, so slavishly; and to shake off this dependence—this is where Lermontov's genius manifested itself. (Anna Akhmatova, as reported by Lidia Chukovskaya)[2]

In most ascriptions of the Russian literary canon, Mikhail Yuryevich Lermontov (1814–1841) is often heralded as the second brightest star in the constellation of Russian poets, overshadowed only by the luminous and perspicacious genius of Aleksandr Sergeyevich Pushkin (1799–1837). Pushkin revolutionized Russian literature. Never before had low-register Russian vernacular been so enthralling.[3] In the words of Andrei Sinyavsky, until Pushkin, "there was almost no light Russian

Portrait of M. Yu. Lermontov by P. E. Zabolotsky, 1837. Held in the Tretyakov State Gallery in Moscow.

verse...and suddenly out of the blue, there appeared curtsies and turns comparable to nothing and no one, speed, onslaught, bounciness, the ability to prance, to gallop, to take hurdles, and to do splits."[4] Pushkin's rich literary repertoire and multifaceted narrative inclinations made his works especially prized by the Russian literate elite, but especially so by the budding genius of Lermontov.

Lermontov found in Pushkin a kind of role model, whose writing could serve as a paradigmatic literary basis, from which his own unique deliberations could emanate new artistic synergies, ideas, and sensations and whose personal conduct eerily foreshadowed Lermontov's own fall from grace in Russian society, his political exile, and his death from a gunshot wound incurred during a duel.[5] Already in the 1830s, the aesthetic tastes and sensibilities of Russia's literate elite started shifting away from lyrical verse productions, to longer prose works, including short stories, serialized articles, and novels.[6]

The consideration that the felicitous philosophical poetry of Fyodor Tyutchev passed almost completely unnoticed in 1836 indicated a symptom of a growing general feeling that the popular zenith of poetry had passed.[7] Before verse started to surrender its pre-eminence to the story, the novel, and the age of Realism, poets thrived in the invigorating environment of Romanticism and the sympathetic critical proximity of fellow artists endeavoring to perform the same craft.[8] Toward the end of Lermontov's flash-like literary career, one that spanned only roughly a dozen years, the seemingly innumerable audience that had once flocked to lyrical verse and afforded poets divine inspiration and encouragement, seemed utterly absent already by 1836.

Even Pushkin started focusing more on prose in order to address the changing tastes of his readers and consumer trends in the emerging Russian literary marketplace.[9] Both Lermontov and Tyutchev experienced the waning of a cultural ambience and public preference for lyricism that had all but disappeared when Lermontov first attained the recognition of Russian readers. In this vein, it is not surprising that Lermontov's literary tour de force, *A Hero of Our Time* [*Geroj nashego vremeni*], culminated in the artistic medium of the novel. Upon closer inspection, the work's prosaic devices are "'cross-fertilized' with countervailing poetic ones: euphonic repetitions, popular sayings whose meanings and sounds, i.e., paronomasia, could be literally realized in a story's plot or themes in the conveyance of proportionality and symmetry that aligned with the author's poetic thinking."[10]

Lermontov was something of a child prodigy and his prowess in verse started manifesting itself when he was only in his early teens. His talents developed during the uneasy and tumultuous historical period between the reigns of Tsar Aleksandr I, the benevolent liberator of Europe and conqueror of Napoleon, and Tsar Nikolai I, the austere despot, who engineered all of Russia's domestic and international policies to conform with predominant principles of nationalism, autocracy, and orthodoxy.[11] When Tsar Aleksander I died in December of 1825, a group of Russian aristocrats made an abortive attempt to overthrow the regime and to deny Nikolai I ascension to the throne in the hopes of initiating widespread constitutional and parliamentary reforms.[12]

Those who carried out the abortive attempt have come to be known as the Decembrists. Five of them were hanged in 1826, and 120 were given harsh sentences of forced labor in Siberian mines.[13] After the quelling of the Decembrist uprising, Tsar Nikolai I employed ruthless and meticulous secret police forces, comprised often of Prussian immigrants from the neighboring Baltic states, to conduct surveillance of state subjects in the interests of preserving unquestioning allegiance to his regime, enforcing strict censorship measures, and propagating information intended to enhance the reputation and directives of the state.[14] Against the backdrop of these oppressive reforms, the emergence of outstanding Russian authors, such as Ivan Krylov (1769–1844), Vasily Zhukovsky (1783–1852), Konstantin Batyushkov (1787–1855), Pushkin (1799–1837), Evgeny Baratynsky (1800–1844), Nikolai Gogol (1809–1852), and Lermontov (1814–1841), coalesced in the early flowering of a Golden Age of Russian literature.[15]

Alexander Herzen once commented, "[t]he history of Russian literature is little more than a catalogue of political martyrs and exiles."[16] That is, while Nicholas I's reign coincided with the fulfillment of a Golden Age of Russian Literature, it also condemned authors to harsh sentences of political exile, forced labor, and military service, usually in foreign locales on the imperial peripheries, places generally marked by uneasy terrain, severe climate, and hostile local populations. To avoid the persecution of state censors, authors developed unique ways of voicing their criticism of the state through the employed devices of allusion, abstraction, metaphor, and Aesopian language, or the seemingly benign expression of concealed disparagements through artistic satire, irony, purposeful misdirection, and juxtaposition.[17] The twentieth-century Russian poet, critic, and essayist Lev Losev even goes so far as to attribute Tsar Nikolai I's strict censorship measures as the primary catalyst that prodded the conception of the Russian Golden Age.[18] Voicing too direct a criticism of the state and its leaders could result in strict penalty, even death, and as such, Russian authors were forced to adapt creatively and adeptly to continue the espousal of their veiled sociopolitical commentaries.

As Lermontov started finding his literary voice at the outset of the 1830s, he came to embody an author of transition. The Decembrist Revolt was still fresh in the memory of Russian literary elite, however, as Lermontov was only eleven years old when the uprising was quelled, the aristocratic peers constituting his generation largely decided to align themselves with the state, rather than to continue to push for the reforms that the revolutionaries initially conceived. In his embittered 1838 poem, "Meditation" ["*Duma*"], Lermontov lamented, "Sadly do I gaze upon our generation!", angrily reproaching its members for being "shamefully indifferent to good and evil,… ignominiously fearful before danger/ And before power—contemptible slaves."[19] In this regard, Lermontov represents an individual set apart from his generation, an individual lost in a bewildering liminal state of the threshold that is neither here nor there. His writing style came to embody a unique, amorphous form, irrevocably torn between the ages of Romanticism and Realism, and the frequently divergent authorial tenets of poetry and prose.[20]

Aside from his established legacies in the media of published books, poems, and letters, Lermontov also possessed exciting talents in the realms of painting, music, and drama.[21] His personality is one that seemingly refutes any singular label or absolute contextual predilection for genre. Considering his multifaceted artistic perspectives, uncanny abilities to synthesize discordant styles, and repudiation of overarching milieus, be they generational, artistic, spiritual, or otherwise, Lermontov's role in Russian literature is seemingly that an indefinable phantom that came to fruition only as the era of Romanticism faded in the eclipse of another's unfolding, yielding to the rise of the Russian novel and the astute psychological insight of Dostoevsky (1821–1881) and Tolstoy (1828–1910).

While Lermontov spent most of his life in Russia, he is most closely associated with the Caucasus, or the mountainous region situated between the Black and Caspian Seas, "the dazzling mosaic of ethnic groups and rival clans," the crossroads of empires, the fault lines of civilizations, a rocky borderland torn between contentious considerations of Muslim versus Christian, Asian versus European, and East versus West, where neither traveler nor permanent resident enjoyed verifiable assurances of safe passage.[22] As a boy, Lermontov visited relatives in the Caucasus on several occasions, and here, he learned of the grandeur and wild beauty of the mountain scenery.[23] The trips made a lasting impression on his artistic consciousness and provided him with themes and landscapes that he would revisit countless times not only in his work, but also in his forced exile and military service in the Life Guard Hussars and line regiments during the Caucasian Conquest, when Russian military forces occupied the region from 1817–1864.[24]

Lermontov was born on October 2, 1814 in Moscow, but spent most of his adolescence on his grandmother's estate at Tarkhany outside Penza, about 400 miles to the southeast of Moscow.[25] His father was a descendant of the Scottish adventurer, Captain George Learmont, who, in the early seventeenth century, entered Russian military service. The poet and his father, however, seem to have been largely ignorant of this ancestry.[26] Lermontov's father, Yuri, served as a small squire and then low-ranking army officer, and there

Above: "A view of Tiflis," completed by M. Yu. Lermontov in 1837.
Held in the State Literary Museum in Moscow.

seems to have been considerable social inequality when he started courting the sixteen-year-old Mlle Arseniev, the daughter of E.A. Arsenieva (Stolypina by her maiden name), a wealthy landowner and influential aristocrat in Moscovite society.

When Lermontov was just three years old, his mother passed away, and he went to live permanently on his grandmother's estate outside Penza. Lermontov's grandmother deliberately limited interactions between father and son because she worried that the boy's father would attempt to appropriate her grandson and raise him in debaucherous settings away from her care and supervision. Lermontov often heard disparaging comments about his father from his grandmother, Mme Arsenieff, who referred to the man as a "strange and depraved creature."[27] Under his grandmother's doting, Lermontov was thoroughly educated, spoiled, and bereft of adventure as a child.[28]

Lermontov was just thirteen when he began reading and writing verse. His diverse educational pursuits and independent research interests exposed him to the foremost literary productions of his time, including, most notably, the Romantic writings of Byron. Lord Byron (1788–1824) was first mentioned in the Russian periodical

Above: "Recollections of the Caucasus," completed by M. Yu. Lermontov
in 1838. Held in the State Literary Museum in Moscow.

press in 1815, and his works grew into a major force in society and
literary culture, as he came to embody the most ostentatious and
notorious of all the major Romantics.[29] Byron's texts were translated
into dozens of languages, launching his celebrity cult-status and
generating international critical acclaim for his most influential
works, *Don Juan*, *Childe Harold's Pilgrimmage*, and *The Corsair*.[30]

Byronism became a fashionable behavioral model in Russia and,
as an ideology, featured elements of proud rebelliousness (versus God,
the social order, civilization, tyranny, etc.), aristocratic arrogance,
melancholy, love of nature, misanthropy, passionate excess, and
demonism.[31] In various contexts, manifestations of Byronism could
foreground political aspiration, social upheaval, and individual
isolation.[32] The twentieth-century Russian literary historian Viktor
Zhirmunsky categorized "the romantic Byronic *poema* by thematic
and compositional features such as a disillusioned hero, an exotic
setting, and fragmentariness."[33] Byronism exerted great influence
on the mindsets of Russian authors, including Pushkin, Aleksandr
Bestuzhev-Marlinsky, and Lermontov.

In the figure of Byron and his associated protagonists, the predominantly male strata of Russian authors identified particularly with the notion of the superfluous man. The concept resonated with a whole demographic of aristocratic Russian male readers, who had seemingly lost their sense of purpose and belonging in society. Superfluity manifested itself on both internal and external levels. Psychologically, for instance, superfluous men tend to feel lazy, bored, and jaded by the routine ebb and flow of estate life, shallow social gatherings, and conformist expectations of their participation in the administration of the state. Physically, moreover, boundaries of class, religion, appearance, ethnicity, and language, etc. would have discouraged their participation in manual labor, thereby limiting their interaction with the majority of the common folk in the Russian population.

In an 1832 poem, Lermontov establishes his intimate connection to the phenomenon of Byronism manifested in a uniquely Slavic context, by asserting categorically, 'No, I am not Byron, I am another unknown chosen one, like the wanderer persecuted by the world, but only with a Russian soul.'[34] For Lermontov, Byron's identity was established as a historical personage, whose creative works and biography marked him for a large group of readers as emblematic of the human condition, but the truth of his personality itself seemed every bit as enigmatic as the human existence it aimed to symbolize.[35] The far-reaching acclaim of Byron's life-text, moreover, served as a type of yardstick for Lermontov's own potential destiny.[36] While the models derived from Byron's writing afforded Lermontov's literary endeavors vibrant themes, compelling plot scenarios, and symbolic imagery, the Russian author adopted and adapted such features and made them his own by grounding them in the contexts of his own unique spiritual dilemmas, exotic travels in the unforgiving setting of the Caucasus, and interjecting elements of Slavic folklore, Eastern orthodoxy, intertwined vernacular and biblical aphorisms, and widely held superstitions.[37]

In his 1836 poem, "The Sail," for example, Lermontov draws on a comparison between a 'lonely sail flashing white / amidst the blue fog of the sea,' and his own quest for something unknowable in the perplexing environs of life.[38] The iambic tetrameter rhythm and alternating feminine-masculine rhyme scheme of the work alludes to the preferred prosodic features of Pushkin. When read deliberately and melodically, moreover, the aural delivery of the poem seems reminiscent of a Russian Orthodox hymn. While this particular work is devoid of explicit vocabulary selections that demonstrate a correspondence with Old Church Slavonic, both Lermontov and Pushkin would commonly employ archaic lexical items in their verse to reiterate the superimposition of biblical language and imagery in the re-imagined contexts of their literary creations.

Operating with the device of metonymy, moreover, the image of 'the sail' infers the entire vessel of the small caravel, which, in turn, seems to reflect the author's own wayward authorial personality. While no specific geographic body of water is mentioned in the text, it seems likely that the ship is traversing the Black Sea, perhaps traveling from the seaside village of Taman, a locale that Lermontov revisits in *A Hero of Our Time* and casts jarringly in the descriptive likeness of an epicenter of Gothic supernaturalism. In the novel, the narrator Pechorin stumbles into "Taman…the nastiest little hole of all the seaports in Russia," and mistakes a group of smugglers for witches and demons.

Throughout the progression of "The Sail," Lermontov goes on to frame the rhetorical questions, "What does he seek in foreign lands? / What did he leave behind at home?"[39] In response to such open-ended metaphysical quandaries, Lermontov provides his readers only with equivocal answers defined by negation rather than positive affirmation: "Alas, it seeks not happiness, / Nor happiness does it escape."[40] After enduring the "heaving of the waves, the whistling of the wind, and the bending and creaking of the mast," the poem's narrative reaches a kind of calm resolution, marked by the sudden appearance of "bright azure currents below / [and] a golden ray of sun above."[41] Despite this temporary reprieve from foreboding troubles, Lermontov imparts that the ship has seemingly oriented itself once more into the chaos of the ocean's wrath: "rebellious, it seeks out a storm / As if in storms in could find peace!"[42] In this mode of Byronic agitation and dissatisfaction with the comfortable and serene, Lermontov reaffirms his preference for conflict, as though the salvation of both author and ship depends not on tranquility and calm, but on struggle, suffering, and sacrifice.

In his subsequent 1841 poem, "I Go Out on the Road Alone," Lermontov altered his conception of the salvation that he so desperately sought previously in "The Sail," nevertheless challenging head-on prevailing metaphysical preaching maintained by the Orthodox Church and organized religion, more generally. Instead of seeking out the mutinous storm as he previously expressed in "The Sail," Lermontov orients his supreme desire as the manifestation of eternal sleep in "a dark oak grove, forever green, where all night and all day, the life force dozing in his breast would be soothed by voices sweet singing to him of love, as well as the rustling and bending of the dark trees."[43] Although ostensibly, the pleasant imagery seems fairly benign compared to the rowdy storm that the ship in "The Sail" willingly seeks out, the poem proffers a tacit challenge to Christianity in the ascribed negation of heaven and hell, and generally all descriptions of the afterlife promoted by popular religion. With the utmost subtlety, Lermontov espouses a direct challenge to the heavenly kingdom of God, preferring instead the natural setting of the sacred oak grove.

Oaks in Russian folklore hold special significance. In the context of pre-Christian Slavic paganism, oaks were generally associated with the patriarchal thunder god, *Perun*.[44] Lermontov effectively carves out for himself a new liminal space, where he would prefer to spend all of eternity. He rejects conceptions of heaven and hell associated with broader religious interpretations of Christianity, Judaism, and Islam, and situates his everlasting idyllic metaphysical existence among his bygone, spiritual Slavic forefathers. As if to add insult to injury in confronting the religions that he has spurned with placid and confident vitriol, Lermontov rejects all considerations of optimism, piety, and atonement in professing, "I see no hope in years to come/ [and] have no regrets for things gone by. / All that I seek is peace and freedom! / To lose myself in sleep!" Despite the inflammatory overtones of the poem in relation to institutionalized religion, Lermontov creates for himself a vision of the afterlife that is wholly and independently his own and successfully persuades readers to contemplate their own spiritual destinies in similar terms.

While Lermontov had already been developing his prowess in verse for several years, it was not until 1837 that he achieved lasting literary fame. In reconciling the death of Pushkin in the fateful duel with the skilled French mercenary Georges-Charles de Heeckeren d'Anthès, Lermontov found suitable motivation for espousing his vehement objection to the mistreatment of the country's foremost literary genius and the overbearing policies of the autocratic state, more generally. While the scars of the Napoleonic Wars were still fresh in the minds of aristocratic Russian readership, Lermontov drew special attention to the foreign status of Tsar Nikolai I's guards and henchmen at court in the interests of nurturing public dissatisfaction and instigating social disobedience. Lermontov achieved almost instant fame and notoriety for defending the honor of his fallen hero and indicting court society for inciting the poet to the bloody confrontation.[45] His angst culminated in the production of the inflammatory lyrical elegy, "The Death of a Poet":

> The murderer with cool calculated aim / Leveled the blow from which there was no rescue; / His empty barren heart beat equably, / Nor did the pistol once shake in his hand. / And wherefore need we wonder? From an alien clime, / Like a hundred other vagrants/ Cast by a cruel fate upon our shore, / Greedy hunters after rank and pelf, / With sneering insolence he despised/ The language and the faith of a foreign land:/ What cared he to spare the darling of our fame, / Or how could his craven soul divine / Against whom his murderous hand was raised? / But all lament is idle, / the stern decree of fate has been fulfilled/ Hushed for ever is the sound of his wild song, / Never shall the echo of his sweet notes be heard again;/ Dark and narrow is the poet's grave, / And on his lips is laid the seal of death.[46]

Fearing that Pushkin's burial might be made excuse for popular demonstration, the autocratic government carried out his interment as hastily and quietly as possible.[47] These measures aroused the contempt of Pushkin's friends, acquaintances, and admirers.[48]

The poem circulated around the imperial capital of St. Petersburg in handwritten copies, and when the work came to the attention of the authorities, Lermontov was swiftly arrested, tried, and transferred to the Caucasus.[49] When N.A. Stoliepan reviled Pushkin's memory in Lermontov's company, he added sixteen lines attacking "the haughty descendants of sires illustrious," calling these conservatives in league with the autocratic state, "the sworn foes and butchers of liberty, genius, and fame."[50] When the poem began to circulate around the Petersburg court, Tsar Nikolai I did not respond enthusiastically.[51] The diatribe resulted in an immediate sentence of exile and mandatory military service on the frontlines of the Caucasian Conquest in 1837.[52] While he first enlisted with the Nizhnegorodsky Dragoons, he later ended up among the ranks of the Life Guard Hussars.[53]

Roughly a year after the publication "The Death of a Poet," Lermontov enjoyed a temporary respite from his political exile and mandatory military service in the form of pardon, obtained largely due to his grandmother's influential aristocratic connections and further pleas to Tsarist authorities.[54] By the beginning of 1838, he was back in Petersburg, this time in the popular limelight as he entertained the attentions of aristocratic circles and publishers of literary periodicals.[55] His return to St. Petersburg ushered in the most prolific years of his tragically short literary career.

In 1840, Lermontov published two volumes of his poems and his most widely recognized novel, *The Hero of Our Time*, in book form.[56] His notoriety and fame did not prevent the young author from joining a secret political debating society, composed mainly of fellow officers, called by the number of its members, "The Sixteen."[57] Emboldened by his newfound literary prestige, and still seething from the apparent domestic injustices carried out by Tsar Nikolai I's foreign enforcers, Lermontov was arrested a second time for engaging in a duel with the son of the French ambassador and was sent to a line regiment in the Caucasus on orders directly from the Imperial despot himself.[58] While he earned commendations for bravery in battle, Lermontov ultimately met his end in a duel like his fallen idol, Pushkin. He was shot down by a former schoolmate, N.S. Martynov, who had often served as the butt for the poet's harsh badinage.[59]

Lermontov is most known for his novel, *A Hero of Our Time*, a dizzying travelogue of the Caucasus, offering tales of love and betrayal, commentary on fate and the vicissitudes of fortune, and rich ethnographic descriptions of the people and locales of the exotic landscape. The text encapsulates some of the earliest and most effective experiments in the narrative form and method relative to the broad trajectory of Russian literature. By manipulating the *syuzhet*—the synchronic order in which the events of a story are said to unfold in conformance with the linear reading experience of a given narrative—and the *fabula*—the order in which the characters involved in the stories experience their surroundings and engage their associated conflicts—Lermontov devises a vibrantly complex text that almost categorically refutes the possibility for a sufficient understanding of the exciting tale in a single reading.

The story opens with a preface of an unnamed narrator, assumed to be an unwieldy amalgamation of the protagonist Pechorin and Lermontov himself. Character and author seem to merge into a single entity, affording the text a more life-like experience of the Caucasus and its associated misadventures. At the outset of this preface, the narrator compares "his literate public to some country bumpkin who hears a conversation between two diplomats from opposing courts and goes away convinced that each is betraying his government for the sake of an intimate mutual friendship."[60] This mode of ironic narrative continues persistently throughout the novel, imparting sarcasm and cynicism directed seemingly at the members of Lermontov's own reading audience.

The multiplicity of the narrators in the story provides the text with divergent experiences, contemplations, and perspectives. At certain moments in the text, however, similarities between the voices involved purposely mislead readers into thinking that a single individual perhaps is responsible for capturing the associated dissimilar vantage points. The first narrator is an unnamed Russian traveler who meets the aging soldier, Maksim Maksimich, in a Caucasian outpost. Maksimich relates his 'friendship' with Pechorin

---

and amuses his guest with the story of *Bela*, where the character of Pechorin makes his first appearance before both the unnamed traveler and the book's reading audience. This simultaneous experience of the story contributes to the tale's self-ascribed credibility. The initial conception of Pechorin is cast through Maksim Maksimich's eyes, a device that imparts a generally favorable presentation of the protagonist, who later, through Pechorin's own travel diaries, reveals himself as a depraved, incorrigible wanderer. In *Bela*, Maksim Maksimich relates the macho exploits and conniving schemes of Pechorin in seizing the Caucasian beauty of his fancy, Bela.

According to the yarn imparted by Maksim, Bela was an exotic Caucasian maiden set to marry Kazbich, a fierce Circassian warrior. Before the consummation of the marriage, however, Pechorin manages to strike a deal with Azamat, who abducts his own sister as a bride for the Russian soldier in exchange for Kazbich's superlative horse. The pair executes the plan flawlessly, as both get what they want: Pechorin obtaining Bela and Azamat landing the horse. There is collateral damage, however, when Kazbich murders Azamat's father, thinking that the boy carried out the theft with his paternal blessing, and also in the interests of summoning Azamat from the other side of the Kuban River with the prize steed. Pechorin keeps Bela as his imprisoned wife at the Russian outpost, eventually convincing her to entertain sexual relations, alluded to colorfully and ambiguously by the bumbling narrator, Maksim Maksimich.

Pechorin and Bela's relationship comes to a abrupt halt, however, when the young beauty is struck by a Russian bullet intended for Kazbich, who attempts to steal her back from Perchorin and to return her into his marital custody. There is an uneasy parallel drawn between the Kazbich's horse and Bela, whose eyes are compared to those of the steed that Azamat so desires. Vladimir Nabokov, who championed the work overall and even completed his own English translation, noted condescendingly, "Lermontov was singularly inept in his descriptions of women."[61] While the issue of gender relations is indeed one-sided, chauvinistic, and misogynistic, the depiction of the female characters through the vantage points of the male characters says more about the associated men in the story than it does about the women.[62] Nabokov goes on to dismiss Bela as "an Oriental beauty on the lid of a box of Turkish delight," Mary as the "generalized young thing of novelettes," and Vera as "a mere phantom."[63] In merging various literary genres and stock characters, Lermontov manipulates the presentation of stereotypical female roles featured repeatedly in mainstream Russian literature set forth by predominantly male authors.

The text furthermore presents readers with a puzzling amalgamation of genres, juxtaposing a society tale in "Princess Mary," with a Gothic ghost story in "Taman," an exotic adventure tale in "Bela," a metaphysical parable in "The Fatalist," a war story in "Maksim Maksimich." If we consider the *fabula* of the story, or the chronological ordering of the events experienced by the associated cast, the second chapter, "Taman," occurs first, the fourth chapter, "Princess Mary," occurs second, the fifth chapter, "The Fatalist," occurs third, the first chapter, "Bela," occurs fourth, and the second chapter, "Maksim Maksimich," occurs fifth. The discovery of Pechorin's diary presented in the last three chapters of the book provides readers with an intimate look into the protagonist's most personal feelings and deliberations, nevertheless marked by indifferent affectations in order to coincide with his self-ascribed reputation of the protagonist as a Romantic Byronic superfluous man.

While Pechorin seems to be a character of immense intrigue, status, and even popularity, he is a master rogue, capable of implanting ideas in peoples' heads. In the words of Helena Goscilo, "his most outstanding asset is his capacity for stirring others' imaginations."[64] Despite the espoused estimations of Pechorin's honor and masculine exploits through both his own and Maksim Maksimich's presentation, details in the text seem to indicate contradictory depictions of the protagonist as effeminate, vulnerable, and lost.[65] Regardless of all of his unnecessary acts of violence and thoughtless scheming, he elicits the pity of readers because he is doomed to live out the effervescent Byronic storyline of a man cast apart from society, doomed to endure a cruel and lonely world governed by the misfortunes of fate and the whims of fancy.

«Парус»

Белеет парус одинокий
В тумане моря голубом!
Что ищет он в стране далекой?
Что кинул он в краю родном?

A lonely sail is flashing white
Amidst the blue fog of the sea!
What does it seek in foreign lands?
What did it leave behind at home?

Играют волны- ветер свищет,
И мачта гнется и скрыпит…
Увы, - он счастия не ищет
И не от счастия бежит!

Waves heave, wind whistles,
The mast, it bends and creaks…
Alas, it seeks not happiness
Nor happiness does it escape!

Под ним струя светлей лазури,
Над ним луч солнца золотой…
А он мятежный, просит бури,
Как будто в бурях есть покой.[66]

Below, a current azure bright,
Above, a golden ray of sun…
Rebellious, it seeks out a storm
As if in storms it could find peace!

Выхожу один я на дорогу;
Сквозь туман кремнистый путь блестит
Ночь тиха. Пустыня внемлет богу,
И звезда с звездою говорит.

Alone I set out on the road;
The flinty path is sparkling in the mist;
The night is still. The desert harks to God,
And star with star converses.

В небесах торжественно и чудно!
Спит земля в сиянье голубом…
Что же мне так больно и так трудно?
Жду ль чего? Жалею ли о чём?

The vault is overwhelmed with solemn wonder.
The earth in cobalt aura slumbers…
Why do I feel so pained and troubled?
What do I harbor: hope, regrets?

Уж не жду от жизни ничего я,
И не жаль мне прошлого ничуть;
Я ищу свободы и покоя!
Я б хотел забыться и заснуть!

I see no hope in years to come,
Have no regrets for things gone by.
All that I seek is peace and freedom!
To lose myself and sleep!

Но не тем холодным сном могилы…
Я б желал навеки так заснуть,
Чтоб в груди дремали жизни силы,
Чтоб дыша вздымалась тихо грудь;

But not the frozen slumber of the grave…
I'd like eternal sleep to leave
My life force dozing in my breast
Gently with my breath to rise and fall;

Чтоб всю ночь, весь день мой слух лелея,
Про любовь мне сладкий голос пел,
Надо мной чтоб вечно зеленея
Тёмный дуб склонялся и шумел.

By night and day, my hearing would be soothed
By voices sweet, singing to me of love.
And over me, forever green,
A dark oak tree would bend and rustle.

1841[67]

1841

Notes

1. M. Yu. Lermontov, "Prayer" ["*Molitva*"], 1830, accessed in *The Complete Works of Lermontov,* [*Polnoe sobranie sochinenij Lermontova*], tom 1 stikhotvoreniya, chast' 2 (St. Peterburg: A. F. Marx: 1891), 112. The opening lines of ""Prayer" ["*Molitva*"] (1830) translated by the author.

2. As cited in Anatoly Lieberman, *Mikhail Lermontov: Major Poetical Works*, (Minneapolis: Univ. of Minnesota Pr., 1983), 8.

3. Tatiana Wolff, *Pushkin on Literature,* Ed. & Trans. Tatiana Wolf (Stanford, CA: Stanford UP, 1998), 180.

4. Andrei Sinyavsky, *Strolls with Pushkin.* Trans. C.T. Nepomnyashchyy and S.I. Yastremski, (New Haven: Yale UP, 1993) 51. See also: Tatiana Wolff, *Pushkin on Literature,* ed. and trans. Tatiana Wolf (Stanford: Stanford UP, 1998), 180.

5. Victor Terras, *Handbook of Russian Literature* (New Haven: Yale UP, 1990), 248–250, 356-358.

6. Paul Foote, "Introduction" to *Hero of Our Time* by M. Yu. Lermontov, (New York: Penguin Putnam, 2001), xiii.

7. D.S. Mirsky, *A History of Russian Literature: From Its Beginnings to 1900*, (New York: Random House, 1958), 136.

8. Ibid. See also: Paul Foote, "Introduction" to *Hero of Our Time* by M. Yu. Lermontov, (New York: Penguin Putnam, 2001), xiii. See also: Priscilla Meyer, *How the Russians Read the French: Lermontov, Dostoevsky, Tolstoy,* (Madison: University of Wisconsin Press, 2010), 36.

9. Wolf Schmid, "'*Nisxozhdenie*' *k proze,*" in *The Pushkin Handbook*, Ed. David Bethea, (Madison: U of Wisconsin, 2005), 210. When considering the holistic trajectory of Pushkin's corpus of work, a marked change seems to have occurred just before 1830. While the author continued to make significant headway in the realm of verse, he started shifting his attentions to the arena of prose and the prospect of merging genres, including the creation of narrative national epics, imaginative travelogues, fairytales, dramatic tragedies, and his exceptional novel in verse, *Eugene Onegin*. Wolf Schmid and David Bethea identify this process of "prosaicization" that started long before prose proper appeared:

> At the same time, the process was not one-sided: as prosaic tendencies developed, they became 'cross-fertilized' with countervailing poetic ones: euphonic repetitions, popular sayings whose meanings (and sounds, i.e., paronomasia) could be literally realized in a story's plot or themes, in other words, the "proportionality and symmetry" that Pushkin aligned with poetic thinking. We see this criss-crossing of prosaic and poetic tendencies most vividly in the *Belkin Tales,* although they can be

perceived as well in such outstanding later prose works as "The Queen of Spades" and *The Captain's Daughter* (210).

10. Ibid.

11. Nicholas Valentine Riasanovsky, *Russian Identities a Historical Survey,* (Oxford: Oxford UP, 2005), 125–130. See Also: Anatole Gregory Mazour, *The First Russian Revolution, 1825: The Decembrist Movement, its Origins, Development, and Significance*, (Stanford: Stanford UP, 1937), 100–106.

12. Anatoly Lieberman, *Mikhail Lermontov: Major Poetical Works*, (Minneapolis: Univ. of Minnesota Pr., 1983), 3.

13. Ibid.

14. Alexander von Benckendorff, a Baltic German from Reval, or modern-day Tallinn, was commissioned by Tsar Nikolai I to serve as the first Chief of Gendarms and Executive Director of the Third Section from 1826 to 1844. The foreign status of Benckendorff and his Baltic entourage perhaps contributed to their perceived abilities to carry out brutal punishments, employ cutting-edge surveillance and interrogation methods, and maintain imperviousness to local corruption; Ronald Hingley, *The Russian Secret Police: Muscovite, Imperial, and Soviet Political Security Operations,* (Simon & Schuster, New York: 1970), 31–33; See also: Robert J. Goldstein, *War for the Public Mind: Political Censorship in Nineteenth-Century Europe* (Westport, CT: Praeger, 2000), 242–243. See also: Charles D. Hazen, *Europe Since 1815,* (New York: H. Holt and Co., 1910), 651.

15. Victor Terras, *Handbook of Russian Literature,* (New Haven: Yale UP, 1990), 38 {Baratynsky}, 174 {Gogol}, 248 {Lermontov}, 236 {Krylov}, 356 {Pushkin}, and 531 {Zhukovsky}.

16. Charles Edward Turner, *Studies in Russian Literature,* (New York: Kraus, 1971), 330.

17. Beate Müller, *Censorship & Cultural Regulation in the Modern Age,* (New York: Rodopi, 2004), 5, 29. See also: Lev Losev, *On the Beneficence of Censorship: Aesopian Language in Modern Russian Literature,* (Munich: Otto Sagner, 1984), x.

18. Lev Losev, *On the Beneficence of Censorship: Aesopian Language in Modern Russian Literature,* (Munich: Otto Sagner, 1984), x.

19. M. Yu. Lermontov, "Duma" ["*Meditation*"], 1838, accessed in *The Complete Works of Lermontov, [Polnoe sobranie sochinenij Lermontova]*, tom 1 stikhotvoreniya, chast' 1 (St. Peterburg: A. F. Marx: 1891), 20. See also: M. Yu. Lermontov, "Meditation" ["*Duma*"], 1838. Accessed online at http://lib.ru/LITRA/LERMONTOW/pss1.txt. Translated and cited by Elizabeth Cheresh Allen in *A Fallen Idol Is Still a God: Lermontov and the Quandaries of Cultural Transition*, (Stanford, Stanford UP, 2007), 1.

20. Elizabeth Cheresh Allen, *A Fallen Idol Is Still a God: Lermontov and the Quandaries of Cultural Transition,* (Stanford: Stanford UP, 2006), 19.

21. David Powelstock, *Becoming Mikhail Lermontov: The Ironies of Romantic Individualism in Nicholas I's Russia*, (Evanston, IL: Northwestern UP, 2005), 51. See also: Victor Terras, *Handbook of Russian Literature* (New Haven: Yale UP, 1990), 248–250. Lermontov started drawing at a very early age. He developed into a talented painter, especially proficient in landscapes in a Romantic style reminiscent of Caspar David Friedrich. During his education at the School of Ensigns of the Guards and of Cavalry Cadets, Lermontov graduated as a cavalry-rank cornet and received his commission in the Life Guard Hussars. In these youthful years, he produced several bawdy songs and pornographic poems. Throughout Lermontov's career, he wrote five plays. His chief dramatic work, "The Masquerade" ("Maskard," 1835), is the only one the poet attempted to have published and performed, but he encountered difficulties with censorship.

22. Lesley Blanch, *Sabres of Paradise: Conquest and Vengeance in the Caucasus,* (London: L.B. Tauris & Co. Ltd., 2004), x.

23. Paul Foote, "Introduction" to *Hero of Our Time* by M. Yu. Lermontov, (New York: Penguin Putnam, 2001), xiii-xiv. See also: D.S. Mirsky, *A History of Russian Literature: From Its Beginnings to 1900*, (New York, Random House: 1958), 137.

24. Jane Burbank, Mark Von Hagen, and A. V. Remnev, *Russian Empire: Space, People, Power, 1700-1930,* (Indiana-Michigan Series in Russian and East European Studies: Indiana UP, 2007), 240, 257. See also: Susan Layton, *Russian Literature and Empire: Conquest of the Caucasus from Pushkin to Tolstoy,* (Cambridge: Cambridge UP, 1995), 1.

25. Charles Edward Turner, *Studies in Russian Literature,* (London: Sampson Low, Marston, Searle, & Rivington, 1882; rpt. New York: Kraus, 1971), 318–319.

26. D.S. Mirsky, *A History of Russian Literature: From Its Beginnings to 1900*, (New York, Random House: 1958), 137.

27. Charles Edward Turner, *Studies in Russian Literature,* (New York: Kraus, 1971), 319.

28. D.S. Mirsky, *A History of Russian Literature: From Its Beginnings to 1900*, (New York, Random House: 1958), 137. See also: Victor Terras, *Handbook of Russian Literature,* (New Haven: Yale UP, 1990), 70.

29. Victor Terras, *Handbook of Russian Literature,* (New Haven: Yale UP, 1990), 70.

30. Ibid.

31. Ibid.

32. Ibid.

33. V.M. Zhirmunskii, *Bairon I Pushkin,* (Leningrad: Nauka, 1978), 28–29, 43–48, 292–331. As cited in Susan Layton, *Russian Literature and Empire: Conquest of the Caucasus from Pushkin to Tolstoy,* (Cambridge: Cambridge UP, 995), 17, 298.

34. M. Yu. Lermontov, *Complete Collected Works of Lermontov*, [*Polnoe sobranie sochinenij*], Ed. B. Eikhenbaum, Tom 1, (Moskva: Gos. Izd-vo khudozh. lit-ry, 1941), 235. See also: M. Yu. Lermontov, "No, I'm not Byron" [*"Nyet, ya nye Bajron"*], 1832. Translated by the author. Accessed online at http://febweb.ru/feb/lermont/texts/lerm06/vol02/le2-033-.htm.

35. David Powelstock, *Becoming Mikhail Lermontov: The Ironies of Romantic Individualism in Nicholas I's Russia*, (Evanston, IL: Northwestern UP, 2005), 79.

36. Ibid. 80

37. Ibid. 79–82

38. M. Yu. Lermontov, *Complete Collected Works of Lermontov*, [*Polnoe sobranie sochinenij*], Ed. B. Eikhenbaum, Tom 1, (Moskva: Gos. Izd-vo khudozh. lit-ry, 1941), 235. See also: M. Yu. Lermontov, "The Sail" [*"Parus"*], Trans. Ilya Kutik. Accessed online at http://web.mmlc. northwestern.edu/~mdenner/Demo/texts/sail.html.

39. Ibid.

40. Ibid.

41. Ibid.

42. Ibid.

43. Ibid. 351. See also: M. Yu. Lermontov, "I go out on the road alone" [*"Vykhozhu odin ya na dorogu"*], Trans. by Ilya Kutik. Accessed online at http://web.mmlc.northwestern.edu/~mdenner/Demo/texts/road_alone.html .

44. J. P. Mallory and Douglas Q. Adams, *Encyclopedia of Indo-European Culture*, (London: Fitzroy Dearborn, 1997), 582.

45. Victor Terras, *Handbook of Russian Literature,* (New Haven: Yale UP, 1990), 249. See also: Charles Edward Turner, *Studies in Russian Literature,* (New York: Kraus, 1971), 326–330.

46. M. I. Lermontov, *Complete Works*, Vol. I, 43. As cited in Charles Edward Turner, *Studies in Russian Literature,* (New York: Kraus, 1971), 328–329; See also: M. Yu. Lermontov, *Sobrani Sochinenii v chetrekh tomakh* (Moscow: Khudozhestvennaia literatura, 1983–84), Vol. II, 346–348. As cited in Susan Layton, *Russian Literature and Empire: Conquest of the Caucasus from Pushkin to Tolstoy,* (Cambridge: Cambridge UP, 1995), 138, 339; See also: appendix of Lermontov's works in David Powelstock,

Becoming Mikhail Lermontov: The Ironies of Romantic Individualist and Nicholas I's Russia, (Evanston: Northwestern UP, 2005), 475–476.

47. Ibid.

48. Ibid.

49. Ibid.

50. Ibid.

51. Charles Edward Turner, *Studies in Russian Literature,* (New York: Kraus, 1971), 329.

52. John Jr. Mersereau, Mikhail Lermontov (Carbondale, Southern Illinois University Press. 1962), 18–22.

53. Ibid.

54. Victor Terras, *Handbook of Russian Literature,* (New Haven: Yale UP, 1990), 249. See also: David Powelstock, *Becoming Mikhail Lermontov: The Ironies of Romantic Individualism in Nicholas I's Russia*, (Evanston, IL: Northwestern UP, 2005), 233.

55. Ibid. See also: D.S. Mirsky, *A History of Russian Literature: From Its Beginnings to 1900*, (New York, Random House: 1958), 137.

56. Ibid.

57. Ibid.

58. Ibid.

59. Ibid.

60. M. Yu. Lermontov, *Hero of our Time,* Trans. Paul Foote, (New York: Penguin Putnam, 2001), 1.

61. V. V. Nabokov, Foreword to *A Hero of Our Time* by Mikhail Lermontov, Trans. V.V. Nabokov, (New York: Anchor Books, 1958), v–xix. As cited in Elizabeth Cheresh Allen, *A Fallen Idol Is Still a God: Lermontov and the Quandaries of Cultural Transition,* (Stanford: Stanford UP, 2006), 260.

62. Ibid.

63. Ibid.

64. Helena Goscilo, "From Dissolution to Synthesis: The Use of Genre in Lermontov's Prose." Diss. Indiana U, 1976, 256. As cited in Elizabeth Cheresh Allen, *A Fallen Idol Is Still a God: Lermontov and the Quandaries of Cultural Transition,* (Stanford: Stanford UP, 2006), 260.

65. M. Yu. Lermontov, *Hero of our Time,* Trans. Paul Foote, (New York: Penguin Putnam, 2001), 26.

66. M. Yu. Lermontov, *Complete Collected Works of Lermontov*, [*Polnoe sobranie sochinenij*], Ed. B. Eikhenbaum, Tom 1, (Moskva: Gos. Izd-vo khudozh. lit-ry, 1941), 235. See also: M. Yu. Lermontov, "The Sail"

[*"Parus"*]. Translated by Ilya Kutik. Accessed online at http://web.mmlc. northwestern.edu/~mdenner/Demo/texts/sail.html.

67. Ibid. 351. See also: M. Yu. Lermontov, "I go out on the road alone" [*"Vykhozhu odin ya na dorogu"*]. Trans. Ilya Kutik. Accessed online at http://web.mmlc.northwestern.edu/~mdenner/Demo/texts/road_alone.html.

Works Cited

Allen, Elizabeth Cheresh. *A Fallen Idol Is Still a God: Lermontov and the Quandaries of Cultural Transition*. Stanford, CA: Stanford UP, 2007.

Blanch, Lesley. *Sabres of Paradise: Conquest and Vengeance in the Caucasus*. London: L.B. Tauris & Co. Ltd., 2004.

Burbank, Jane, Mark Von Hagen, and A. V. Remnev. *Russian Empire: Space, People, Power, 1700–1930*. Bloomington, IN: Indiana UP, 2007.

Foote, Paul. Introduction. *Hero of Our Time*. By M. Yu. Lermontov. Trans. Paul Foote. New York: Penguin Putnam, 2001.

Goldstein, Robert J. *War for the Public Mind: Political Censorship in Nineteenth Century Europe*. Westport, CT: Praeger, 2000.

Goscilo, Helena. "From Dissolution to Synthesis: The Use of Genre in Lermontov's Prose." Diss. Indiana U, 1976.

Hazen, Charles D. *Europe Since 1815*. New York: H. Holt and Co., 1910.

Hingley, Ronald. *The Russian Secret Police: Muscovite, Imperial, and Soviet Political Security Operations*. New York: Simon & Schuster, 1970.

Layton, Susan. *Russian Literature and Empire: Conquest of the Caucasus from Pushkin to Tolstoy*. Cambridge, UK: Cambridge UP, 1995.

Lermontov, M. Yu. *Complete Collected Works of Lermontov* [*Polnoe sobraniesochinenij*]. Ed. B. Eikhenbaum. Tom 1. Moskva: Gos. Izd-vo khudozh. lit-ry,1941.

_____. *Hero of our Time*. Trans. Paul Foote. New York: Penguin Putnam, 2001.

_____. "I go out on the road alone" [*"Vykhozhu odin ya na dorogu"*].Trans. Ilya Kutik. 16 Jan. 2003. Web. 30 Nov. 2013. <http://web.mmlc.northwestern. edu/~mdenner/Demo/texts/road_alone.html >

_____. "Duma" [*"Meditation"*] *The Complete Works of Lermontov,*[*Polnoe sobranie sochinenij Lermontova*]. Tom 1 stikhotvoreniya. Chast' 1. St. Peterburg: A. F. Marx: 1891.

_____. "No, I'm Not Byron" [*"Nyet, ya nye Bajron"*]. 1832. *Fundamental Digital Library of Russian Literature and Folklore*. Gorky Institute of World Literature. 27 Feb. 2007. Web. 30 Nov. 2013. < http://feb-web.ru/ feb/lermont/texts/lerm06/vol02/le2-033-.htm>

_____. *Sobrani Sochinenii v chetrekh tomakh.* Moscow: Khudozhestvennaia literatura, 1983–84.

_____. "The Sail" [*"Parus"*]. Trans. Ilya Kutik. 16 Jan. 2003. Web. 30 Nov. 2013. <http://web.mmlc.northwestern.edu/~mdenner/Demo/texts/sail.html>.

Lieberman, Anatoly. *Mikhail Lermontov: Major Poetical Works.* Minneapolis: U of Minnesota P 1983.

Losev, Lev. *On the Beneficence of Censorship: Aesopian Language in Modern Russian Literature.* Munich: Otto Sagner, 1984.

Mazour, Anatole Gregory. *The First Russian Revolution, 1825: The Decembrist Movement, Its Origins, Development, and Significance.* Stanford, CA: Stanford UP, 1937.

Mersereau, John Jr. *Mikhail Lermontov.* Carbondale, IL: Southern Illinois UP, 1962.

Meyer, Priscilla. *How the Russians Read the French: Lermontov, Dostoevsky, Tolstoy.* Madison, WI: U of Wisconsin P, 2010.

Mirsky, D.S. *A History of Russian Literature: From Its Beginnings to 1900.* New York: Random House, 1958.

Müller, Beate. *Censorship & Cultural Regulation in the Modern Age.* New York: Rodopi, 2004.

Nabokov, V.V. Foreword. *A Hero of Our Time.* By Mikhail Lermontov. Trans. V.V. Nabokov. New York: Anchor Books, 1958.

k. *Becoming Mikhail Lermontov: The Ironies of Romantic Individualism in Nicholas I's Russia.* Evanston, IL: Northwestern UP, 2005.

Riasanovsky, Nicholas Valentine. *Russian Identities a Historical Survey.* Oxford, UK: Oxford UP, 2005.

Schmid, Wolf. *"Nisxozhdenie' k proze."* *The Pushkin Handbook.* Ed. David Bethea. Madison, WI: U of Wisconsin, 2005.

Sinyavsky, Andrei. *Strolls with Pushkin.* Trans. C.T. Nepomnyashchyy and S.I. Yastremski. New Haven, CT: Yale UP, 1993.

Terras, Victor. *Handbook of Russian Literature.* New Haven, CT: Yale UP, 1990.

Turner, Charles Edward. *Studies in Russian Literature.* 1882. New York: Kraus, 1971.

Wolff, Tatiana. *Pushkin on Literature.* Ed. & Trans. Tatiana Wolf. Stanford, CA: Stanford UP, 1998.

Zhirmunskii, V.M. *Bairon I Pushkin.* 1924. Leningrad: Nauka, 1978.

Romanticism, the Caucasus, and Russian Orientalism _____

Rachel Stauffer

The Russian Romantics, a group predominantly composed of young male authors from approximately the 1810s to the 1840s, contributed significantly to the products of Russia's Golden Age, particularly to the Golden Age of Poetry, as Donald Rayfield discusses in his chapter in this volume. Alexander Pushkin and Mikhail Lermontov top the list as the most well-known Russian Romantics and are still revered in contemporary Russia. Their characters, Onegin and Pechorin, respectively, represent one of the most common character types in both the real and fictional worlds of Russian Romanticism: the superfluous man, or *lishnij chelovek* [лишный человек]. Hugh McLean defines this term as: "a traditional designation for a series of characters in Russian literature who are perceived—or regard themselves—as being in a state of disharmony with the world around them, rejecting it or being rejected by it" (McLean 454). McLean also supports the existence of superfluous men in the real world of nineteenth-century Russia as well as in the fictional realm, calling the superfluous man "evidence of complex interaction between 'art' and 'life'" (McLean 454). The superfluous man is bored with everything, hopelessly Byronic, and endlessly searching for a respite from the monotony of life. He gambles, pursues women for the thrill of conquest, excessively eats and drinks, and engages in duels. In real life, Pushkin and Lermontov both died as the outcome of injuries sustained in duels, Pushkin at age 37 and Lermontov at only 27. Literary superfluous men, like Pushkin and Lermontov, often find themselves in the mountainous region of the Caucasus, the nineteenth-century exotic playground and spa of the Russian elite. The landscapes of the steppe frontier and the Caucasus, as depicted by Pushkin and Lermontov, are often used to parallel characters' emotions. When characters are happy, the Caucasus and the steppe frontier serve to inspire and awe. When characters are sad or lonely, the Caucasus and the steppe frontier are isolating, imposing, or violent landscapes. In this chapter, we will consider the Romantic writings of Pushkin and Lermontov with an eye towards understanding the superfluous man and his depictions of the Caucasus in both poetry and prose. A larger question of Orientalism emerges in this examination, and this is an issue that is worthy of our attention as well, particularly since this volume concentrates on the Golden Age of Russian literature, broadly speaking, the nineteenth century, and the nineteenth century is coincidentally a pivotal period in Russian expansion, conquest, and Christianization, most notably in the Crimea and the North and South Caucasus regions. The implications of Russia's conquest of the Caucasus during the nineteenth century are still highly relevant to contemporary affairs and Russia's relations with the people and nations of this important geographic crossroads between Europe and Asia.

Alexander Sergeevich Pushkin (1799–1837) is Russia's national poet. He is decidedly more famous in Russia than in the West, but his works have stood the test of time. Mikhail Yurievich Lermontov (1814–1841), similarly, is a beloved poet and author in Russia. Pushkin's *Eugene Onegin* [*Евгений Онегин,* 1825–32], his most famous poetic work, is a *roman v stikhakh,* 'novel in verse.' During Russia's Golden Age, poetry achieved high status as a primary form of literary expression, and Pushkin's novel in verse was the first of its kind at the time in the Russian tradition. It seems worthwhile to mention here that the greatest work of Georgian literature (composed in the Republic of Georgia, in the South Caucasus region), *The Knight in the Panther's Skin* [ვეფხისტყაოსანი, *Vepxistqaosani,* 1196–1207] by Shota Rustaveli, is a work of verse with over 6,000 lines, written in the thirteenth century, during Georgia's Golden Age. Its form is, perhaps, less specified as a novel in verse, but its composition (with meter and an AAAA rhyme scheme, known as the Rustavelian quatrain) seven hundred years before Russia's Golden Age is worth mentioning, particularly considering the emphasis here on Russian depictions of the Caucasus. As we will see, such depictions often assume the Georgians and other peoples of the Caucasus region to be inferior to the Russians, or somehow less evolved artistically or intellectually (as is common among the Orientalist perspectives of the time).

Mikhail Yurievich Lermontov (1814–1841) was also a poet, although his novel, *Hero of Our Time* [*Герой нашего времени, Geroj nashego vremeni*, 1840]—unlike Pushkin's major work—is written in prose, and is an extraordinarily complex and unique work of literature for its time. Composed of five major parts, including a diary said to have been found by the narrator after the main character Pechorin's death, the novel's structural complexity and metafictive prowess are truly unique. One of its sections, purportedly from Pechorin's diary, "Princess Mary", takes place in Pyatigorsk, in the North Caucasus, among high society Russians vacationing and taking in the mineral waters well-known to the area.

Both Pushkin and Lermontov lived the lifestyles of superfluous men, evident in the Byronic sentiments expressed throughout their works. After all, the Romantic period in Russia was dedicated to the artist's expression of his innermost feelings, and doing so in a way that was aesthetically appealing, while acknowledging the unique qualifications of the artist to do exactly this. Emotional experience and Byronic lifestyle seemed to go hand in hand. The Romantic period is one artistic result of Russia's proud and nationalistic defeat of Napoleon in 1812, an event that created a generation of heroes, not unlike the superfluous men. The very nature of the hero was that of an unattainable ideal, similar to Napoleon's quest for world domination. Romantic heroes were to embody typical Neoclassical features and virtues, including heroism, honor, general good looks, and a sense of duty to self and nation.

Pushkin and Lermontov both idealize and denigrate the Caucasus in their texts. Pushkin's most famous work, *Eugene Onegin*, does not take place in the Caucasus, but several of Pushkin's works do, and he also kept a travelogue during his exile to the Caucasus in the late 1820s. Here, we will discuss short and long works of verse including *The Fountain of Bakchisarai* [*Бакчисарайский фонтан, Bakchisaraiskii fontan*, 1822], written during Pushkin's first exile to the Caucasus, and his revised-for-publication version of his travelogue, *Journey to Arzrum at the Time of the 1829*

Campaign [*Путешествие в Арзрум во время похода 1829 года*, *Puteshestvie v Arzrum vo vremja pokhoda 1829 goda*, 1829]. Our briefer discussion of Lermontov will focus predominantly on verse and *Hero of Our Time*.

In Pushkin's travelogues from the later 1820s, most notably *Journey to Arzrum*, the poet makes generalized observations that provide needed separation between Europe (including Russia) from Asia (Georgia, Turkey, anything directly north or south of the Caucasus Mountains):

> The crossing from Europe to Asia becomes more perceptible from hour to hour: the forests disappear, the hills smooth over, the grass thickens and grows sturdily; birds appear that are unfamiliar in our forests; eagles sit on the knolls that mark the main road, as if on guard, and proudly look at the travelers.[1]

This passage in the first chapter sets the tone for the travelogue, clearly dividing the European Russia of Pushkin's imagination from the non-European steppe frontier under observation. The observation about eagles is not without significance. The Imperial emblem of Russia, imported from Byzantium, was the double-headed eagle. Here the eagles "as if on guard, proudly look at the travelers." This seems a rather strategic turn of phrase, suggesting that the Russians, the eagles here, are on watch in the region, which, as a result of the Russian conquest was a contemporaneous truth. The landscape of the steppe frontiers of the Russian south does differ significantly from that of European Russia, as Pushkin describes. Similarly, the forest is traditionally the foundation of East Slavic culture, while the steppe is representative of non-Slavic, often Turkic, groups. As David Schimmelpenninck van der Oye emphasizes:

> Long before they thought of East and West, Europe and Asia, or Christian and pagan, for the people who eventually became the Russians, forest and steppe defined their notion of self and other. The East Slavs, from whom Russians derive their ancestry, first settled Europe's wooded northeastern periphery sometime in the latter half of our era's first millennium. (12)

Pushkin's observation of how "the forests disappear" and "the hills smooth over" represents this same division of forest and steppe, West and East, self and other. Though a seemingly innocuous and picturesque description, certainly the implications of this short passage carry heavy cultural and temporal significance, setting the stage to assert Russian dominance, culturally imagined and militarily executed, throughout the entire region.

The Russian conquest of the steppe frontier and Caucasus was initiated in the sixteenth century with Ivan the Terrible's expansion of Muscovy south to the Tatar region of Kazan'. By the nineteenth century, as Michael Khodarkovsky observes, "Russia was now destined to bring Civilization and Christianity to the numerous non-Christian peoples who would become part of the 'glorious and rising' empire" (184). Russia's self-imposed duty to Christianize, stemming from its self-designation in the fifteenth century as the Third Rome, was still a driving force of expansion. Schimmelpenninck van der Oye also observes that the first department of Asiatic languages was founded in St. Petersburg in 1855, by which time the conquest of the Caucasus was well underway. The languages taught in that department reflect two different cultural influences: first, the conquest of the Caucasus, represented by the opportunity for students (often elite, wealthy European Russians) to study languages of the Caucasus; and second, a persistent emphasis on converting non-Christians to Christianity, evidenced by the offering of languages of the Arab-Islamic world, Central Asia, and East Asia (Schimmelpenninck van der Oye 173). This point just emphasizes that, like most conquest and colonialization, Russia's drive to, using Khodarkovsky's terminology, "civilize" the Caucasus was intentional and calculated. The Russians' perception of themselves as European, however geographically gerrymandered, emerged with the founding of St. Petersburg in 1703. By the end of the eighteenth century, Catherine the Great (German by birth) had developed ties with the Georgians, who were seeking alliances to aid in their consistent struggle against the Ottoman Turks, as Khodarkovsky describes:

Surrounded by the Muslim peoples of the Caucasus and compelled to pay tribute intermittently to the Persians or the Ottomans, the Georgians often invoked the image of defiled Christianity to solicit Russian help. They appealed to Moscow to liberate them from the Turks, who had captured much of their land, and from the shamkhal and his people, described as 'infidel dogs, who capture Christians at night and then convert them to Islam' (36).

As a Christian nation, Georgia, in theory, had a common heritage with Russia, as Khodarkovsky acknowledges:

At a time when religion and state sovereignty were not and could not be clearly separated […] the Russian envoys were always prepared to argue for Russian sovereignty over Western Georgia 'because it was a Christian country'. They also heard similar arguments from the Ottomans, who insisted that the Circassians and the Kumyks were Muslims and therefore subjects of the Ottoman Empire (36).

The drive to Christianize is not to be underestimated as a motivating factor in Russia's interests in the region because here we see that, while the Russians staked claims to the Christian areas, they also sought to Christianize the Islamic areas in their path (which, consequently, was viewed as a potential threat by the Islamic power dominating points north and south of the Caucasus). Additionally, the divide between Christian and Muslim further contributes to the other binary oppositions (e.g. Europe and Asia, self and other, West and East) involved in Russia's imagined and evolving identity in the Caucasus.

In *Journey to Arzrum*, there are several passages that convey Russocentric and pro-conquest points of view. For example, after a young Kalmyk girl generously offers him food, which he eats, Pushkin comments, "I do not think that any other national cuisine could possibly be anymore repulsive."[2] Similarly, Pushkin finds the bathing facilities in the natural springs to be vastly improved in comparison to his first visit to the Caucasus, most likely these improvements are the result of Russian (read: European) influence and gentrification: "In my time the baths were located in little shacks which had been constructed in a hurry…Now splendid bathhouses and buildings have been built"[3] (Pushkin 417–8). Pushkin's preference for the more Westernized facilities indicates a stronger idealization of Russian or European tendencies, rather than of Asian or non-Western ones. Pushkin extolls the virtues of General Ermolov, the main *conquistador* of the initial conquest of the Caucasus, and, at the same time, he mentions the "order, cleanliness, beauty"[4] that have emerged as a result of the conquest (418). As Katya Hokanson has noted, "Gogol describes Pushkin's virtuosity in portraying foreign places as a facet of his ability to describe things perfectly, but as a Russian would see them" (341). Additionally, Ian Helfant suggests, "Just as Russia's troops were expected to conquer territory and subdue Muslim peoples, so Russian authors were expected to validate these conquests through literary incarnations of imperialist ideology" (367–369). For these reasons alone, not to mention controversial questions of authorial intent, we should not judge Pushkin too harshly for his Orientalist statements about the steppe and the Caucasus. At the same time, most critics acknowledge that the depictions of the Caucasian landscapes Pushkin included in his fictional Romantic works are in stark contrast with his impressions as a tourist in his travelogues. Ian Helfant describes the latter as "embedded in the rich context of orientalist discourse in Pushkin's day" (Helfant 367). Helfant and other critics maintain that *Journey to Arzrum* contains a combination of Pushkin's personal observations with approved political rhetoric about the Caucasus, rather than a singular message of Pushkin's own observations and opinions. With this in mind, perhaps we do not have to be so hard on Pushkin for his Orientalist tendencies, considering that he was exiled to the Caucasus by the very government he praises in the text.

As Monika Greenleaf has observed, the publication of *Journey to Arzrum* coincided with a general trend towards publishing travel journals, particularly depicting travel to non-Russian and non-Western destinations, a trend with a clear function: "In describing Asia, Russian travelers were not only inventing and propagating their version of 'eastern' geography, but also establishing Russia's right to be identified with the practitioners of orientalism" (945).

In order to prevent being defined as the Orient itself, Russia had to convey an Orientalist stance, thus defining itself, before Orientalists would undertake that very task.

Pushkin's poem, *The Fountain of Bakchisaray*, tells a folk legend from the Crimea depicting a love triangle among a Khan (Girey), a young Polish princess captive (Marija), and a Georgian woman of the Khan's harem (Zarema). Zarema had previously been the Khan's favorite until Marija was captured. (Here we are reminded of the Georgians' claims that the Muslims captured Christians at night, as mentioned by Khodarkovsky). Since Marija's arrival at the palace, the Khan has no interest in Zarema. The Khan never has his way with Marija and never makes her join the harem, but he is distracted by her sadness in captivity. In the end, we learn that Marija has died, possibly killed by Zarema, who has threatened her. When Zarema threatens Marija, she claims that if Marija does not "return Girey to Zarema" she will have to use a dagger on her because she was "born near the Caucasus".[5] The opposition between the beautiful, virginal, Western Slavic (Polish) Christian figure of Marija and the violent, harem-dwelling, Georgian (in the Russian view, non-Western), Islamic Zarema provides obvious contrast in line with the existing binary oppositions we have mentioned, but why Zarema must be from the Caucasus, that is, why the Caucasus must be the origin of her violence, so to speak, is less clear. It is possible that Pushkin's rhetoric here is designed to support the Russian Empire's conquest of the Caucasus, although it also could be less strategic or purposeful, designed merely to add a detail relevant to the Russian reader.

Mikhail Lermontov, our other Romantic superfluous man under consideration in this chapter, spent time in the Caucasus as a child with family and as an adult in exile. For him the Caucasus region was both idyllic and inspiring, as well as savage and uncivilized. In *Hero of Our Time*, Lermontov masterfully incorporates the landscape of the Caucasus to reflect the feelings and experiences of Pechorin, both the positive and the negative. Upon arrival in Pyatigorsk at the beginning of "Princess Mary" in *Hero of Our Time*, Pechorin writes:

When I opened the window, my room was filled with the smell of flowers growing in the modest front garden. The stems of the blooming cherry blossoms watching me through the windows, and the wind occasionally scattering my desk with their white petals. The view on three sides is perfect. To the west the five-headed Beshtau is dark blue like 'the last cloud in a dissipating storm'; to the north Mashuk rises up, like a shaggy Persian hat, and it covers this entire part of the horizon; to the east it is happier: below in front of me the clean new little city strikes the eye, the sounds of the healing springs, the sound of the multilingual crowd—and there, further, the mountains tower even darker blue and foggier, and on the edge of the horizon stretches a silver belt of snowy peaks, beginning with Kazbek and ending with the two-headed Elbrus…It is so joyful to live in such a land! A sort of gratifying feeling is flowing through all of my veins. The air is clean and fresh, like the kiss of a child; the sun is bright, the sky deep blue—what more could you want? Here why do we even have passions, desires, regrets?[6] (Lermontov 361).

Pechorin's elatedness here, his inflated state of joy, is mirrored in the sights, sounds, and acquaintance with the peaks of the mountains, which he names. The bright sun and the blue sky resemble fixed epithets found in Russian folk songs, fairy tales, and epics, perhaps suggesting that Pechorin is in his most natural and primal state in Pyatigorsk, lamenting his own Romantic tendencies towards "passions, desires, regrets." The Caucasus here serves as the backdrop for clearly and purely Romantic motifs, as an impenetrably wild and incomparably beautiful site.

Lermontov's reverence for this untamed beauty is not only present in *Hero of Our Time*. Because of the significant amount of time Lermontov spent in the Caucasus, both as a child and as an adult in exile, the mountains appear throughout his works of poetry. In one of his most famous poems, "Сон", "*Son*" 'The Dream' (1841), the mountains take on a more sinister and foreign nature, as the narrator, in a valley, lies dying from a gunshot wound:

I was lying alone on the valley's sand,
The cliffs' ledges crowding all around,

And the sun burned their yellow heights,
And burned me—but I slept in a deathly dream.
And I dreamed in radiant fires
The evening fire in my native land
Among young women, decorated in flowers
Carried on a joyful conversation about me.[7]

Here, the mountains impose on the narrator's space, the sun's brightness burns him, in contrast to the sun in Pechorin's description. He dreams of his "native land," Russia, longing for home, rather than the place where this "deathly dream" occurs. The barrenness of the Caucasian valley, covered with sand, is opposed to the flowers decorating the young Russian women in his imagination. In a more politicized poem following his exile to the Caucasus, Lermontov bids farewell to Russia, deeming it more uncivilized than the Caucasus:

Goodbye unwashed Russia,
Country of slaves, country of masters,
And you all, fully uniformed in blue,
And you, their devoted people.

Maybe behind the wall of the Caucasus
I will escape the notice of your *pashas*,
From their all-seeing eye,
From their all hearing ears.[8]

Here, Lermontov reverses Russia with the Caucasus and steppe frontiers, turning away from Russia, describing it as the country of slaves and masters, possibly because of the conquest. The Caucasus Mountains here offer anonymity, protection, and freedom from the "all seeing eye" and "all hearing ears" of the Imperial Government. Not unlike this poem, in another work of verse, Lermontov depicts the steppe frontier as cruel, difficult, and unforgiving, describing the journey of a leaf on its way to the Black Sea "it rolled along the steppe, persecuted by a cruel storm / It withered and faded from the cold, heat, and sadness / and then finally rolled its way to the Black Sea."[9] Just as Pechorin's elatedness mirrors the beauty of the Caucasus on

---

his arrival to Pyatigorsk, so does Lermontov's unintended exile in the Caucasus ruminate on his depictions of Russia as the savage nation and of the lonely leaf, traversing its barren and unforgiving landscapes, finding solace at the shores of the Black Sea.

Whereas Lermontov and his superfluous characters tend to reflect their emotions through the natural façade of the Caucasus, Pushkin's depictions of the Caucasus are a bit more direct, less Romanticized, and at times, even portraying the landscapes as inconvenient or overrated. Pushkin's perception is sometimes less a Romantic or idealized one, and more one of a weary or homesick exile. That said, he is still enthralled with the mystic, impressive, and overbearing qualities of the Caucasus region, as witnessed in some of his poems. Pushkin was exiled twice to the Caucasus. During the first visit, he was inspired to write *Prisoner of the Caucasus* [*Кавказский пленник, Kavkazskij plennik,* 1820–21], a work of verse about a Russian held prisoner by Chechens. This particular text has stood the test of time, even made into a film by Sergei Bodrov as recently as 1996, highlighting Russia's original conquest and more recent conflict in Chechnya. Pushkin wrote his first impressions of the Caucasus in a letter:

> I regret, my friend, that you were not with me to see the magnificent chain of these mountains; their icy heights, which from a distance, during sunrise, appear as strange clouds, multicoloured and still; I regret that you were not with me to climb the sharp-edged peak of Beshtu, with its summit comprised of five hills, or Mashuk, or Iron, Stone and Snake Mountains. The Caucasian region, the torrid boundary of Asia, arouses interest in all respects. [The Russian General] Ermolov has filled it with his name and beneficent genius. The savage Circassians have become timorous; their ancient audacity is disappearing. The roads are becoming less dangerous by the hour, and the numerous convoys are becoming superfluous. It is to be hoped that this conquered land, which until now has brought no real benefit to Russia, will soon form a bridge between us and the Persians for safe trading, that it will not be an obstacle to us in future wars—and that perhaps we will carry out Napoleon's chimerical plan of conquering India (Bethea 380).

Pushkin's commentary here is polarized between savagery and beauty, but does not oppose the conquest of the Caucasus by the Russians. Susan Layton, an authority on Russian literary perceptions of the Caucasus writes:

> If we listen to the full range of Russian voices from young Pushkin's era, we hear not one, but two discursive tendencies in utterances about Caucasian mountain peoples. Persistent throughout the nineteenth century, these two tendencies shared some diction ('wild') and concepts (mountaineers are martial by nature), but diverged in their value judgments of the uncivilized foreigners. Many Russian officials and military commanders insisted on Asian alterity by characterizing the Caucasian tribes as ignoble brutes... But the image of the ignoble mountaineer faced stiff competition from the noble mountaineers first invented in Pushkin's 'Prisoner of the Caucasus'. Throughout the nineteenth century, in fact, the bad savage was fighting a losing battle to displace romanticism's heroic tribes in the minds of Russian readers [...] Romantic literature's colorful mountaineers undoubtedly provided enjoyment, although not of a consistently mindless sort. Moreover, no Russian author ever uttered a protest sufficiently powerful to prevent the conquest of the Caucasus (Layton, "Nineteenth-Century Russian..." 82–3).

Indeed, the Russian Romantics, especially Pushkin and Lermontov, even if they had wanted to protest the conquest, would have been unlikely to say anything against the reigning mentality of the Empire—both were exiled to the Caucasus by that same leadership. Emerging into literature in such a climate, it is not surprising that Pushkin and Lermontov both come across in their depictions of the Caucasus as Russocentric or Orientalist. Simultaneously, as Layton cites, Pushkin was well aware of Russia's unstable geographical association with Europe and was quoted as saying, "Good old Russia! So it really does belong to Europe. And I'd always thought that this was just a mistake of the geographers" (Layton, *Russian Literature* 86). Even today, we divide Russia into two parts: European Russia, west of the Ural Mountains, and Asiatic Russia, east of the Ural Mountains. Georgia considers itself to be part of Europe. The highest peak in Europe is accepted globally as Mount Elbrus, located in the Caucasus. When Russia draws the maps, however, occasionally the line between Europe and Asia sometimes begins north of the Urals, and then traverses westward, placing Georgia and points to the south and to the west in Asia rather than in Europe.

No matter the misperceptions or strategically-woven political messages about the region on the part of Pushkin or Lermontov, the steppe and the Caucasus play an important role in the establishment of Russian identity during the Romantic period. The untamed wilds of the Caucasian nations and tribes represent the freedom lost by both authors in their exile to the region. The idyllic, over-the-top, and idealistic portrayals of the mountains and the unbridled horses and women coincide with the grandiose heroism and unmatched beauty so characteristic of Russian Romantic works. The Caucasus Mountains provide an ideal backdrop to reflect the emotions, battles, and triumphs of superfluous men. In poetry and in prose, the mountains' superfluousness mirrors that of these Romantic heroes—untethered and wild, yet bound to Imperial and societal convention. Undoubtedly, the ties of the Caucasus to Greco-Roman civilizations appealed to these Romantics as well as to a neoclassic theme: the legend of Prometheus chained to Mount Kazbek, the journey of Jason and the Argonauts to the Land of the Golden Fleece, then Colchis, now Western Georgia, as well as a new perception of the Caucasus as the new Parnassus, the new peaks of inspiration. The Caucasus offered Pushkin and Lermontov a unique vantage point for their writing, unmatched by the cityscapes and society that more frequently surrounded them, while it also sustained the conquest of the region, which more definitively associated Russia with the West, fulfilling its obligation to fortify Christianity over Islam, West over East, civilization over savagery, forest over steppe, and most importantly, self over other.

Notes

1. "Переход от Европы к Азии делается час от часу чувствительнее: леса исчезают, холмы сглаживаются, трава густеет и являет большую силу

растительности; показываются птицы, неведомые в наших лесах; орлы сидят на кочках, означающих большую дорогу, как будто на страже, и гордо смотрят на путешественников" (Pushkin 417).

2. «Не думаю, чтобы другая народная кухня могла произвести что-нибудь гаже".

3. "…в мое время ванны находились в лачужках, наскоро построенных… Нынче выстроены великолепные ванны и дома".

4. "Везде чистенькие дорожки, зеленые лавочки, правильные цветники, мостики, павильоны. Ключи обделаны, выложены камнем; на стенах ванн прибиты предписания от полиции; везде порядок, чистота, красивость..." Everywhere there are pretty little paths, little green benches, proper little flowers, little bridges, pavilions. The springs finished off with stone; nailed on the walls of the bathhouses are orders from the police; everywhere there is order, cleanliness, and beauty…"

5. "Зарему возвратить Гирею... / Но слушай: если я должна / Тебе... кинжалом я владею, / Я близ Кавказа рождена".

6. "...когда я открыл окно, моя комната наполнилась запахом цветов, растущих в скромном палисаднике. Ветки цветущих черешен смотрят мне в окна, и ветер иногда усыпает мой письменный стол их белыми лепестками. Вид с трех сторон у меня чудесный. На запад пятиглавый Бешту синеет, как «последняя туча рассеянной бури»; на север поднимается Машук, как мохнатая персидская шапка, и закрывает всю эту часть небосклона; на восток смотреть веселее: внизу передо мною пестреет чистенький, новенький городок, шумят целебные ключи, шумит разноязычная толпа, — а там, дальше, амфитеатром громоздятся горы все синее и туманнее, а на краю горизонта тянется серебряная цепь снеговых вершин, начинаясь Казбеком и оканчиваясь двуглавым Эльборусом...Весело жить в такой земле! Какое-то отрадное чувство разлито во всех моих жилах. Воздух чист и свеж, как поцелуй ребенка; солнце ярко, небо синл—чего бы, кажется, больше? зачем тут страсти, желания, сожаления?" (Lermontov)

7. Лежал один я на песке долины. / Уступы скал теснилися кругом, / И солнце жгло их желтые вершины / И жгло меня - но спал я мертвым сном. / И снился мне сияющий огнями / Вечерний пир в родимой стороне. / Меж юных жен, увенчанных цветами, / Шел разговор веселый обо мне. (*Bilingual Anthology of Russian Verse*).

8. Прощай, немытая Россия / Страна рабов, страна господ, / И вы, мундиры голубые, / И ты, им преданный народ. / Быть может, за стеной Кавказа / Укроюсь от твоих пашей, / От их всевидящего глаза, / От их всеслышащих ушей (Stikhi.ru).

---

9. И в степь укатился, жестокою бурей гонимый; / Засох и увял он от холода, зноя и горя / И вот наконец докатился до Черного моря (*Bilingual Anthology of Russian Verse*).

Works Cited

Bethea, David. *The Pushkin Handbook*. Madison, WI: U of Wisconsin P, 2005.

Fuller, Dana. "M. Iu. Lermontov". *Bilingual Anthology of Russian Verse*. Northwestern University. 16 Jan. 2003. Web. 7 Oct. 2013. <http://max.mmlc.northwestern.edu/~mdenner/Demo/poetpage/lermontov.html>.

Greenleaf, Monika. "Pushkin's 'Journey to Arzrum': The Poet at the Border." *Slavic Review* 50.4 (Winter 1991): 940–953.

Helfant, Ian. "Sculpting a Persona: The Path from Pushkin's Caucasian Journal to *Puteshestvie v Arzrum*". *Russian Review* 56. 3 (Jul. 1997): 366–382.

Hokanson, Katya. "Literary Imperialism, Narodnost' and Pushkin's Invention of the Caucasus". *Russian Review* 53.3 (July 1994): 336–352.

Khodarkovsky, Michael. *Russia's Steppe Frontier: The Making of a Colonial Empire, 1500–1800*. Bloomington: Indiana UP, 2002.

Layton, Susan. "Nineteenth-Century Russian Mythologies of Caucasian Savagery." In *Russia's Orient: Imperial Borderlands and Peoples, 1700-1917*. Eds. Daniel R. Brower and Edward J. Lazzerini. Bloomington, IN: Indiana UP, 1997.

_____. *Russian Literature and Empire*. Cambridge, UK: Cambridge UP, 1994.

Lermontov, Mikhail. *Geroj nashego vremeni* [*Hero of Our Time*]. In *Poemy. Geroj nashego vremeni*. Nazran', Ingushetian Republic: Izdatel'stvo AST, 1999.

McLean, Hugh. "Superfluous man". *Handbook of Russian Literature*. Ed. Victor Terras. New Haven, CT: Yale UP, 1985.

Pushkin, Alexander. *Puteshestvie v Arzrum: Vo vremja poxoda 1829 goda*. In *Sobranie sochinenij v 10 tomax*. PVB, 2002. Web. 10 Oct. 2013. <http://rvb.ru/ pushkin/01text/ 06prose/ 01prose/ 0870.htm?start=0&length=all>

Schimmelpenninck van der Oye, David. *Russian Orientalism*. New Haven, CT: Yale UP, 2010.

Stikhi.ru. "Proshchai nemytaja Rossija". 2011. Web. 7 Oct. 2013. <http://www.stihi.ru/2011/09/28/2913>.

Nikolai Gogol's Complex Relationship with Food: Between Romanticism and Realism

Rachel Stauffer

Nikolai Vasilievich Gogol (1809–1852) is one of the most beloved authors in Russia. Ukrainian by birth, Gogol moved to St. Petersburg at age 19 and worked diligently to break into the emergent literary scene, befriending Pushkin, and quickly making his mark on the literary world with his unusual stories based on life in rural Ukraine, quite a departure from the urban, educated population in St. Petersburg, in *Evenings on a Farm Near Dikanka* [*Вечера на хуторе близ Диканьки*, *Vechera na khutore bliz Dikan'ki*, 1832] and *Mirgorod* [*Миргород*, 1835]. Ranging from tales of the mundane to the fantastically supernatural, Gogol's depictions of rural life were unlike anything being published at the time. Indeed, his oeuvre is distinctive in the context of his contemporaries' works. Gogol emerged onto the St. Petersburg literary scene at the height of Pushkin's fame. Romantic themes, lofty ideals, superfluous heroes, and the high society drama of the elite were normal themes. Gogol is somewhat anomalous—not a Romantic author in the proscribed sense, but also not entirely fully Realist, in comparison to authors like Dostoevsky and Tolstoy. However, his works, perhaps more than those of any other author of this period, certainly set the stage for Russian Realism. Gogol's Petersburg stories, such as *The Overcoat* [*Шинель*, *Shinel'*, 1842], represent an important shift in Russian literature, to which future literary geniuses, such as Dostoevsky, were paying close attention. For example, the hero of *The Overcoat*, Akakii Akakievich Bashmachkin, a civil servant, lives a life completely devoid of the society functions and spontaneous duels of Romantic superfluous men. Akakii Akakievich lives a much more humble and monotonous life, a type of existence not previously depicted or valued in Russian literature. For the purpose of comparison, the following passage from Mikhail Lermontov (1814–1841) describing Grigorii Pechorin, a quintessential Romantic hero in the appropriately titled novel, *Hero of Our Time* [*Герой нашего времени*, *Geroj nashego vremeni*, 1839–1841], will serve as an example of the life of a Romantic hero, the typical representative of Russian Romanticism in the 1810s to 1840s:

> When he left, a terrible sadness burdened my heart. What if fate had brought us together again in the Caucasus, or if she purposely came here while knowing that she would run into me? ...and how we would run into each other?... and then, if she knew this...My feelings have never deceived me. There is no person in this world over whom the past has as much power, as it does over me: every memory about every past sadness or happiness resounds in my soul [...]...I am stupidly created: I forget nothing – nothing! (Lermontov 373).[1]

Here, Pechorin battles his emotional self, wishing he could feel less fearful of his emotions and their consequences. Akakii Akakievich, on the other hand, on a day-to-day basis, feels very little, or at least the narrator provides little insight into his emotional state:

> Arriving home, he sat down at the same hour at the table, quickly gulped down his cabbage soup and ate a slice of mutton with onion, not at all noticing their taste, he ate all of this with flies or with whatever else God sent at the time. Once he had noticed that his stomach had started to swell, he got up from the table, took out a jar with ink and copied papers that had been brought home.[2]

The only emotion Akakii Akakevich feels throughout the text is typically associated with his new overcoat—its creation, its acquisition, and later, its absence as the result of theft. When he makes a payment on the coat to the tailor and realizes that he will really, truly have a new coat, "his heart," Gogol writes, "begins to beat."[3] The essence of Gogol's character in "The Overcoat" is less emotional and more physical. This physicality is represented by the coat itself as well as by Akakii Akakievich's typically emotionless state. But to Akakii Akakievich, the coat is not only a coat, it represents an achievement, an improvement to life, especially considering the St. Petersburg cold, and this is important to Akakii Akakievich, who is not independently wealthy and subsequently is unconcerned with the problems of someone like the Romantic hero Pechorin, who is concerned about his emotional state and simultaneously wrapped up in the drama of high society. It is because of *The Overcoat* that the critic Vissarion Belinsky, an important critic of the time, "interpreted Gogol very freely as having pioneered the down-to-earth and socially conscious depiction of Russian life that he wished to encourage" (Frank 12). Akakii Akakevich, in contrast to Pechorin, represented the real people of Russia who struggled unnecessarily with bureaucracy, faced daily financial hardship, and had no possibility of achieving higher social status. This character's emergence set forth a general movement toward Realism, the depiction of everyone and everything. Gogol is, for this reason, sometimes considered the founder of Russian Realism.

Works of Russian Realism depict the parts of society once omitted from or considered taboo in works of Romanticism, including lower social classes, like for example, the peasant class, as depicted in Turgenev's *Hunter's Sketches* [*Записки охотника, Zapiski oxotnika*, 1852]. Gogol's work is typically not constrained to a literary period and is widely accepted as an anomaly that is neither Romantic, nor Realist. Renato Poggioli has noted, "Prince Mirsky separates the 'age of Realism' from the 'age of Gogol'" (Poggioli 253). Hugh McLean has pointed out that "after Belinsky's death the very term 'natural school' was outlawed by the censorship, but a substitute was soon found, the 'Gogolian trend' (*gogolevskoe napravlenie*)" (McLean 366). In his *History of Russian Literature*, Victor Terras discusses Gogol in his chapter on the Romantic period because, in strict temporal terms, this is where Gogol falls in the chronology, but in thematic terms, Gogol is far from it. Here we will assume that Gogol is anomalous, but falls more readily into the category of pre-Realism or the Natural School. McLean describes Realism as follows, which is the approach to Realism that this chapter will engage:

Where *romanticism* stressed the exceptional, the larger-than-life, the heroic, Realism concentrated on the everyday, the average, the 'typical.' Where Romanticism treated the individual as unique and independently valuable, Realism perceived human beings as integral parts both of the system of nature and of society. Romanticism portrayed its heroes' behavior as motivated by their own ideas, passions, aspirations, and will; Realism viewed peoples' lives as largely determined by social or biological forces beyond their control. The romantic author had no compunctions about obtruding his own reactions and reflections into his narrative; the realist author felt constrained to remain objective, dispassionate, to 'let the facts speak for themselves'. Proud of his title of 'artist', the romantic author saw no reason to deny that his works were his own creation, the products of his imagination and even of inspiration vouchsafed from on high; for the realist, however, imagination connoted invention and even falsehood, and he deployed every technical means at his disposal to create the illusion that his fiction was fact...by no means all the 'realistic'features were exhibited in every realist's work... nevertheless a sufficient concentration and conscious exploitation of them is present in the 19th century to justify calling it the classic period of Realism (McLean 364).

McLean's definition is useful in this analysis because it suggests polar distinctions between Realism and Romanticism rather than offering the option of a gray area, which is sometimes where Gogol is placed on the broader spectrum—neither Romantic nor Realist— or sometimes as both.

Gogol's early work, mostly short stories, is difficult to categorize as purely Realist. It depicts the Ukrainian countryside, integrating folk belief, rural life, and legends consistent with East Slavic folklore and dual belief [*двоеверие, dvoeverie*]. Elements of the supernatural or mystical intermingle with ordinary people in otherwise routine existence. The mundane, quotidian quality of characters' lives is often interrupted by an unprecedented encounter with something or someone not of the physical world, often supernatural. In his famous story "Vii" ["Вий," published in *Mirgorod*], a monk wanders onto a farmstead and is overpowered by an old woman who, in a scene filled with sexual innuendo and physical sensations, casts a spell on him and the two literally fly through the air throughout the night. When the spell is broken and the monk has both feet on the ground, he beats the old woman nearly to death, only to see that she has somehow transformed into a beautiful young maiden. The young maiden subsequently dies from the beating and, on her deathbed, requests that this particular monk read the prayers at church over her body for three nights once she has died. The monk agrees to this odd request, and each night, the young maiden's corpse comes alive and the church is haunted by progressively terrifying ghosts, goblins, and the undead, the last of which, Vii, allegedly the king of the dwarves, scares him to death.

In Gogol's story, "The Nose" ["Hoc", *Nos*, written 1835–36], a seemingly normal day begins with a barber finding a human nose in his loaf of bread. He has no idea how he got the nose, so he gets rid of it in order to avoid being accused of a crime. Meanwhile, Major Kovalev, a client of the same barber, wakes up normally, looks in the mirror, and discovers that his nose is missing. Kovalev searches around St. Petersburg for his nose, only to find it in an officer's uniform of a higher rank, attending church, and acting as though it has no idea who Kovalev is. Hilarity ensues, and the nose is eventually arrested for trying to cross the border into Latvia without a passport. At the end of the story, the narrator acknowledges its absurdity, which does not clarify anything for the reader who, particularly in Gogol's time, must have been simultaneously enamored of and bewildered by this text. Even in the short story "The Overcoat," Akakii Akakievich dies and returns from the dead as a ghost who haunts St. Petersburg and steals overcoats. The supernatural and fantastic elements of Gogol's works have often caused confusion as to whether he should be categorized under Russian Romanticism or Russian Realism. In this chapter, we will consider an important theme that does conform to the ideas of Realism throughout Gogol's work: food. As Vladimir Nabokov noted about Gogol, "The belly is the belle of his stories, the nose is their beau" (3). The physical connotation of food, along with Gogol's consistent inclusion of it in his works, as well as his own troubled relationship with it in real life, all coalesce and help us see him as more Realist than Romantic.

The theme of food and eating recurs consistently in the majority of Gogol's works. The canon of scholarship on this topic widely acknowledges the colorful assortment of characters who occupy and devote themselves wholly to the preparation and consumption of vividly described delicacies: magical *varenniki* that dip themselves in sour cream and propel themselves into mouths; an abundance of little pies (*pirozhki, pirogi*); and dozens upon dozens of scenes in which characters dine together on traditional Ukrainian and Russian fare. Gogol's food imagery is not only appetizing in its description and often enchanted in its presentation, but it also reflects the real life irony of Gogol's own love for and eventual rejection of the same sustenance. By self-imposed starvation, Gogol denied himself the very same enjoyment his characters derive from the pleasure of food. He starved himself to death, dying at the all-too-early age of 42. Nabokov describes Gogol's death and his lifelong attitude towards food:

> Absolute bodily exhaustion in result of a private hunger strike (by means of which his morbid melancholy had tried to counter the Devil) culminated in acute anemia of the brain (together, probably with gastroenteritis through inanition) – and the treatment he was subjected to, a vigorous purging and bloodletting, hastened the death of an organism already gravely impaired by the effects of malaria and malnutrition [...] In the months preceding his death he had starved himself so thoroughly that he had destroyed the prodigious capacity his stomach had once been blessed with; for none had sucked in such a number of macaroni or eaten so many cherry pies as this thin little man (1–3).

Not discounting the tragic truth of Gogol's troubled relationship with food, as a theme in his works, it is widely acknowledged. Much of the existing criticism looks to Freudian psychoanalysis to interpret Gogol's obsession with food as an oral fixation. While these interpretations are useful in their own way, and even though they coincide beautifully with a Freudian perspective, here we will consider Gogol's food imagery through a different lens: by looking at the significance of food imagery in terms of its role in the larger context of the Golden Age, specifically, Gogol's place between Romanticism and Realism.

One of the defining traits of Realism is the acknowledgement of human physicality and bodily function, McLean's "biological forces." The physical needs of human beings emerge as themes in Russian literature only during the Realist period. As Belinsky observed, this physicality is part of Gogol's universal appeal to readers, both Russian and foreign, even though he is also undeniably nationalist:

> Gogol strictly adheres in his writings to the sphere of Russian *zhitejskij* [everyday, life's] activity [. . .] For the poet who wants his genius to be recognized everywhere and by everyone, and not only by those who are his fellow countrymen, nationality is the first, but not the only condition: it is still essential that he who is *national* is at the same time *global*, that is, that of his creations, nationality is the form, the body, the fruit, the physiognomy, the differentiation of the spiritual and physical world, of common human ideas. (Belinsky 16)

Ronald D. LeBlanc, one of the authorities in the area of food, eating, and gastronomy in nineteenth- and twentieth-century Russian literature discusses the contrasts in food imagery between Romanticism and Realism:

> Whatever the ultimate cause of this obsession with gastronomy, the fact remains that in Russian literature of the modern era the kind of food that is artistically represented – and the manner in which that food is produced, prepared, served, and consumed – invariably tells us as much about the personality and psychological profile of the eater, as well as the sociology and cultural values of the world that he or she inhabits...Historically considered, one of the primary functions that food imagery fulfilled within secular literature in Russia was initially to break some of the lingering aesthetic taboos against corporeality that had been established during the neoclassical

period. These taboos had long regulated the choice of the appropriate subject matter and the proper artistic method to represent the human body in what was considered to be serious literature...In the classic nineteenth-century Russian novel, the enjoyment of food and drink is often used by realist writers as a way to condemn the banality of those philistines who care more for stuffing their bellies than for developing their minds or elevating their souls ("Food, Orality, and Nostalgia..." 247–8).

Two important elements of LeBlanc's statement here are the tradition of food as a taboo subject in literature, and the role of food as a satirical device, which 'condemns the banality' of society's endless physical motivation to consume. In a seemingly unrelated article, "Food in the Rus' *Primary Chronicle*," Horace Lunt remarks on one essential role of food during Russia's early days: "Eating habits and food are used in many cultures as symbolic signals for identifying outsiders, i.e., 'others,' who are potentially threatening to one's community" (Lunt 25).[4] Lunt here implies that food is a representation of national identity and, therefore, a reflection of traditional customs and local culinary specialties. Therefore, food can be considered a nationalistic construct, which, according to Belinsky, is a necessary component of Realist literature. This paper comes from Glants and Toomre's volume *Food in Russian History and Culture*, a book that, as a whole, conveys the degree to which food is a cultural and historical construct in Russia, emphasizing that the Russians are unique among other world cultures because of an uncommonly deep *national* appreciation for food. Therefore, we can surmise that the use of food as subject matter in Russian literature is not only keenly purposeful in Gogol's works because it touches the Russian reader on a personal level, but it also shows the reader that the author is not an outsider—that he or she truly understands the nature of Russian reality. Beyond his own personal obsession with it, Gogol would find food to be a useful conduit for the expression of Russian reality.

The many images of food in Gogol have already been examined in great detail in works of scholarship. Here we will consider many of the same works that are most commonly analyzed by critics when it comes to Gogol's food imagery, while adding that the imagery serves to perform a function of realist art, as McLean puts it, "...[to perceive] human beings as integral parts both of the system of nature and of society...; [to view] peoples' lives as largely determined by social or biological forces beyond their control..." (McLean 366). Natalie Kolb-Seletski's 1970 article "Gastronomy, Gogol, and His Fiction" nicely summarizes the depth to which food is described in Gogol's works:

> It would seem that no matter which of Gogol's literary works one considers – *Evenings on a Farm Near Dikan'ka*, short stories that make up the *Mirgorod* collection, the Petersburg stories, *Rome*, the comedies *The Inspector General* and *The Marriage* or *Dead Souls* – one finds everywhere not only heroes who like to eat well but unforgettable descriptions of mouth-watering appetizers, robust dinners, lusty banquets, savory suppers, breakfasts, midmorning and midnight snacks, and epicurean feasts fit for a king..." (Kolb-Seletski 35-6).

LeBlanc has published entire articles devoted to food and its role in Gogol, conducting what is probably the most in-depth analysis to date of food imagery in Gogol's novel, *Dead Souls* [*Мертвые души, Mertvye dushi*, 1842] and his play, *The Inspector General* [*Ревизор, Revizor*, 1836]. In LeBlanc's article "Dinner With Chichikov", LeBlanc makes a powerful observation about food as a fictional device in *Dead Souls*:

> Andrej Bely tabulates a total of eighty-six different culinary dishes mentioned in Gogol's Petersburg stories, his stage comedies, and *Dead Souls*. Indeed the references to food and eating are so numerous in this last work that Bely suggests we might well call Gogol's epic poem not an *Iliad* but rather a *Gobble-iad*, and that the true hero of this work might well be considered the 'belly'. What is the point of these numerous references to food and eating in *Dead Souls*? Are they merely reflections of the author's own gastronomical obsessions? Or do they serve instead some specific

narrative function within the text? . . . The fictional meal, as we shall come to see, serves as a particularly useful device which allows the author to comment at length both upon the psychology of his characters and upon the nature of the fictional world they inhabit... (*Dinner with Chichikov* 68).

In their research, Kolb-Seletski and LeBlanc both recognize that food is playing a textually significant role that contributes to the reader's understanding of the characters' psychological compositions and the settings in which they exist. The vivid and true-to-life food imagery in Gogol's works not only adds to the plot and the setting, but also shows the author's unique manner of connecting art and reality.

In the prologue to Gogol's *Dikan'ka Tales*, the narrator of the tales, Rudi Pan'ko, provides the reader with a list of vocabulary to aid in the understanding of certain folk terms so that the readers "will not think poorly of" him (Gogol 12). The list for the first half of the *Dikan'ka Tales* consists of approximately seventy-five words, of which roughly one-third is related to food or vessels for eating or drinking. One term even refers to a stomach sickness. In the prologue to the second cycle, there are approximately sixty terms, many repeated from the first list, and of those included, around twenty-five percent relate to food or vessels for food. Later Realist authors, such as Ivan Turgenev and Nikolay Nekrasov used the physiological sketch as a medium to show the diverse facets of society in St. Petersburg in a journalistic, almost scientific, writing style. While they did not specifically include lists of vocabulary in their assessments of these parts of Petersburg society, it would seem that what Gogol is trying to do with the *Dikan'ka Tales* is similar. The author is trying to show the Ukrainian, or rural way of life, to an elite class of readers in Moscow and St. Petersburg. Gogol purposefully constructs these lists of vocabulary as a means of making the content of the stories represent the ethnicity of their characters while also pointing out to the educated urban reader that he is an outsider to rural life. As a result, he succeeds in presenting Belinsky's requisite Realist *nationality*. The fact that food terminology is a hefty portion of which the vocabulary lists consist only goes to show further evidence that food, *nationality*, and Realism are all connected in Gogol's works.

The *Dikan'ka Tales* are full of food imagery. Aleksandr Obolensky summarizes these in great detail in his book *Food-Notes on Gogol*. About "The Sorochinsky Fair" ["Сорочинская ярмарка", *Sorochinskaja jarmarka*], Obolensky mentions food images, such as the descriptions of fresh fruit, fish, and grain corresponding to the late summer harvest; the fair itself gives off the smell of all kinds of food; a main character is named the Ukrainian word for onion; and the author also gives us a description of a sunset made of "melons and pumpkins" (Obolensky 15). While Obolensky's analysis of the *Dikan'ka Tales* does claim to focus on food imagery, he seeks to link Gogol's food images with the fantastic and especially with the supernatural and demonic. Growing up in rural Ukraine, where folk belief still abounds, it is likely that folk legends, specifically in *memorate* and *fabulate* forms were abundant throughout Gogol's early life. Ukrainian folklore is full of these cautionary tales and legends about witches, devils, the undead, and place spirits, and as a result of growing up surrounded by such tales, it is possible that Gogol on some level, even as an adult, was a believer in such things. If we accept that Gogol had some sort of belief in the fantastic, that food imagery is representative of *universality* and *physicality*, and that food is often associated with the diabolical and supernatural, then the nature of food as a Realist construct in Gogol's works is even more conceivable. The fact that Gogol takes a true entity such as food and links it to what most would consider a liminal or fictional entity, the supernatural, he manages to combine the two worlds, creating a sort of middle ground that is neither completely real, nor completely unreal. He blurs the line between what is of this world and what is not so perfectly that the reader can never be sure that the world presented is without ties to the real world.

The *Mirgorod* stories represent similarly transitional ground, primarily between rural and urban life. Written between the *Dikan'ka Tales* and *Petersburg Tales*, the stories still take place in the Ukrainian countryside, but there is a merger of the two worlds as characters travel between the country and the city. Obolensky claims: "Devils and witches are here left behind, except for one brief scene when the devil appears in the form of a brown sow. Mirgorod, the writer implies ironically, is a quite ordinary small town, and his heroes are quite ordinary, even typical characters..." (Obolensky 39). There is no over-the-top, heroic or grandiose idealism in these tales such as would be found in Romanticism, only the tedium of everyday life. The supernatural that does exist in these stories, such as in "Vii", again indicates that it and the real world are interrelated in Gogol's mind. Daniel Rancour-Laferriere has even suggested that the supernatural creature in "Vii" is nothing more than a monstrous interpretation of Gogol's own relationship with his father.[5] While this interpretation is psychoanalytical at its core, it is still possible to relate the real world familial situation with the fantastic in the story. Obolensky, regarding the transitional nature of the Mirgorod cycle, claims that "there is the unity provided by the kind of food mentioned in Gogol's writings, which changes as the locale changes...Just as a transition can be felt in the style of the *Mirgorod* stories from that of the *Dikan'ka Tales*, so too there is a transition in the foods which the characters in *Mirgorod* prefer" (Obolensky 49). For example, the role of food in "Old World Landowners" ["Старосветские помещики", *Starosvetskie pomeshchiki*, published in *Mirgorod*], in contrast to earlier texts, has *no* magical significance. The two characters in this story eat whenever and whatever they feel like eating, and this has them eating throughout the story. The notion of banal routine goes back to LeBlanc: "In the classic nineteenth-century Russian novel, the enjoyment of food and drink is often used by Realist writers as a way to condemn the banality of those philistines who care more for stuffing their bellies than for developing their minds or elevating their souls..." (*Food, Orality, and Nostalgia* 248). *Mirgorod* exemplifies this point beautifully with the story "Starosvetskie pomeshchiki," and the further biographical connection to it and to "Vii" support the notion that this cycle, too, is Realist, although its perspective on food is slightly different.

Returning to Gogol's most well-known tales, "The Nose" and "The Overcoat," we find less food imagery, but consistency in its presence and role as a Realist construct. Although less prominent, food plays as much a Realist role in these works as in *Mirgorod* and the *Dikan'ka Tales*. Whereas these aforementioned story cycles show a strong sense of *nationality*, Gogol's later stories illustrate the concepts of *universality* and *physicality* to, arguably, the greatest degree in Gogol's work. "The Nose" begins with breakfast. The author opens the story with a sensual feast: "Ivan Jakovlevich woke up rather early and smelled hot bread. . .—Today I, Praskov'ja Osipovna, will not be drinking any coffee...instead I would like to have a slice of hot bread with onion..." (Gogol, 313). Not only does the above scene tempt the appetite of the reader, but also initiates the story by engaging the character's sense of smell, which in a story called "The Nose", is naturally not an accidental nod to physicality. Beyond this opening scene, there are a number of descriptions that deal specifically with food images. Kovalev enters a *konditerskaia*, a store that sells sweets, so that he can look in the mirror; an upset Kovalev mentions that it's okay for a woman selling oranges to be without a nose, but it is inappropriate for a man such as himself; upon trying to place an ad in the paper to have his nose returned, he shows his noseless face to the man in charge of placing ads, who describes the smooth spot as a freshly cooked *blin*, a Russian crepe-like pancake, an important national and ritual food; and a police officer with whom Kovalev speaks has a sweet tooth. The importance of food imagery in this story is central to the plot for two reasons. The first is that the sense of smell and, therefore, the nose are closely related to the sense of taste and the act of eating. Secondly, the content of this story, a man waking up to find his nose masquerading about town as a General is so unrealistic that food serves as an anchor by which the story's content relates to a real life situation. Gogol concludes the story by saying "Say what you like, but similar occurrences take place in the world—rarely, but they do happen" (Gogol 344).

In "The Overcoat," as discussed at the beginning of this chapter, eating is an everyday, banal task, such that, once Akakii Akakievich decides to have a new overcoat made for himself, the financial burden of the coat requires him to spend less money on food. As already cited, the early scene of Akakii Akakievich eating is routinized, habitual, and not at all a positive or satisfying experience. It comes as no surprise, then, that to Akakii Akakievich, the burden of hunger is an annoyance, but not a devastating consequence. The joy that Akakii Akakievich takes in the projected warmth of his new overcoat far outweighs his hunger: "he even became completely accustomed to being hungry in the evenings; but to make up for it, he was nourished from within, carrying in his thoughts the everlasting idea of his future overcoat."[6] In "The Overcoat," considered by many to be the most Realist of Gogol's works, we see the role of hunger outweighing the role of food, an appropriate transition in the context of the author's own changing views on the subject in the later stages of his life, and certainly a more Realist approach to the socioeconomic imbalances present in nineteenth-century Russian urban society.

Notes

1. Когда он ушел, то ужасная грусть стеснила мое сердце. Судьба ли нас свела опять на Кавказе, или она нарочно сюда приехала, зная, что меня встретит?... и как мы встретимся?.. и потом, она ли это?... Мои предчувствия меня никогда не обманывали. Нет в мире человека, над которым прошедшее приобретало бы такую власть, как надо мною: всякое напоминание о минувшей печали или радости болезненно ударяет в мою душу [...]...Я глупо создан: ничего не забываю, - ничего!

2. Приходя домой, он садился тот же час за стол, хлебал наскоро свои щи и ел кусок говядины с луком, вовсе не замечая их вкуса, ел все это с мухами и со всем тем, что ни посылал Бог на ту пору. Заметивши, что желудок начинал пучиться, вставал из-за стола, вынимал баночку с чернилами и переписывал бумаги, принесенные на дом. Gogol, Nikolai. "Shinel." *Alexei Komarov's Internet Library.* Added to web from Gogol', N.V. *Cobranie cochinenij v devjati tomax.* Vol 3. Moscow: Russkaya Kniga, 1994. <http://ilibrary.ru/text/980/p.1/index.html>

3. "Сердце его, вообще весьма покойное, начало биться". Ibid. "His heart, generally quite quiet, began to beat." The word 'pokojnoe' can also be used to refer to someone or something that has died, e.g., deceased, or the late so-and-so. This short, but complex line may subtly suggest that Akakii Akakievich is not really alive until he receives the new overcoat, and the end of the story suggests that he cannot live without it.

4.   Lunt, Horace G. "Food in the Rus' *Primary Chronicle*". *Food in Russian History and Culture*. Eds. Musya Glants and Joyce Toomre. Bloomington, IN: Indiana UP, 1997.

5.   Rancour-Laferriere, Daniel. "The Identity of Gogol's *Vij*." *Harvard Ukrainian Studies* 2.2 (June 1978): 211–234.

6.   Gogol, Nikolai. "Shinel." *Alexei Komarov's Internet Library*. Added to web from Gogol', N.V. *Cobranie cochinenij v devjati tomax*. Vol 3. Moscow: Russkaya Kniga, 1994. <http://ilibrary.ru/text/980/p.1/index.html>

Works Cited

Belinsky, Vissarion. *Mysli i zametki o russkoj literature* [Thoughts and notes about Russian literature]. Google Book: Livres, 2013.

Frank, Joseph. *Between Religion and Rationality: Essays in Russian Literature and Culture*. Princeton, NJ: Princeton UP, 2010.

Gogol, Nikolai V. *Vechera na khutore bliz Dikan'ki*. Moscow: Izdatel'stvo ACT, 2004.

Kolb-Seletski, Natalie. "Gastronomy, Gogol, and His Fiction." *Slavic Review* 29.1 (Mar 1970): 35–57.

LeBlanc, Ronald D. "Dinner with Chichikov: The Fictional Meal as Narrative Device in Gogol's *Dead Souls*." *Modern Language Studies* 18.4 (Autumn 1988): 68–80.

_____. "Food, Orality, and Nostalgia for Childhood: Gastronomic Slavophilism in Midnineteenth- Century Russian Fiction." *The Russian Review* 58 (April 1999): 244–267.

Lunt, Horace G. "Food in the Rus' *Primary Chronicle*." *Food in Russian History and Culture*. Eds. Musya Glants and Joyce Toomre. Bloomington, IN: Indiana UP: 1997.

McLean, Hugh. "Realism." *A Handbook of Russian Literature*. Ed. Victor Terras. New Haven, CT: Yale UP, 1985.

Nabokov, Vladimir. *Nikolai Gogol*. New York: New Directions Publishing, 1961.

Obolensky, Aleksandr. *Food-Notes on Gogol*. Winnipeg, Manitoba: Trident Press, 1972.

Poggioli, Renato. "Realism in Russia." *Comparative Literature* 3.3 (Summer 1951): 253–267.

Ivan Turgenev: An Advocate of Russian Realism _____

Frank Jacob

One of the most important Russian writers of the Golden Age was Ivan Sergeevich Turgenev (1818–1883), who definitely ranks on top with other exponents of Russian Realism of the nineteenth century. According to some, next to Tolstoy and Dostoevsky, Turgenev is the most famous Russian author (Thieme 9; Woodward 1). Although Russian, he identified himself with Western culture and acted more like a spectator who wrote about Russia while living in Germany or France (Zûñiga 9). Even if he saw himself as a Westerner while staying in close contact with the literary circles of France—as his close friendship with Flaubert illustrates (Beaumont)—he wrote about his home: Russia. Due to this, works like *Rudin*, *A Nest of the Gentry*, *On the Eve*, and *Fathers and Sons* are "generally recognized as Turgenev's most notable contribution to Russian and world literature" (Woodward i).

His works provide the reader with a "subtle breeze of internal pain, frustration and melancholy" (Zûñiga 10) because "the great nineteenth-century chronicler of Russian society" (Wilkinson 2) bore witness to the step-by-step downfall of the Russian gentry, while contributing a detailed, as well as realistic, description of the suffering agrarian population of Tsarist Russia (Zûñiga 13). Despite the fact that Turgenev is an influential Russian figure in this period—during which the country was undergoing a transformative process—in the West, his works are overshadowed by Tolstoy and Dostoevsky, who are more widely read than Turgenev (Thieme 9). In Russia, Pushkin and Gogol are perhaps more widely read than Turgenev as well. This seems to be especially unjust because works like *A Sportsman's Sketches* [Записки охотника, *Zapiski okhotnika,* 1852] influenced his literary heirs and because Turgenev set standards in prose fiction that Dostoevsky and Tolstoy openly challenged and more or less secretly emulated (Orwin 37). But it was not only Russian writers who were inspired by the breathtaking effect of Turgenev's realistic writings because even world-famous

Western authors like Hemingway were remarkably influenced by the Russian writer with regard to their later literary oeuvres (Wilkinson 1–3). Consequently, and despite the fact that Turgenev did not see himself as a master of literature (Tussing 35), his contribution to Russia's Golden Age cannot be omitted. Moreover, he did not just write novels, narratives, and novellas, but also lyrics as well as twelve dramas (1843–1852), of which the first were more aligned with the ideals of Russian Romanticism—the artistic and literary movement Turgenev eschewed, since he wrote more realist works in the following decades (Koschmal 1). Regarding his motives, which are traceable through all his works, he was mainly focused on the common man, whom he described in detail, but his works were influenced by many other sources of inspiration.

Following this insight, the subsequent chapter will not only present a biography of the important Russian writer, something which has already been done in detail (Pritchett; Shapiro; Troyat; Yarmolinsky), but will also use another approach to characterize Turgenev, as well as his works. To achieve this aim, a short biographical sketch will complement the characteristics of Turgenev's realism in the following section. Furthermore, decisive motives behind Turgenev's works will be analyzed in order to determine which events or thoughts inspired the author and what he tried to achieve by writing about the appropriate topics. For this, motives aroused by Turgenev's family, his experiences of love, a fascination with the supernatural, and his observation of political grievances of the nineteenth-century agrarian Russia will be taken into account to show what factors were responsible for Turgenev's own evolution into the realist advocate against an antiquated social system—a system of which he originally benefitted by virtue of his birth.

A Short Biography

Turgenev was born on November 9, 1818 near Oryol, a city around 200 miles southwest of Moscow. His mother was Varvara Petrovna Lutovinova, a rich noble woman, while his father Sergei Nikolaevich Turgenev had served as a colonel in the Russian cavalry before settling at his wife's estate at Spasskoye. For the education of the children, the family moved to Moscow, where Turgenev was taught by private tutors. In 1833, he started to study philology at Moscow University. This city, in which Western and Eastern cultures met, made an enduring impression on him (Zúñiga 31). In 1834, he moved to St. Petersburg to continue his studies in Russia's then capital and became part of the emerging literary circles there. In contrast to Moscow, the intellectual influence of Western thought was stronger because of St. Petersburg's status as a port city and its perceived role as Russia's window to the West. Turgenev belonged to the faction of the intelligentsia known as the Westernizers, who were influenced by French Naturalism. By contrast, their antagonists, the Slavophiles, favored a stronger Pan-Slavism, or a preference for adopting a more Russocentric, rather than Eurocentric, approach to literature and the arts.

In 1834, Turgenev started writing lyrics, and in the same year, finished his first work, *Steno* [Стемно], a Romantic, poetic drama influenced by the works of the English poet Lord Byron. Hence, Turgenev started his literary career as a representative of Russian Romanticism, and the 100 poems he wrote before 1837 reflect this influence. This romantic phase reputedly influenced Turgenev's subsequent career because, even if the master himself didn't like his early works, the realist Turgenev was "a child of the ending romantic and idealistic period" (Nohejl 113).

After graduating from St. Petersburg University in 1837, Turgenev left Russia to finish his education in Europe, a common practice among most members of the gentry. He enrolled at Berlin University to study philosophy (Woodward 3). Ultimately, he stayed in Germany for ten years (with interruptions), building a significant acquaintance with this country as well as deep friendships with Germans and Russians he met there. Michael Bakunin, with whose sister Turgenev had a liaison in later years, was one such Russian he met in Germany. Karl August Varnhagen, Bettina von Arnim, and Alexander von Humboldt would become his friends as well (Zúñiga 37). His readings of Hegel and Schopenhauer (Masing-Delic 14; McLaughlin; Thieme 9; Tussing Orwin 37–38) influenced him in a decisive way, and the young man became a realist, whose "enemy was serfdom" (Zûñiga 88). Due to this Western influence, Turgenev wrote mainly about his home country, but in a very critical and realistic style.

In 1841, Turgenev returned to Russia, where he continued writing poetry and also completing his master's degree at St. Petersburg University. One year later, his illegitimate daughter Paulinette—the child of Turgenev and a female serf—was born, and Turgenev befriended Alexander Herzen, an important Russian writer, philosopher, and publicist of the time. He also got to know Vissarion Belinsky, another important literary critic, who would connect Turgenev with other likeminded writers and people in the Russian intelligentsia. In 1843 in St. Petersburg, Turgenev's life took a new path when he met the soprano singer Pauline Viardot-Garcia. Turgenev fanatically loved this woman, who saw him just as a friend. He wrote her letters over a long period and followed her and her husband through Europe. He even lived together with the family, which also provided his illegitimate daughter with an education and family life. In Baden-Baden he built a house next to them and lived with them in Château Courtavenel and later in Paris. Turgenev longed to be close to Pauline, who was one of the most important women in the writer's life (Zûñiga 73–83).

Belinsky introduced Turgenev to Dostoevsky, who had recently published *Poor Folk* [*Бедные люди, Bednye ljudi*, 1846], and envy as well as antipathy defined their relationship from Turgenev's side (Zûñiga 47). After translating Byron and Goethe into Russian, Turgenev returned to Germany in 1847 to be close to Pauline Viardot. For the next several years, he wrote the physiological sketches, based on the French *physiologie*, which were published in 1852 under the title *A Sportsman's Sketches,* published as well in the journal *Sovremennik* (*The Contemporary*), an important publication of the time. The publication of these works made Turgenev famous. In these texts he described Russian rural life in a very detailed way. The aim of the *physiologie* or the *physiological sketch* was to depict scenes of everyday life as realistically as possible, with almost a photographic or scientific quality about them. Readers in general and the critics in particular loved the accuracy of character descriptions in these narratives. From 1848 to 1850, Turgenev lived in Paris to be close to Pauline Viardot, but had to return to Russia because his mother had become ill and was near death. If not for this, the Russian authorities could have seen him exiled much longer. In fact, the authorities had begun to dislike Turgenev's inconveniently realistic depiction of Russia because Turgenev described the reality, especially of those who were not part of the prosperous gentry, but poor and suppressed by the ruling classes.

In 1849, his drama *Breakfast at the Chief's* [*Завтрак у предводителя, Zavtrak u predvoditelia*] was censored and the dramatic play *A Month in the Country* [*Месяц в деревне, Mesiats v derevne*], which he finished in 1850, was also censored due to its original title *The Student* [*Студент*]. In 1852, Turgenev's *A Sportsman's Sketches* [*Записки охотника, Zapiski okhotnika*] were published in two volumes, and in the same year, he also wrote Gogol's obituary. As a result of both, he was imprisoned for one month and later exiled to the estate at Spasskoye until 1853, when he was allowed to return to St. Petersburg. Due to the Crimean War (1853–1856), however, he was not allowed to leave Russia. Despite the war, *A Sportsman's Sketches* was translated into French and published in France, perhaps owing to the opposition between France and Tsarist Russia in the Crimean War. After the war, Turgenev was able to leave Russia again and lived in exile in Baden-Baden or Paris until his death, visiting Russia only a few times (Zúñiga 135). During the following decades of exile, he would publish his most famous works of Russian Realism like *Rudin* [*Рудин*, 1857] and *Fathers and Sons* [*Отцы и дети, Otsy i deti*, 1862]. He remained in contact with Russian friends and other Russians, who were living in France or Germany, like Nikolai Trubetskoy in Paris. Through these contacts, he was provided with news from Russia through journals or through debates on the actual political circumstances (Waddington 203–210).

In 1859, one of his most famous novels, *Home of the Gentry* [*Дворянское гнездо, Dvorjanskoe gnezdo*] was published, followed by his essay "Hamlet and Don Quixote" [*Гамлет и Дон Кихот*,

1860]—originally a public speech delivered in St. Petersburg—and the narrative *First Love* [*Первая любовь, Pervaia Liubov*, 1860]. Despite his many successes, in that same year, he was accused of plagiarism by the writer Ivan A. Goncharov, but was not found to be at fault. Goncharov accused Turgenev of having taken characters and situations from his work *The Precipice* [Обрыв, *Obryv*, 1869] for *A Nest of Gentryfolk* because Turgenev was one of Goncharov's literary friends, who had been allowed to read the work prior to its publication. When Turgenev later agreed to remove one chapter from his novel Goncharov was validated and accused Turgenev of stealing his ideas. In March 1860, the "literary judges made a compromise pronouncement that since both drew their themes from the same Russian background, certain similarities of incidents and thoughts were inevitable" (Scalapino 170). The issue, although technically resolved, ended the friendship between the two writers.

In 1862, Turgenev moved from Paris to Baden-Baden to follow the Viardots. From then on, he lived in Germany, only travelling to Paris or to Russia on occasion. In Russia, his collected works were published for the first time in 1865. In 1871, he moved to Paris again, where he met Gustave Flaubert and George Sand. He became part of the French literary circles in Paris and lived with the Viardots in a villa in Bougival. Turgenev continued writing until his death in Paris on September 3, 1883 at the age of 65. Despite the fact that Turgenev spent most of his time as a writer outside of Russia, his writing provides detailed descriptions of Russian society in the nineteenth century. He contributed significantly to the development of Russian Realism and the precise uniqueness of Turgenev's contributions in this regard should not be overlooked.

Turgenev's Realism

In Russian history, the nineteenth century is of special importance because many significant social and economic reforms transformed the nation in many ways (Zink 9). Among the intelligentsia, growing dissatisfaction with the stark contrast between the ideals of Romanticism and actual social reality served as a catalyst for a more "human literature" (Zúñiga 37). Alexei Koltsov, Nikolai Nekrasov, and Nikolai Gogol were among Realism's first representatives. Theirs and other works marked the beginning of the Russian Realism, which would become an important era in the Golden Age of literary Russia.

Turgenev, Dostoevsky, and Tolstoy became the "major creators of Russian psychological prose" (Tussing Orwin 21). This trend emerged as a result of European influences, specifically German philosophy of the 1830s (e.g., Johann Gottlieb Fichte, Friedrich Wilhelm Schelling, and Georg Wilhelm Friedrich Hegel) and French Naturalism. Due to this, these three writers became part of a philosophically well-educated class that would dominate Russian literary development during its Golden Age. While Dostoevsky, Tolstoy, and Turgenev are the most famous ones, there were even more representatives of the mentioned class—e.g. Gogol or Chekhov—who were producing influential pieces of Russian literature in the nineteenth century. Many people of the Russian gentry often went to Western Europe to complete their studies. The experience of a Western education in Germany or France, which became common for the sons of the Russian gentry, highly influenced Russian Realism in the latter half of the nineteenth century, and subsequently, *vice versa*. The philosophy of Hegel and others made the young Russians think about the situation in their country from the perspective of an outsider, which contributed to many of the young men becoming critical of Tsarist Russia's political system. Similarly, Turgenev's later works apparently showed "an underlying tone of disenchantment and gentle frustration" consistent with Western philosophers of the time, such as Hegel or Schopenhauer (Heier 92). In contrast to Russian Romanticism, new topics were dominating the literary field: society and its internal pressure, poverty, and serfdom (Zink 11–12). Orwin aptly asserts that "the reality of subjectivity is a cardinal principle of all great works of Russian psychological realism" (Tussing Orwin 5). As a consequence of the growing revolutionary potential of Russia's poor people:

The rise of psychological realism [in the 19th century] demanded new narrative techniques to convey complicated emotional experiences. Novelists discovered that dialogue was an intricate semiotic system in which direct speech had to be supplemented with information on, for example, the interlocutors' speech characteristics, their mood and gestures (Hellgren 130).

Turgenev contributed to this new movement, using dialogue techniques he had employed during his early phase of drama writing. He described circumstances or people by using long dialogues. One example is of Fedya, Kostya, and Pavlusha in "Bezhin Meadow" [«Бежин луг», *Bezhin lug*] appearing in Turgenev's *Sportsman's Sketches*, as in the following conversation, which highlights this new approach to dialogue:

"Boys," he began after a short silence, "something bad happened."
"Oh, what?" asked Kostya hurriedly.
"I heard Vasya's voice." They all seemed to shudder.
"What do you mean? What do you mean?" stammered Kostya.
"I don't know. Only I went to stoop down to the water; suddenly I hear my name called in Vasya's voice, as though it came from below water,
'Pavlusha, Pavlusha, come here.' I came away. But I fetched the water, though."
"Ah, God have mercy upon us!" said the boys, crossing themselves.
"It was the water-spirit calling you, Pavlusha," said Fedya; "we were just talking of Vasya."
"Ah, it's a bad omen," said Ilyusha, deliberately.
"Well, never mind, don't bother about it," Pavlusha declared stoutly, and he sat down again; "no one can escape his fate."
The boys were still. It was clear that Pavlusha's words had produced a strong impression on them.
They began to lie down before the fire as though preparing to go to sleep.
"What is that?" asked Kostya, suddenly lifting his head.
Pavlusha listened. "It's the curlews flying and whistling." "Where are they flying to?"
"To a land where, they say, there is no winter."

"But is there such a land?"

"Yes."

"Is it far away?"

"Far, far away, beyond the warm seas." (*Bezhin Meadow* 13–14).

The writer used generalizations in all his novels, which depicted what Turgenev himself saw as unchangeable rules of life. Turgenev's works are often clearly "creations of a writer who is concerned less with the tragedies of individuals than with the tragedy of the human condition" (Woodward 2). Among his favorite themes, Turgenev was interested in the meaning of life and the interrelationship of mankind and his environment. The depiction of injustice in his works typically reflects the injustice of human life, which means that "the world of Turgenev's novels is a world that precludes all freedom of action" (Woodward 10). Due to this setting, it is not surprising that his characters are "doomed to oblivion" (Heier 93). His heroes generally struggle between rationality and emotion. One of his most described characters is "the ruthless, amoral, unprincipled egoist" (Woodward 5), such as Darya Mikhailovna in *Rudin*, Varvara Pavlovna in *A Nest of Gentlefolk*, and *Nikolai Artemievich* in *On the Eve* [*Накануне*, *Nakanunje*, 1860]. The protagonists to these antagonistic egoist figures, Turgenev's heroes, such as Dmitrii Nikolaevich Rudin, are mainly driven by higher ideals or ideas, for which they would willingly die.

Especially with regard to these characters, Turgenev could be seen as an intermediary between the West and Russia. But he was also able to influence Western perceptions of Russia (Brang 4). While he often included more negative stereotypes when he wrote about Russia or the Russians, he did not omit positive aspects. The value of the Russian soul was described as often as the abilities and generosity of the Russian people (Brang 11). In his non-fiction, Turgenev rejected negative stereotypes and advocated for tolerance and the overcoming of national and religious borders, which divided the East and West of Europe. Consequently, the European perception of Russia was partially defined by Turgenev's writing. Since 1854, Turgenev's major works were translated into French and published abroad. This made Turgenev a well-known Russian writer, who was also accessible to a broader Western audience. Despite his realistic images of daily life in agrarian Russia, which made him famous in Europe, Turgenev was influenced by his own experiences as well as the rapid social, philosophical, and political developments of the nineteenth century. These influences are traceable in the major motives of Turgenev's writings.

Turgenev's Motives and Their Origins

Some motives in Turgenev's works are a consequence of his own experiences in childhood. He suffered at the hands of his mother, Varvara, who ruled the home like a tyrant. As a consequence of her harsh treatment of both her child and the serfs on her estate, Turgenev became a voice against the Russian system of serfdom. His mother became an archetype of the dominant women who forced Turgenev's heroes into depressions or agony. Aunt Marfa in the *A Nest of Gentlefolk,* like many of his other female figures, reflects Turgenev's childhood trauma inflicted by his mother (Zûñiga 17–22). Unfortunately, it was not only his dictatorial mother who influenced the writer's novels and narratives—Turgenev's father was a model for some of his son's all-too-realistic depictions of the gentry as well.

Sergei Turgenev was six years younger than his wife and as an officer of the cavalry could not provide much money or land when he married Varvara. Due to this, he did not interfere in matters of finance or the estate. He was reputed to have been involved with the estate's young female serfs as well. The role of a philanderer found its literary expression in Turgenev's novella *First Love.* Vladimir Petrovich, the hero of this shorter text is a reflection of Turgenev himself, stating: "I lived in Moscow with my parents. They had taken a country house for the summer near the Kalouga gate, facing the Neskutchny gardens. I was preparing for the university, but did not work much and was in no hurry" (Turgenev, *Short Prose* 467). He falls in love with Princess Zasyekina but learns that the object of his affection is not interested in him because she has fallen in love with his father, Pyotr Vasilyevich. The moment Vladimir acknowledges this fact, he is able to provide the reader with a deep insight into Turgenev's own experiences:

> Suddenly, before my very eyes, the impossible happened. My father suddenly lifted the whip, with which he had been switching the dust off his coat, and I heard a sharp blow on that arm, bare to the elbow. I could scarcely restrain myself from crying out; while Zinaïda shuddered, looked without a word at my father, and slowly raising her arm to her lips, kissed the streak of red upon it. My father flung away the whip, and running quickly up the steps, dashed into the house.... Zinaïda turned round, and with outstretched arms and downcast head, she too moved away from the window. My heart sinking with panic, with a sort of awe-struck horror, I rushed back, and running down the lane, almost letting go my hold of Electric, went back to the bank of the river. I could not think clearly of anything. I knew that my cold and reserved father was sometimes seized by fits of fury; and all the same, I could never comprehend what I had just seen.... (Ibid. 516)

Love and the resulting dispute between heart and mind are central motives in Turgenev's writing, as he often shows the reader cases of unrequited love and power struggles in human relationships. Hobbes' principle, *homo homini lupus est,* [man is a wolf to [his fellow] man] is visible in Turgenev's romantic relationships between men and women (Woodward 2–5). His play *A Month in the Country* described the unrequited love of a man for a gentry-woman, and in his first novel *Rudin*, Turgenev essentially described his own liaison with Tatyana Bakunin, who was desperately in love with Turgenev, for whom the feeling was not mutual. The main character, Dmitrii Rudin, finds refuge in philosophy and ideas because he is not able to succeed in real life. Consequently, he is not willing to start a romantic relationship with a young woman, which could definitely be a reflection of Turgenev's own decision regarding Tatyana's advances (Zûñiga 58–60). Rudin is described like a discursive Hamlet, who is going to die in the French Revolution of 1830. Turgenev therefore created a "living archetype" (Zûñiga 65) who resembled both Bakunin and Turgenev.

Love triangles are also abundant in Turgenev's works, stemming from his relationship with the Viardots. In *Nest of the Gentryfolk*, he seems to depict this relationship because a woman disrupts the romantic relationship of an ideal couple (Zûñiga 152–154), much like what Turgenev probably thought of Viardot's husband. Hence, Turgenev had always been working with his own experiences, which explains the supernatural themes that emerge in his texts.

Turgenev had a special interest in the supernatural and the psychological aspects of human existence. Dreams were an essential part of his narratives and show that Turgenev was willing to examine the deepest roots of the human mind. In his story *Klara Milich* [*Клара Милич*, 1883], he takes on themes of a supernatural orientation (Nemere 116–144). The story involves a young student, Jakov Aratov, and an actress named Klara, who commits suicide during a play. Before her suicide, Klara's advances were unwelcome to Aratov. However, shortly after her death, Aratov becomes addicted to the dead woman, who returns to him in his dreams. Aratov believes that, while dreaming, he is able to communicate with Klara, and his obsession for her grows by the day. Finally, he is dying, and his death is "an ecstasy of love" (Nemere 116). The end of Aratov's physical life becomes the ultimate climax of life. He finally talks about his own death with pleasure: "Well; what then? If I must die, let me die. Death has no terrors for me now. It cannot, then, annihilate me? On the contrary, only thus and there can I be happy … as I have not been happy in life, as she has not…. We are both pure! Oh, that kiss!" (Turgenev, Short Prose 50). In this story, the conflict between science and the supernatural is represented through Aratov and Aratov's father, who studied, but was also interested in occult practices, like alchemy. The theme and characters represent this conflict, suggesting Turgenev's interest in or personal experience with this very subject.

In contrast to the previously mentioned motives (family, love, the supernatural), a more commonly observed theme of Turgenev's works was political. Most young writers or political activists of the Russian intelligentsia had recognized that the problem of their home country was serfdom, "a relic of feudalism" (Zink 24). As a consequence, younger writers did not continue writing about peripheral regions, in which Russian imperialism would succeed (Layton 258). Instead, they concentrated on the agrarian society of the Tsarist Empire. After the failed uprising of the Decembrists in 1825, any hope for increasing democratization was eliminated. Nicholas I asserted his authority, tightening restrictions on literature, using censorship and the secret police to suppress any subversive factions of Russian society. Foreign journals and books were banned, and plays, like some of Turgenev's dramas already mentioned above, were forbidden. Turgenev, who had worked in the office of the internal ministry between 1843 and 1845, was among the first to suggest the abolition of serfdom. During his work for the ministry, he wrote a description of the existing agrarian system and proposed to change this situation.

Later, he befriended Vissarion Belinsky, publishing in Belinsky's journals at the time when Belinsky was developing the foundations of Realism by writing about Gogol and Pushkin (Zûñiga 47). Turgenev published detailed descriptions of peasant life in *A Sportsman's Sketches* (Tussing Orwin 38–39), showing the good and the bad sides of serfdom and the struggles of the peasant class. These texts may have influenced Alexander II, who emancipated the serfs in 1861 (Zûñiga 124). But in 1852, the *Sketches*, in combination with his long stay abroad, his friendship with the publicist Herzen, and his obituary on Gogol brought Turgenev to prison and later into banishment. (Zûñiga 125) Despite this suppression by the authorities, the proponents of the Realist movement continued to promote agrarian emancipation (Zink 12–13). Realist literature was an important contributor, since Realist depictions of the peasants described "no abstract population, no metaphysical definitions but concrete people and events" (Zink 30). In so doing, the literature promoted a sort of nationalism that facilitated societal change. The Soviet writer Sergei Mikhailovich Golitsyn (1909–1989) later described this influence in the following way:

> [The] 1860s was the critical turning point at which the progressive movement was led astray. It was in that crucial decade that the well-

intentioned patricians who predominated in progressive circles yielded their authority to plebeians. Consequently, for the first time, radicals not only offered idealistic programs for political and social reform but threatened to destroy the fabric of Russian society (Pozefsky 103).

Turgenev's literature was similarly transformative, making the figure of the "nihilist into a social ideal" (Pozefsky 104) when his heroes became representatives of the younger generation involved in social protest in the later nineteenth century. In *Fathers and Sons*, he described this conflict between the fathers, who were part of the old, imperial Tsarist society, a feudalist autocracy, and the sons, the Western-influenced intelligentsia longing for a freer Russia (Zúñiga 177). Turgenev's contribution to the beginnings of liberalization in Russia was immense, because his writing provided the image of Russia as itself, rather than as an unattainable, European ideal. Furthermore, he was able to interconnect the intelligentsia of Eastern and Western Europe by virtue of his status in the societies of both cultural spaces.

Conclusion

Turgenev's impact and influence on the latter half of the nineteenth century and the continued evolution of literature in the Golden Age is worthy of recognition. His collected works provide thousands of pages of different literary genres, motives, and characters. While Turgenev is not as famous as Dostoevsky or Tolstoy in the West, he was nevertheless very important in the development of Russian literature. Turgenev's works, at first part of Russian Romanticism, became the essential literary sources of Russian Realism and definitely belong to the heritage of the Golden Age of Russian literature.

Turgenev was influenced by the issues of his time as well as by his own experiences with his family, the serfdom, and the gentry. He aimed to describe the truth, even if it was not positive or complimentary towards members of society, including those at his own social level. Turgenev, who lived most of his life outside of Russia, was a unique spectator. Well-versed in the politics of Russia and the West, he could provide accurate reflections of daily life in nineteenth-century Russia that would impact the way that Russian authors depicted reality.

Works Cited

Beaumont, Barbara. *Flaubert and Turgenev: A Friendship in Letters: The Complete Correspondence*. New York: WW Norton & Co, 1985.

Brang, Peter. "Images and Mirages in Turgenevs Darstellung der Nationalcharaktere. Klischeezertrümmerung oder Trendverstärkung?" *Ivan S. Turgenev. Leben, Werk und Wirkung*. Ed. Peter Thiergen. Munich: Verlag Otto Sagner, 1995. 1–25. Vorträge und Abhandlungen zur Slavistik. Bd. 27.

Heier, Edmund. *Comparative Literary Studies: Lermontov, Turgenev, Goncharov, Tolstoj, Blok—Lavater, Lessing, Schiller, Grillparzer*. Munich: Verlag Otto Sagner, 2000. Vorträge und Abhandlungen zur Slavistik. Vol. 39.

Hellgren, Ludmilla. *Dialogues in Turgenev's Novels. Speech-Introductory Devices*. Stockholm: Almqvist & Wiksell International, 1980. Stockholm Studies in Russian Literature. Vol. 12.

Koschmal, Walter. *Das poetische System der Dramen von I. S. Turgenevs. Studien zu einer pragmatischen Dramenanalyse*. Munich: Verlag Otto Sagner, 1983. Slavistische Beiträge. Bd. 166.

Layton, Susan. *Russian Literature and Empire. Conquest of the Caucasus from Pushkin to Tolstoy*. Cambridge, UK: Cambridge UP, 1994.

Masing-Delic, Irene. "The Music of Ecstasy and the Picture of Harmony: Nietzsche's Dionysius and Apollo in Turgenev's 'Song of Triumphant Love.'" *Exotic Moscow under Western Eyes*. Ed. Irene Masing-Delic. Boston: Academic Studies Press, 2009. 3–18.

McLaughlin, Sigrid. *Schopenhauer in Rußland. Zur literarischen Rezeption bei Turgenev*. Wiesbaden: Harrassowitz, 1984.

Nemere, Maja. *Verführerische Lektüren in der Prosa des russischen Realismus*. Frankfurt am Main et al.: Peter Lang, 2011. Slavische Literaturen. Bd. 44.

Nohejl, Regine. "Das lyrische Frühwerk als Schlüssel zum Schaffen Turgenevs." *Ivan S. Turgenev. Leben, Werk und Wirkung*. Ed. Peter Thiergen. München: Verlag Otto Sagner, 1995. 109-136. Vorträge und Abhandlungen zur Slavistik. Bd. 27.

Pozefsky, Peter C. *The Nihilist Imagination. Dimitrii Pisarev and the Cultural Origins of Russian Radicalism (1860–1868)*. New York: Peter Lang, 2003. Middlebury Studies in Russian Language and Literature. Vol. 27.

Pritchett, V. S. *The Gentle Barbarian: The Work and Life of Turgenev*. New York: Ecco Press, 1986.

Schapiro, Leonard. *Turgenev: His Life and Times*. Cambridge, MA: Harvard UP, 1982.

Thieme, Galina. *Ivan Turgenev und die deutsche Literatur*. Frankfurt am Main: Peter Lang, 2000. Heidelberger Publikationen zur Slavistik, Literaturwissenschaftliche Reihe. Bd. 15.

Troyat, Henri. *Turgenev: A Biography by the Author of Chekhov*. Boston: Dutton Adult, 1988.

Turgenev, Ivan: *Bezhin Meadow*. London: Heinemann, 1897. Web. 30 Nov. 2013. <http://ebooks.z0ro.com/ebooks/Russia/Turgenev/Bezhin%20Meadow%20 Turgenev.pdf>.

Turgenev, Ivan: *Ivan Turgenev's Short Prose Works*. Trans. Constance Garnett. Pennsylvania State University. Web. 30 Nov. 2013. <http://www2.hn.psu. edu/faculty/jmanis/turgenev/Turgenev-ShortStories6x9.pdf>

Tussing Orwin, Donna. *Consequences of Consciousness. Turgenev, Dostoevsky, and Tolstoy*. Stanford, CA: Stanford UP, 2007.

Waddington, Patrick. "Turgenev and his Russian Friends at Fontainbleau: The Trubetskoy-Orlov Family." *Ivan S. Turgenev. Leben, Werk und Wirkung*. Ed. Peter Thiergen. *Vorträge und Abhandlungen zur Slavistik*, Vol. 27. München: Verlag Otto Sagner, 1995. 203–225.

Wilkinson, Myler. *Hemmingway and Turgenev: The Nature of Literary Influence*. Ann Arbor, MI: UMI Research Press, 1986.

Woodward, James B. *Metaphysical Conflict. A Study on the Major Novels of Ivan Turgenev*. Munich: Otto Sagner, 1990.

Yarmolinsky, Avraham: Turgenev: *The Man, His Art and His Age*. London: Octagon, 1977.

Zink, Andrea. *Wie aus Bauern Russen wurden. Die Konstruktion des Volkes in der Literatur des russischen Realismus 1860–1880*. Basler Studien zur Kulturgeschichte Osteuropas, Vol. 18. Zurich: Pano Verlag, 2009.

Zúñiga, Juan Eduardo. *Iwan S. Turgenjew. Eine Biographie*. Frankfurt am Main/ Leipzig: Insel Verlag, 2001.

The Life, Works, and Times of Fyodor Dostoevsky: Realism in the Golden Age _____

Tatyana Kovalevskaya

"A human being is a mystery which must be solved."
—Fyodor Dostoevsky

Fyodor Mikhailovich Dostoevsky was born on November 11, 1821 to the family of Mikhail Dostoevsky, a doctor in St. Mary's Hospital for the Poor in Moscow. Born in the small apartment his father had been given in a wing of the hospital building, Dostoevsky lived in Moscow until 1837 when, upon the death of his mother, he went to St. Petersburg to study at the Engineering School. The school was housed in Mikhailovsky Palace, originally built as the principal residence of Emperor Paul I, who had been afraid of plots against his life and had envisioned the palace as his stronghold. In an all-too-coincidental twist, Paul was assassinated there in 1801, after only five years on the throne. It was widely rumored that the assassination had been carried out with the knowledge and consent of Paul's eldest son, the future emperor Alexander I. Not coincidentally, the subject of patricide remained an important theme throughout Dostoevsky's life.

Although Dostoevsky was trained to be an engineer, a literary career always seemed more attractive to him. In 1845, his novel *The Poor Folk* landed before Nikolai Nekrasov, a famous poet, who, ecstatic, took the manuscript to Vissarion Belinsky, one of the most influential critics of the time, exclaiming, "a new Gogol appeared!" (Dostoevsky 1465). Belinsky was a little skeptical at first, yet he, too, admired the young writer's first work. *The Poor Folk* (Бедные люди, Bednye ljudi, 1846) is a novel in letters exchanged between a small-time official, Makar Devushkin, and a young girl, Varenka Dobroselova. The image of a small-time official in his small-time and excruciatingly poor life takes the readers, indeed, back to Nikolai Gogol and his famous character Akakii Akakievich Bashmachkin from "The Overcoat" [Шинель, Shinel', 1842], with its message of compassion for the downtrodden. "The little person," as such characters came to be known, became a staple of the Russian literature in the nineteenth century.

Dostoevsky continues Gogol's tradition by depicting the social ills that plague people like Devushkin, yet he puts his own spin on the social message so typically inferred from Gogol's writings. Makar Devushkin reads "The Overcoat" and revolts against Gogol's portrayal of Bashmachkin. Devushkin sees in Gogol not the social diatribe against the cruel and inhumane treatment of the underprivileged, but yet another example of that very cruelty and inhumanity. In Devushkin's view, in describing the privations Bashmachkin is prepared to suffer to get a new overcoat, Gogol mocks his character. Moreover, Gogol's character has no desires beyond an actual overcoat, which takes the place of a real human companion. Devushkin, on the other hand, is capable of devotion and love, as he meekly humors Varenka's every whim because she is suffering, too, even though she is casually cruel to him. Whereas Bashmachkin dreams of his future overcoat as a life companion, Devushkin sells his uniform to aid a real, living, breathing human being he thinks is in need of help. Gogol, in Devushkin's view, dehumanizes the "little person," while Devushkin, through actions aimed at benefiting other people, establishes his own human dignity. The theme of humanity found in every human being, no matter how undeserving or ridiculous outwardly, will run throughout Dostoevsky's works, including his last great novel, *The Brothers Karamazov* [Братья Карамазовы, Brat'ja Karamazovy, 1880]. Devushkin also sees true understanding of the "little person" in Alexander Pushkin and his story "The Station Master" [Станционный смотритель, Stantsionnij smotritel', 1831].

The epistolary genre chosen by Dostoevsky for his first novel serves two purposes. Firstly, it links *The Poor Folk* to such famous novels in letters as P. Ch. de Laclos' *Dangerous Liaisons*, J. J. Rousseau's *Julie*, or the *New Heloise*, S. Richardson's *Clarissa*, J. W. von Goethe's *The Sorrows of Young Werther*, warning the readers to expect a sentimental novel, yet with a dash of melancholy or even cruelty. Secondly, it disguises the authorial voice, permitting the characters to speak for themselves. About the readers' reception of his narrative technique in *The Poor Folk*, Dostoevsky wrote, "They are used to seeing the author's physiognomy in everything, but I never showed mine" (Dostoevsky 28–1:117). The technique of letting the characters' competing voices speak for themselves with little or no imposed authorial message will become Dostoevsky's trademark in his later works, even those written in the traditional third-person narrative.

Dostoevsky's next works met with diminished critical welcome. In 1846, he published *The Double* [Двойник, Dvojnik], a story of another small-time official, Golyadkin, who goes mad thinking that he is haunted by a doppelgдnger, who eventually assumes his identity and takes his place in life. The readers never learn whether the replacement actually occured, or was, indeed, a result of Golyadkin's insanity. The theme of doubles— characters who starkly reflect each other's particular traits and even complement each other in plot mechanics—becomes another of Dostoevsky's trademarks throughout his writing career. Critics found the story to be too drawn-out, and some condemned it as an inept imitation of Gogol's fantastic stories "The Nose" [Hoc, Nos, 1836] and "Diary of a Madman" [Записки сумасшедшего, Zapiski sumasshedshego, 1835]

In general, Dostoevsky's early writings already demonstrate the topics that will preoccupy him in his later and most famous works. The tale "The Landlady" ["Хозяйка", "Khozyaika", 1847] touches on the subject of freedom as a burden for an average human, who yearns to shift that burden onto someone else. The short story, "Mr. Prokharchin" ["Господин Прохарчин", "Gospodin Prokharchin", 1846], puts yet another twist on the theme of the "little person." Prokharchin, a dirt-poor official, is discovered upon his death to have amassed a large fortune hidden in his torn mattress. This is a nod to Pushkin and his Covetous Knight from the eponymous work. For Pushkin's knight, possession of money is more important than the joys the money can afford. At the same time, in Dostoevsky's story, the money is viewed as a potential for acquiring a different identity, for becoming a master instead of a slave. Mr. Prokharchin is a little person who is searching for power he could wield over others. At the same time, witnessing a fire, Mr. Prokharchin suddenly discovers that other people around him are living, suffering human beings, and the shock of compassion proves too difficult an ordeal for him. These themes will all appear again and again in Dostoevsky's later works.

In his early years, Dostoevsky adhered to liberal views and participated in the activities of a politically active group led by Mikhail Petrashevsky. In 1849, Dostoevsky was arrested for having an illegal printing press in his possession. He was sentenced to death, led to the Semyonov Square in St. Petersburg with a group of fellow inmates. Just as he was awaiting execution, his death sentence was commuted, and he was instead sent to Omsk hard labor prison for four years. These four years in Siberia changed Dostoevsky. He himself spoke about the rebirth of convictions he experienced in prison. His political views changed from avowedly liberal to deeply conservative, yet in his literary works, he continued to explore the themes and subjects he had undertaken prior to his prison experience. After prison, he was eventually able to settle in St. Petersburg, where he lived until his death in 1881. The city, too, as in Gogol's stories, became a character in his works.

In 1861–62, Dostoevsky published *Notes from the House of the Dead* [Записки из мертвого дома, Zapiski iz mortvogo doma], a fictionalized account of his prison years. A fictitious narrator, Goryanchikov, whose crime is one of passion, not politics, retells Dostoevsky's own experiences. *Notes from the House of the Dead* continues the theme of dehumanized humanity. This time, dehumanization doesn't always come as a result of societal oppression. Political prisoners aside, the murderers described in the novel chose to sever themselves from humanity through their own willfully committed crimes. A large number of those criminals were Russian peasants, traditionally referred to in Russia as "the people" (narod), and here lies Dostoevsky's startling discovery. "The people" were something of a sacred cow for a faction of the Russian intellectuals. Still motivated by Rousseauist ideals of the natural man, a large share of intellectuals viewed the Russian peasants (at that time, mostly serfs, that is, property of their landlord or the state) as the bearers of the true spirit of morality and Christianity. Those were the views specifically proclaimed by the so-called Slavophiles and the related native soil movement.

Adherents of this movement called for the return to the "native soil," to the national roots, and saw "the people" as the depository of the true Christian faith (the Orthodoxy) and the Christian spirit of unity embodied in the traditional social organization of peasants into communes with their collective responsibility. Although Dostoevsky subscribed to those views, he discovered that the peasants he encountered in the labor prison lacked the comprehension of the cornerstone of Christianity that he himself considered the most essential part of it: human free will and the responsibility it entails. Dostoevsky was deeply religious, and it is impossible to discuss his works in separation from his Christian faith. The central part of the loosely structured *Notes from the House of the Dead*, which is more a series of sketches than a novel with a continuous plot, is the chapter "Akul'ka's Husband. A Story," which tells a seemingly incomprehensible tale of the murder of saintly Akul'ka by her husband. This is a motiveless crime that baffles even the murderer, who tells his own story to his listener and the readers alike. *Notes from the House of the Dead* implicitly questions the salvific essence of the Russian peasantry, and it will take Dostoevsky more than a decade to come to terms with his prison revelations.

In 1864, Dostoevsky published one of his seminal works, *Notes from the Underground* [Записки из подполья, Zapiski iz podpol'ja]. The first part is a heated argument against the popular utilitarian philosophy of the time. Influential writers and literary critics (literature in Russia has traditionally done triple duty as philosophy and theology, too), such as Nikolay Chernyshevsky, the author of *What Is To Be Done?* [Что делать? Chto delat'? 1863], Nekrasov, and Dmitry Pisarev, a critic who proclaimed that boots are greater than Shakespeare, proposed the utilitarian nature of everything and the theory of reasonable egotism as the mainspring of human action. Human beings, according to these proponents of utilitarian philosophy, are always guided by their material benefits, and once it is explained to them where their true benefit lies, they will behave in such a manner as to achieve it. The nameless Underground Man, writing in the first person, declares that a person's freedom is his ultimate desire, and in order to feel truly free, a person must be ready to do anything, even to cause grievous harm to themselves. Such an understanding of free will separates the Underground Man from the entire world. The novel explores human loneliness conceived on a metaphysical scale, a loneliness that stems from the inability to form a meaningful relationship of equals. In the Underground Man's view, love is only "the right to tyrannize" (Jackson 183). His underground is of his own making, and no matter how badly he wants to leave it, his philosophy keeps him prisoner to it.

Notes from Underground was censored heavily and in ways unexpected by the writer. Dostoevsky complained to his brother, "Censors, pigs as they are, let pass all the make-believe blasphemies, yet excised those parts where I deduced the need for faith and Christ" (Dostoevsky 28–1:73). The manuscript didn't survive, and Dostoevsky himself never restored the excised parts for subsequent publications, so we will never know what the original form of the work was. Yet his reticence in restoring the unequivocally positive message of the novel is interesting, indicating that Dostoevsky prefers to convey his message by having his readers work the meaning out for themselves, proceeding mostly ex adverso.

In 1866, Dostoevsky published *Crime and Punishment* [Преступление и наказание, Prestuplenie i nakazanie], probably his most famous novel, the title of which has become proverbial across the globe. The novel essentially replays the problem of the little person in search of power. The crime from the title, the murder of a vile pawnbroker, committed ostensibly to provide the criminal, Rodion Raskolnikov, with some money, is, in fact, committed to test his idea that there are people in the world who, by virtue of being exceptional beings ("Napoleons," as he calls them) are allowed to break the rules set for the ordinary folk, and Raskolnikov is one of them. "Am I a trembling creature, or do I have the right?" (pt. 5, ch.4) Raskolnikov muses. Raskolnikov doesn't simply do away with society's rules. He sets himself apart from "creatures," i.e. from humans. He appropriates superhuman, godly prerogatives and essentially establishes himself to be a god in his own right, disposing of people as he sees fit.

His crime, however, involves the kind of punishment he cannot bear. That punishment is a complete severance from the humanity. He is unable to maintain meaningful human contact. Raskolnikov's crime is not a simple criminal matter. It turns into a metaphysical transgression, which is emphasized in an important episode in the novel, where he is read the scene of the raising of Lazarus from the Gospels, hinting that he is as dead to humanity as Lazarus, yet even Christ can resurrect him, too. The way out of metaphysical death, however, is not found in a straightforward religious conversion. Raskolnikov is offered the same chance as the Underground Man, the chance of human companionship and love, but, unlike the Underground Man, he evolves, seizing the chance to escape his metaphysical predicament through fully embracing human love and companionship from Sonya Marmeladova, one of society's outcasts, who prostituted herself to save her family from starvation. Sonya's own transgression doesn't sever her human ties, on the contrary. Paradoxically, sin in Dostoevsky often serves as an eye-opening experience, enabling people to truly comprehend and share the suffering of others and find true human companionship. That is the epiphanic breakthrough that enlightens Raskolnikov at the novel's end.

Every detail in Dostoevsky's novel is significant, including characters' names, which are almost invariably meaningful. Raskolnikov's last name comes from the Russian raskol: split, dissent, schism. Sonya's first name is a diminutive from Sophia, "wisdom," traditionally used to denote the wisdom of God, and Marmeladova, comes from marmelad, marmalade, a bitter irony given her actual life.

Crime and Punishment is tightly woven into the fabric of the Russian literary tradition. One of its most unusual characters is the city of St. Petersburg itself, an instigator of Raskolnikov's crime. Dostoevsky continues the so-called St. Petersburg myth in Russian literature, started by Pushkin's poem *The Bronze Horseman* [Медный всадник, Mednyj vsadnik, 1833] in which the city, built at huge human cost in the Baltic coastal swamps on the orders of Peter I (the Bronze Horseman of the title is a famous monument to Peter), is represented as a dual entity, both strikingly beautiful and strikingly cruel, trampling ordinary human lives in the name of the grand idea of a powerful sea-faring empire.

The novel, like all Dostoevsky's works, has a careful and complicated structure. It contains a system of doubles as Raskolnikov's thoughts and actions are reflected in the figures of Arkady Svidrigailov and Petr Luzhin. Moreover, even though the narration is in the third person, Mikhail Bakhtin, one of Russia's most influential twentieth century thinkers and literary scholars, considered *Crime and Punishment* an excellent example of what he called "the polyphonic novel," meaning a novel without a dominant authorial voice, where characters' voices are all given equal weight and substance. Bakhtin considered the ending of the novel a failure, or possibly, a forced imposition. However, it is important to take into account that Bakhtin's time was during the Stalinist purge (1935–1940), which dictated uniformity of thought. Therefore, he tended to overemphasize everything that represented a departure from authority in any shape or form, and his evaluation of the novel's ending might have been influenced by this. Bakhtin's perspective, however, is not entirely inaccurate. Dostoevsky's works are unrivaled in the degree of independence and equality permitted to characters, and this makes his novels both difficult to summarize or explain neatly. It also makes them fascinating as subjects for thought and discussion. Dostoevsky, like no other Russian writer of the Golden Age, forces his readers to think for themselves. He offers them guidance, yet the opposing points of view are expressed with such force and conviction that the readers sometimes fall under their sway completely.

Dostoevsky's next novel is *The Idiot* [Идиот, Idiot, 1868), the subject of heated critical debates. Dostoevsky himself proclaimed that he attempted to depict a "positively beautiful human" (Dostoevsky 28–2:251). Yet this is a story with a tragic ending, in which the alleged positively beautiful human, Prince Myshkin (from the Russian mysh', mouse), fails to help any of the people he strives to help and ends up in a mental hospital in Switzerland, with virtually no hope of recovery. Myshkin is traditionally viewed as a Christ figure, and his apparent failure posits some unfavorable questions for Dostoevsky's religious beliefs. Yet the novel would fare best being read ex adverso. In Dostoevsky's declared goal, the emphasis should be put on the word human. A famous scene in the novel depicts Myshkin and another character, Rogozhin, gazing at the reproduction of the painting *Dead Christ* by Hans Holbein, which is a claustrophobic picture depicting a virtually decomposing body of Christ. "Why, a man's faith might be ruined by looking at that picture!" (pt. 2, ch. 4) Myshkin remarks. The crux of Dostoevsky's declaration and Holbein's painting is the humanity of the positively beautiful being and Christ. Humanity alone is insufficient. Christ's dual nature as both divine and human overcame the purely human decomposition so vividly pictured by Holbein and so conducive to the loss of faith. He was God and man, and He returned to life and saved humankind. Myshkin is purely human, and his humanity is insufficient for the tasks he sets for himself, the tasks of salvation. In this novel, human companionship is viewed as essential for humanity, yet as an obstacle to the universality that marked Christ's mission. After the death of his first wife, Dostoevsky jotted down theological ruminations that concentrate very much on that duality of human companionship, its necessity, and its exclusion of others from the union of the two. Only the divine mystery of the afterlife could transcend that duality. In *The Idiot*, pure humanity is tested and found lacking. *The Idiot* is probably Dostoevsky's most overt, and, in a typically Dostoevskyan way, most disguised apophatic theological argument.

Dostoevsky's next novel was *Demons* [Бесы, Besy, 1871–72]. Dostoevsky mocks his former ideological soulmates from the 1840s. Stepan Verkhovensky is a parody of a typical 1840s liberal, who is

Hans Holbein the Younger. *The Body of the Dead Christ in the Tomb*. 1521–22.
[Kunstmuseum Basel]

pro-Western, politically averse to the regime purely because it is fashionable, and yet he is a coward. His stance on religion is that God needs man, and not vice versa. If Stepan is a kindly enough parody, his son Pyotr is a fairly denigrating parody of 1860s nihilist revolutionaries (based on the historical figure of Sergei Nechaev). Pyotr is probably best described as a self-serving little weasel. The central character, however, is Nikolay Stavrogin, who, as a boy, was Stepan's tutee and who is, consequently, his spiritual son as Pyotr is Stepan's biological offspring. Pyotr espouses revolutionary rhetoric while striving for personal gain. Stavrogin is a metaphysical rebel, continuing the tradition of Raskolnikov, a character who thinks himself above the rest of humanity and believes he possesses the right to dispose of others as he sees fit. Yet Stavrogin is indispensable for Pyotr's designs. He is the ultimate impostor both politically- and metaphysically-speaking, a fact that is emphasized by open parallels with Shakespeare's Henry IV. The novel contains a spate of ideas, some of them crucial to Dostoevsky himself. One of the characters, Kirillov, speaks of turning himself into a god by killing himself without fear, thus presenting another variation of Dostoevsky's traditional theme of an overreaching human being. Another character, Shatov, expounds the idea of Russians as the true God-bearing people, an idea Dostoevsky himself espoused, yet where Dostoevsky speaks of Christianity, Shatov speaks of some sort of a collective popular identity, which he essentially deifies. Dostoevsky's habit of twisting his own cherished ideas and giving them to dubitable characters makes his novels all the more difficult to interpret.

Demons also dwells on the interrelation of the political and the metaphysical. The demons are those who strive to plunge Russia into an ungodly existence under a metaphysical impostor, who takes the place of God and the tsar. Yet, as Stepan prophesizes during his deathbed conversion, Russia's future is that of the possessed from the Gospels, who had the demons driven out of him by Christ and sat at Christ's feet listening to Him. This message didn't endear Demons to the authorities in the USSR, and the novel was tacitly proscribed for its biting satire of the Russian revolutionaries. *Demons* demonstrates that Dostoevsky was both a religious and political thinker for whom religion was the underlying substance of politics.

In order to communicate his thoughts directly to the reader, he initiated the publication called *A Writer's Diary* [Дневник писателя, Dnevnik pisatelja 1873–1881], which contained his direct opinions on a range of subjects, from criminal cases to politics to everyday behavior (one of the articles is called "Something on Lying"), as well as a number of short stories, which became famous in their own right. Dostoevsky was, indeed, viewed as a teacher. People wrote to him seeking advice on various aspects of life. Some scholars claimed that Russia's politics were also heavily influenced by Dostoevsky's thought, and it contributed to the eventual downfall of the monarchy because Dostoevsky miscalculated in his appraisal of the Russian people (Kantor 264–268). *A Writer's Diary*, indeed, contains a short story "The Peasant Marey," which takes up the subject of Dostoevsky's prison experience fifteen years after the fact. Remembering his childhood on the family estate, called Darovoe, Dostoevsky recalls being frightened of a wolf which was never there and being consoled by a peasant named Marey. This consolation comes as a stark revelation of the underlying kindness that shines even through the coarsest outer crust. That memory helped Dostoevsky see the peasant inmates in a new light and recognize their essential humanity even under their scary appearance. Yet it is noteworthy that this memory didn't make it into the *Notes from the House of the Dead*. The answer came fifteen years after the original question.

Another famous short story appearing in the *Diary* is "The Dream of a Ridiculous Man" with its vision of the Golden Age of innocent and pure humankind. In a vision, the nameless Ridiculous Man finds himself among such humans and then corrupts them, turning their world into a copy of our own. When he awakens from his vision, he decides to embark on a quest of sorts to restore the Golden Age and to start by finding a little girl whose plea for help he previously spurned. Once again, the ideal state of humankind is viewed as the state of universal connectedness. In this, Dostoevsky follows the Russian religious tradition of sobornost' (from the

Russian word 'sobor': general assembly, church diet, cathedral), the Christian unity of humankind. Yet this ideal is to be reached through specific, small steps of kindness to the people around us. Attentive readers are reminded of *The Poor Folk* and Devushkin's very specific acts of kindness towards Varenka, without any hope of reward or, sometimes, even basic gratitude.

Dostoevsky's next major novel, *The Adolescent* [Подросток, Podrostok, 1875], picks up the subject of the Golden Age, on which one of the characters dwells extensively. The novel centers around the life of Arkady Dolgoruky, who bears the noble aristocratic last name of his legal father who is, ironically, a liberated serf, while his biological father, the nobleman Versilov, is an unresolved presence in Arkady's life. Arkady goes through the novel nursing his idea of becoming a Rothschild, i.e. becoming rich, without the need to ever display one's riches. He continues the tradition of Pushkin's Covetous Knight and Dostoevsky's own Mr. Prokharchin in that, for him, money is an external means of shaping an independent and influential identity. Arkady feels his humiliating social position acutely and plans to follow the path of all those little people who seek power in order to overcome low social status. Through other characters and in various ways, the novel presents Dostoevsky's

Claude Lorrain. *Landscape with Acis and Galatea*. 1657. Staatliche Kunstsammlungen Dresden. [Dostoevsky referred to this painting as "The Golden Age"]

traditional ideas of human companionship, the religious Christian path, and the true camaraderie found in the Christian unity.

Dostoevsky also continued with his journalistic and public activity. In 1881, a monument to Pushkin was unveiled in Moscow. Dostoevsky delivered a speech on the occasion, and a purely cultural event was turned into a cultural-political statement. Dostoevsky declared Pushkin to be the most important Russian writer, and, in his view, Pushkin most fully embodied a specific Russian trait of being able to internalize and make any other culture his own. Nineteenth-century Russian culture and literature are, indeed, suffused with Western themes and subjects, and they owe far more to the Western cultural tradition than to the native one, a break with which essentially came in the seventeenth century when Peter I re-oriented Russia towards the West and made emulation of the Western models a cultural standard. Yet Dostoevsky believed that Western culture was not mechanically adopted. On the contrary, it became an integral, inalienable part of Russia's own, unique culture and literature, and Pushkin emblematized this process best.

Dostoevsky's final novel, *The Brothers Karamazov* (1879–80), is the first of two novels Dostoevsky planned, but didn't complete, as he died shortly after the publication of the first one. All of his major themes converge here. This is a carefully constructed detective story (Dostoevsky read and highly valued Edgar Allan Poe, the founder of the detective story genre) written with Dostoevsky's traditional goal of keeping his readers interested. His traditional theme of brotherhood receives an almost literal treatment as the novel centers around three Karamazov brothers—Dmitrii, Ivan, and Alyosha— and their presumed illegitimate brother Pavel Smerdyakov. Their relations are far from brotherly, and their depraved, disgusting, and lustful father Fyodor provides more grounds for discussing Dostoevsky's traditional topic of who has the right to decide which human being is undeserving of the right to live. The trial of the alleged murderer of Fyodor provides the courtroom drama of the novel. The patricide associated with Mikhailovsky Palace, where the young Dostoevsky studied, returns as a major theme in this final, and possibly greatest, novel. The system of doubles again serves to highlight the implications of the characters' philosophical stances. Ivan Karamazov, in particular, has a complex web of doubles around him, including his own half-brother Smerdyakov, and it is Smerdyakov who shows him that thought is as powerful as action, and thinking is no mere academic pursuit, but possibly an impetus to act for other people. In the beginning of the novel, Alyosha, the youngest son, is a novice of elder Zosima, a monk who, in the tradition of elders, has complete power over his disciples. One might think that this is shockingly similar to the idea of the select humans, who have the right to dispose of others as they see fit. However, in the relationship of the elder and his novice, the decision to abrogate one's will is made voluntarily in the name of God, not by the select human, but by the ordinary one.

Before his death, Zosima turns Alyosha out into the world, which is Alyosha's true tribulation. Ivan, the middle brother, is the philosophical center of the novel, and he illustrates the so-called "Poem of the Grand Inquisitor," which conveys Dostoevsky's beloved theme of freedom. The grand inquisitor adheres to the theory of greater and lesser human beings, but this time, this theory is coupled with the idea that freedom is the greatest burden imposed by Christ on people, and people are unable to shoulder this kind of responsibility. Therefore, only a select few should take this burden upon themselves, depriving others of liberty and granting them happiness instead. The themes of compassion and human brotherhood also feature prominently in the novel. It is Ivan who rebels against God in protest against the suffering of people, and particularly the suffering of children. And yet he, again, divides humankind into those who should suffer and those who should not. However, it is a universal, all-inclusive compassion that should be the salvific rule of human life. A recent critical volume on *The Brothers Karamazov* holds as one of its main tenets that one of the novel's principal themes is that of apokatastasis, the universal restoration, the universal salvation, which doesn't exclude anyone or anything (Kasatkina 8). Not even the gravest of human sins can exclude people from God's grace, but they should be prepared to accept responsibility, and in their best moments, that responsibility spreads to expiating the sins of others. The universal brotherhood should be achieved not only in word, but also in deed.

Dostoevsky is considered among the greatest psychological writers of all times and one of the greatest Russian novelists and thinkers. His influence on world culture attests to his greatness. Friedrich Nietzsche read Dostoevsky, but he proclaimed the opposite of what Dostoevsky sought to convey. Nietzsche's is an ametaphyiscal world, in which every person is a law onto himself, motivated by a will to power.

French Existentialists Albert Camus and Jean-Paul Sartre were also heavily influenced by Dostoevsky, and Camus wrote on Dostoevsky's works and even adapted *Demons* for the stage under the title *Les Possedés* (*The Possessed*). His adaptation is still being staged in Russia, including by the famous Polish director Andrzej Wajda.

Twentieth-century cinema was profoundly interested in Dostoevsky's works. Their significance was thought to exceed the scope of nineteenth-century Russian culture, as Akira Kurosawa directed *The Idiot* set in twentieth-century Japan, and Italian neo-realist director Luchino Visconti incorporated motifs from Dostoevsky's novels into his films *Rocco e i suoi fratelli* (*Rocco and His Brothers*), heavily influenced by *The Idiot*, and *La caduta degli dei* (*The Damned*), which includes scenes from *Demons*.

Today's popular culture, probably without even realizing it, also incorporates themes and motifs from Dostoevsky, particularly the subject of the division of humans into the select few and the ordinary mass and the subject of freedom as a burden from which humans should be relieved in order to fully enjoy their lives.

In today's Russia, Dostoevsky is often styled as a prophet for his penetrating insights into political and religious human nature. Which of his pronouncements could be considered prophesies that have come true is still subject to debate, though.

Works Cited

Bakhtin, M. M. and Caryl Emerson. *Problems of Dostoevsky's Poetics*. Minneapolis: U of Minnesota P, 1984.

Belknap, R. L. *The Structure of The Brothers Karamazov*. The Hague, Paris: Mouton, 1967.

Dostoevsky, Fyodor. *Polnoe sobranie sochinenii*. Vol. 28. Leningrad: Nauka, 1972–1990. 30 vols.

Jackson, R. L. *Dostoevsky's Quest for Form: A Study of His Philosophy of Art*. New Haven, CT: Yale UP, 1966.

Jackson, R.L. *The Art of Dostoevsky: Deliriums and Nocturnes*. Princeton, NJ: Princeton UP, 1981.

Kantor V.K. *Sudit' Bozh'iu tvar'. Prorocheskii pafos Dostoevskogo*. Moscow: Rosspen, 2010.

Kasatkina T.A. Predislovie. *Roman F.M. Dostoevskogo "Brat'ia Karamazovy:" sovremennoe sostoianie izucheniia*. Moscow: Nauka, 2007.

Knapp, L. *The Annihilation of Inertia: Dostoevsky and Metaphysics*. Evanston, IL: Northwestern UP, 1996.

Miller, R. F. *Dostoevsky and the Idiot: Author, Narrator, and Reader*. Cambridge, MA: Harvard UP, 1981.

Morson, G. S. *Introductory Study: Dostoevsky's Great Experiment. Fyodor Dostoevsky. A Writer's Diary*. Trans. Kenneth Lantz. Evanston, IL: Northwestern UP, 1993.

Scanlan, J. *Dostoevsky the Thinker*. Ithaca, NY and London: Cornell UP, 2002.

The Old Magician in Pursuit of Truth: Lev Tolstoy's Lifelong Search for Meaning _____

Ani Kokobobo

Born in 1828 in Yasnaya Polyana (the Tula region of Russia), Count Lev Tolstoy died in 1910, an old man well into his eighties. He witnessed Russia's long nineteenth century first hand through its various ups and downs. In that span of time, he went from being a literary upstart who boldly sent an unsigned manuscript to a prestigious literary journal of his time, to one of the better-known Russian writers of the nineteenth century, an author who could hang his hat on world literature masterpieces like *War and Peace* [*Война и мир, Vojna i mir*, 1869] and *Anna Karenina* [*Анна Каренина,* 1878]. Indeed, the collection of Tolstoy's works published during the period of the Soviet Union consists of some ninety volumes that could fill many bookshelves. As the observant reader of Russian might note, however, many writings from that collection are not literary. The role of writer was not the only one Tolstoy assumed. During the middle of his life, he fell into a terrible depression that eventually led to the complete reinvention of his spiritual beliefs. In that time, he went from being the "great writer of the Russian land" as Turgenev called him,[1] to a would-be prophet and spiritual moral compass of late Tsarist Russia. As part of his new beliefs, Tolstoy preached the renunciation of wealth, adopting simplicity, vegetarianism, and pacifism. These new beliefs and practices, particularly the renunciation of privilege and wealth, were difficult to reconcile with Tolstoy's own social position as a count and a well-to-do member of the Russian nobility. Conflicts abounded with his wife of many years, Sofia Andreevna, who did not support Tolstoy's emergent moral ideals and was concerned about the welfare of their many children. Their increasing conflict came to a head in 1910 when Tolstoy finally left the estate at Yasnaya Polyana. Due to ill health, he did not go very far and died shortly thereafter at the Astapovo train station near present-day Lipetsk. Countless people gathered to mourn him from all around the country.

Perhaps the best way to describe Tolstoy's long, rich, and colorful life is that it was a passionate, incessant search. "The old magician stands before me, alien to everyone, a solitary traveler searching vainly through all the deserts of thought for an all-embracing truth," writes Maksim Gorky about Tolstoy.[2] Gorky, who had the rare opportunity to spend time with Tolstoy during the latter's final years, identifies the indefatigable process of seeking that occupied Tolstoy's very core throughout much of his life; it determined who he was as a writer and as a man. Above all, as Gorky puts it, Tolstoy sought truth, or, put in another way, a higher meaning to human existence. He eventually identified universal, all-encompassing love for others as this higher meaning. Even so, the findings of this enduring search were less important than the process itself. All his life, Tolstoy never stopped searching. It is his perennial search, his desperate longing for a higher truth that unites the different stages of Tolstoy life; it also defines his writings—whether literary or spiritual. Furthermore, this search shaped the fictional characters to which he gave life. All great Tolstoyan characters—Nikolenka Irtenev, Andrei Bolkonsky, Pierre Bezukhov, and Konstantin Levin—are great seekers.

***

Mapping Tolstoy's lifetime, we can trace a variety of spiritual searches. The earliest of these began when Tolstoy experienced loss at a young age. His mother died in 1830, when Tolstoy was only two years old and could neither speak nor remember her. This first experience with death filled him with a desperate need to find pieces of his lost parent among those who knew her. "The harder little Leo tried to remember his mother, the more she eluded him," writes Henri Troyat in a well-known biography of Tolstoy.[3] Troyat notes that there was hardly even a portrait of Tolstoy's mother while he was growing up, excepting a small silhouette cut out of black paper, from when she was ten or eleven. This picture lacked in details and did a poor job satisfying the child's longing. Instead, Tolstoy's initial, primal search persisted to the end of his life—even as an old man in his eighties, Tolstoy would still long for his *maman*.[4] Similar searches for emotional fulfillment and completion would spring out of this initial search. As Richard Gustafson argues, Tolstoy's life-long search for God, his "quest for perfection," for moral achievement that would transform life on earth into life in the Kingdom of Heaven, all related to his lost mother. "The Kingdom of God returns [Tolstoy] to his mother's embrace," writes Gustafson.[5] "The loving, caring mother whom one does not know is the constant model for Tolstoy's God."[6]

A second loss would compound the initial one, when only a few short years later in 1837, Tolstoy's father also died. Tolstoy and his four siblings (three brothers and a sister) were raised by relatives. For much of the writer's childhood, his brothers were his primary companions, which may have contributed in part to Tolstoy's later elevation of loving brotherhood into a human ideal. The Tolstoy children played many games, some vividly recreated in Tolstoy's novel *Childhood*. One game in particular, called the "ant brotherhood," stands out; the brothers huddled together in a tent during this game, thus forming a brotherhood. The significance of the game relates to a story told by Lev's older brother, Nikolai Tolstoy. The eleven-year-old Nikolai spoke of a little green stick, on which the secret of human happiness was written. The stick was buried near their house. According to Nikolai, once the secret was found, people would be happy and cease to be ill or angry with one another—people would be joined in an "ant brotherhood." This story made an incredible impression on the young Lev, who dreamt of this "ant brotherhood" for much of his life. Indeed, in later years, after his mid-life religious awakening, this "ant brotherhood" assumed the shape of a human brotherhood of love.[7] It is perhaps only fitting that when Tolstoy was an old man, excommunicated by the Russian Church and denied a proper Orthodox burial, he asked to be buried in his estate, by Nikolai's green stick.[8]

While it would take many years for Tolstoy to advocate human brotherhood or higher meaning, his early years were shaped by a search for happiness and purpose in the form of a career or vocation. Tolstoy began to study at the University of Kazan in 1844, beginning as a student in the Oriental Languages department and later transferring into the law department. Unable to meet curriculum requirements, he eventually left in 1847 without a degree. After this failure, Tolstoy returned to his family's estate in order to assume the role of landowner. His endeavors, largely fruitless in the sphere of agriculture, gave rise to a twenty-chapter novelistic fragment, *A Landowner's Morning* [*Утро помещика, Utro pomeshchika,* 1856]. One enterprise followed the other as Tolstoy, partly in response to gambling debts, followed his brother Nikolai into the military. He fought in the Crimean War in Sevastopol in 1854–55. Tolstoy described his wartime experiences in one of his more interesting earlier works of fiction, *Sevastopol Sketches* [*Севастопльские рассказы, Sevastopol' rasskazy,* 1855]. The work, which renders war as an unnecessary and cruel farce, is marked by some of the first stirrings of Tolstoy's later pacifism. As A. N. Wilson argues, participation in a war without real stakes, like the Crimean War—where great European powers were bickering over Ottoman Empire territories—contributed to Tolstoy's later categorical pacifism. He implies that participation in a more meaningful, more patriotic war, like the 1812 battle against Napoleon, or Russia's World War II campaign against Hitler, might have yielded different insights.[9]

While many of these early ventures failed to provide Tolstoy with genuine purpose, they nonetheless showed him things about himself. In particular, the military revealed just how much Tolstoy did not fit within structured and organized systems. As Aylmer Maude, one of Tolstoy's biographers, who became acquainted with the man personally, puts it:

> Tolstoy had no adequate sense of being a responsible member of a complex community with the opinions and wishes of which it is necessary to reckon. On the contrary, his tendency was to recognize with extraordinary vividness a personal duty revealed by the working of his own conscience and intellect, apart from any systematic study of the social state of which he was a member.[10]

Being in the military made it clear that Tolstoy was not the type of person to merge into the crowd.

All in all, despite the lack of success, many of Tolstoy's early endeavors provided the raw material for what would become his true vocation: writing. Tolstoy's free time in the Crimea allowed him the opportunity to write *Childhood* [*Детство, Detstvo,* 1852] the first installment of his debut in Russian *belles lettres:* the trilogy *Childhood, Boyhood,* and *Youth. Childhood* captures the story of a little boy, Nikolenka Irtenev, who shares many biographical details of Tolstoy's life, but who, unlike his author, is able to spend a few precious first years with his mother before she dies. The mother in *Childhood* serves as an ideal of love, spirituality, and faith for the young boy; as a consequence of her death, he is left to search on his own for the meaning of life. In time, this search leads Tolstoy's autobiographical alter ego away from society and toward deeper spiritual meaning and truth. The story was written in a pristine Realist style aimed at capturing every small detail of reality. Published in Nekrasov's journal *The Contemporary*, it proved an overwhelming success on the Russian literary scene. Two other famous Russian writers, Ivan Turgenev and Fyodor Dostoevsky, were full of praise for the piece, which assured its overwhelming success and solidified Tolstoy's reputation. As A. N. Wilson suggests, from this point on, Tolstoy was a writer; his life was defined by "what he [was] or [was] not writing."[11]

Yet this devotion did not, by any means, put an end to Tolstoy's search. In many respects, as committed as he was to writing, Tolstoy never fully gave himself to the profession at the expense of everything else. Rather, he juggled multiple occupations. After the great success of his early works, Tolstoy experienced somewhat of a lull as a writer toward the late 1850s, in large part due to his own unwillingness to become overtly political, while literature was growing politicized on the eve of the 1861 emancipation of the serfs. Several of Tolstoy's works from the late 1850s—*Family Happiness* [*Семейное счастье, Semejnoe schast'je,* 1859], *Albert* [*Альберт,* 1857], and *Lucerne* [*Люцерн,* 1857]—received a chillier reception than his first few works. As a result, for a number of years, Tolstoy renounced authorship despite remaining inwardly devoted to literature.

Tolstoy sought to fill the vacuum by taking up other occupations. Most notably, he taught the peasant children in his village for three years, beginning in the fall of 1859. Influenced by Rousseau, whose portrait he wore around his neck during his adolescent years, Tolstoy did not believe in inculcating peasant children with societal dogma or artificial, strict education. Instead, he saw greater value in the unique experiences of the peasant children and believed that the purpose of education should be to help elucidate these experiences. As Henry Gifford argues, his time as a teacher energized Tolstoy the writer; in particular, we know that he retold the peasant children stories from various sources in world literature (like Homer or Goethe), while encouraging them to share their own creative impulses of storytelling with him.[12] This inherent respect for the peasant and his or her worldview can be instantly gleaned from Tolstoy's essay from this period (1862): "Are the Peasant Children To Learn To Write from Us? Or, Are We To Learn from the Peasant Children?" Tolstoy's answer was that he had a great deal more to learn from the peasant children than they did from him—in particular, the peasant children opened up a world of authenticity and simplicity, which assumed a pivotal role in Tolstoy's fiction.

It should come as no surprise, then, that this foray into education invigorated Tolstoy as a writer. He began writing his epic novel, *War and Peace*, shortly after the essay about the peasant children. One of the longest novels ever written, *War and Peace* took Tolstoy six years to complete (1863–1869). The novel was initially supposed to be called *Decembrists* and focus on the group of individuals who rebelled against Nicholas I's ascension to the throne in 1825. They were exiled to Siberia for their transgressions, and Tolstoy wished to compare these revolutionaries to the revolutionary figures of his time, like Nikolai Chernyshevsky, who had by that time published the novel *What Is To Be Done?* [*Что делать?*, *Chto delat'?*, 1863]. Before turning to the Decembrists, however, Tolstoy felt that he had to first contend with their pre-history—the 1812 French Invasion of Russia by Napoleon. Tolstoy began his historical novel as early as 1805, trying to get to the root of the conflict.

Ultimately, amassing over 150 characters and over 1200 pages, the novel did not make it to 1825, ending in 1813, just beyond Napoleon's unsuccessful invasion of Russia. Tolstoy was too caught up in capturing every detail of life in the years on which he focused and weaving together the linkages between life during the time of war and at peacetime. In between the complex, interwoven fictional storylines, he expounded on his philosophy of history. Despite the novel's relevance to Russian history, many of the original readers of *War and Peace* were confused about the novel's genre; they could not pinpoint who the protagonists were, or where the historical plot ended and the novelistic one began.

As Boris Eikhenbaum notes, the philosophy of history in *War and Peace*, one of the key components of the novel, was devised in response to thinkers of Tolstoy's time, like Chernyshevsky.[13] Among many things, Tolstoy's philosophy of history also served as an anti-revolutionary statement, implying that the only sphere in which we are capable of meaningful change as individuals is within our personal lives. In *War and Peace*, revolutions or large battles, like those of 1805 and 1812 between the Russian and the French, simply happen for no given reason; distinct individuals, even those as megalomaniacal as Napoleon, have no say on the matter. György Lukács, who writes of Tolstoy's "great and truly epic mentality," suggests that *War and Peace* captures "a life based on a community of feeling among simple human beings closely bound to nature, [...] adapted to the great rhythm of nature, which moves according to nature's cycle of birth and death and excludes all structures which are not natural..."[14] 'Family happiness,' the very thing that Tolstoy had unsatisfactorily articulated in the earlier novella by that name, emerges as the central force of *War and Peace*.

It is not surprising that family happiness would assume this role in Tolstoy's epic novel precisely as he was writing *War and Peace*. Literature had always served as a vehicle for Tolstoy to channel and resolve his own life questions. After years of searching, longing for dead parents, or trying to replace the longing for love with either literary or pedagogical ventures, in 1862, at the age of 34, Tolstoy married the beautiful Sonya Behrs. The two were married for 48 years, and Sonya bore Tolstoy thirteen children. She also became his supporter in all endeavors. During the period he was working on *War and Peace*, Sonya assisted him by copying the growing novel by hand seven times. She was the only person capable of decoding Tolstoy's complicated script. Her involvement was so consistent that some scholars have suggested that she may have taken liberties with the narrative. When *War and Peace* was written, the couple was newly married, so Tolstoy felt quite happy in his new family life and echoed much of that happiness in the novel. At least for that period of time, he felt he had finally found what he had been seeking for so many years.

Yet, like the university, or the army, the institution of marriage could no more contain Tolstoy and his rebelliousness. His thinly veiled double in *Anna Karenina*, Konstantin Levin, is described as a wild man who can hardly fit anywhere; Levin breaks with many social conventions, just as Tolstoy himself did. "All his life," writes Shklovsky, "Tolstoy longed to break free; he needed freedom."[15] Tolstoy's paradoxical double status as someone who wanted community yet also longed for freedom, or, in the words of Richard Gustafson, as a "resident and stranger," can be traced throughout his life. Tolstoy's marriage to Sonya has gone down in history as a terrible union, but, as some recent scholars have suggested, Sonya was fully devoted to the author and played a fundamental role in preserving both his health and the legacy of his writing.[16] Their problems sprung from the fact that what she wanted—the best interests of their family above the interests of everyone else—came to be at odds with his moral ideals. Some initial glimpses of the marital tension can already be noted in the epilogue of *War and Peace* where the hero Pierre, despite being satisfied with his family life, nonetheless longs to find meaning outside the home through a political cause.

This dualism is essential to our understanding of Tolstoy the man. In fact, it extends beyond his relationships with other individuals and cultural institutions; it touches the core of his search for meaning. Tolstoy could never hold on to any one person or ideal for long; his thirst for meaning was never permanently satiated.

The tension within him, the paradox between wanting a higher meaning, yet failing to be satisfied with it—his dually constructive and destructive nature—has been often identified by critics over the years. The most exhaustive articulation of this particular dualism is found in a now classic essay by Isaiah Berlin, titled "The Hedgehog and the Fox." In that essay, Berlin characterized Tolstoy as thinker; artist; and, paradoxically, a "destructive intellect" yearning for an overarching synthesis. Tolstoy," he writes, "longed for a universal explanatory principle." Yet, continues Berlin, "Like all penetrating, very imaginative, very clear-sighted analysts who dissect or pulverize in order to reach the indestructible core [...], he continued to kill his rivals' rickety constructions [...] always hoping that the desperately sought for 'real unity' would presently emerge from the destruction of the shams and frauds [...]."[17] Tolstoy's intellectual "pulveriz[ing]" was seen by Berlin as one of the author's most natural inclinations and talents. However, even as he questioned and destroyed at will, the visceral thirst for a foundational principle remained unquenched in Tolstoy. Tolstoy, argues Berlin, "wished more than anything to be stopped by an immovable obstacle, he wished his violent projectiles to be resisted by impregnable fortifications."[18] Berlin's fundamental insight remains true at all stages of Tolstoy's spiritual development.

Tolstoy's search is embodied in the seemingly inexhaustible searches of many of his fictional characters. In *War and Peace*, Pierre Bezukhov's search is so unrelenting that it cannot even end with the novel's conclusion. The search also found manifestation in Tolstoy's second novel, *Anna Karenina* of 1878, which, in his view, was his only suitably novelistic creation. All characters in *Anna Karenina* search for happiness, but Levin is most conscious of the path of seeking. In *Anna Karenina*, we also find some clues to Tolstoy's paradoxical duality. Gloomier than *War and Peace, Anna Karenina* was filled with its author's existential angst, which is channeled into both Anna and Levin.

"I feel that I am perishing—that I am living and dying, that I love life and fear death—how can I be saved."[19] This tortured question, posed by Tolstoy in 1878, provides evidence of a deep spiritual anguish and quagmire—the fear of death. It was this fear that made for the dualism inherent to Tolstoy. Throughout his life, he tried to find some ideal that would grant him spiritual solace in light of death's biggest engines of destruction. *Anna Karenina*, in which questions of death and the meaning of life figure prominently, became a place for him to air his grievances. Characters wrestle with death in the novel—like their authorial creator, they are scared of it and they bargain with it. In one of the more terrifying scenes, Nikolai Levin, the brother of Konstantin, dies, thus reminding Levin and the reader of death's terrible finality and inevitability. Levin, like Tolstoy himself, has many false starts in finding a meaning to life that is more powerful than death's engines of destruction.

Indeed, though *Anna Karenina* is set during peacetime, death punctuates Tolstoy's novel even more than it does *War and Peace*. In part, the reason for this was that, while completing *Anna Karenina* in 1877, Tolstoy's own search for meaning was especially desperate and as yet unfulfilled. Family, which had served as a source of meaning in earlier years, no longer granted the peace and happiness that Tolstoy needed; after all, family members were mortal too and susceptible to death's engines of destruction. Beginning in the late 1870s, Tolstoy was plagued with many agonizing questions about the meaning of his life and even considered suicide. Like Levin, he had to hide rope and weapons in his home for fear that he might hurt himself. Yet also like Levin, and unlike the novel's eponymous heroine Anna, who commits suicide by jumping in front of a train, Tolstoy managed to keep living despite his depression.

Tolstoy's struggle is mirrored in the struggles faced by the novel's characters. Anna has ceased searching for higher meaning and expects nothing but hatred from those around, while Levin continues to search until he manages to find an answer in love. Even though Levin realizes that he will still be angry with others and cannot always be loving, he is committed to trying to be as generous and as good as he can. Reminded of the peasant Platon, who lives for the spirit rather than for the body, Levin realizes that love of others is the only force that can match death—by loving and helping others, rather than focusing on himself and self-interest, he can attain the kind of meaning in life that feels larger than death.

At the end of *Anna Karenina*, Levin's resolution to try to be as loving as he can, despite his failings, did not, unfortunately, come with a resolution for his author. Tolstoy himself, after having created two masterpieces of Russian literature in *War and Peace* and *Anna Karenina* still saw no end to his struggles. In fact, he viewed his previous literary occupation as frivolous and a distraction from the true search for meaning. Repeated bouts of depression, inability to work, and ill health inspired serious thoughts about religion in him. In *A Confession* [*Исповедь, Ispoved'*, 1882], his public declaration of faith, Tolstoy tells of how his troubles led him back to the faith he once held in childhood. That faith directed him to the local Orthodox parish, the most likely venue for nurturing his rekindled religiosity. Around 1877, Tolstoy began to go to church and would even fast regularly in accordance with Orthodox practice. The reconciliation, however, was a tenuous one. Seeking, after all, is not finding. Gradually, as he embarked deeper into his personal religious quest, Tolstoy experienced a profound disillusionment with ecclesiastical authorities. Much to the disapproval of Sonya, this disillusionment compelled him to pull away from the Orthodox faith entirely in 1879. In a work from 1880 denouncing church dogma, Tolstoy writes that: "if [he] had judged Christianity through [church liturgy] alone, [he] would not only have lost faith but would have turned into the fiercest enemy of the faith itself..."[20]

Ultimately, the answer to Tolstoy's search would prove the same idea of love that gave Levin his meaning. After finishing *Anna Karenina*, Tolstoy set to finding God and love through a retranslation of the New Testament gospels. Even as he contemplated faith, traditionally the province of idealists, his destructive intellect was at the forefront. Yet his faith in the goodness of Christianity remained firm, so he took the investigation of this faith into his own hands. Convinced that the canonical Church Slavonic gospels were too polluted by church dogma, Tolstoy spent two years (1880–1882) re-translating the four New Testament gospels from the original Greek. He took the scissors to the gospels, cutting out all the miraculous content and telling a straightforward story of Jesus the man. Only a human Christ, as weak, sad, and as full of longing as the rest of us, could satisfy Tolstoy. He had no use for magical beings unburdened by the fear of death.

Tolstoy's reading of the gospels gave rise to an entire theology based on love. He came to believe that each individual, like Christ, was partly descendent from God. God's spirit had shaped the spiritual makeup of human beings and emancipated them from their animal, physical selves. As such, individuals could attain the Kingdom of God on earth if they lived for this spirit within them. Living for the spirit meant a number of things to Tolstoy. Above all, it meant love and caring for others and doing good deeds, while practicing nonresistance to evil. Jesus' life served as a righteous paradigm for the godly life and thus occupied a crucial role. Along with it, the Sermon on the Mount, which was given much attention in Tolstoy's religious worldview, articulated notions of universal brotherhood of love and non-resistance to evil. These last two concepts constitute the better-known elements of Tolstoianism.

Tolstoy's newly reinvented Christian faith ultimately served as the foundation for his spiritual search during the rest of his life. The truth that Tolstoy had been chasing could finally be reached through Christianity. Works, like the gospel translations, and future writings, like *The Kingdom of God Is Within You* [*Царство божие внутри вас, Tsarstvo bozhije vnutri vas,* 1894] or *Path of Life* [*Путь жизни, Put' zhizni,* 1910], further helped define Tolstoy's religious beliefs and provided spiritual meaning that alleviated, at least for a short time, his fears about death. Through his faith, Tolstoy articulated a vision of an afterlife in spirit. In the course of his spiritual journey, Tolstoy also enriched his spiritual beliefs with concepts from other world religions, including Buddhism and Taoism. In fact, late in his life, Tolstoy believed that, despite differences, all faiths, including Christianity and Islam—as well as Buddhism, Taoism, and other religions—bore elements of a single theological core. In his words, while "religions are different in their outer forms all are the same in their foundational beginnings."[21] Tolstoy's pluralistic religious doctrine is best illustrated in a late religious work, like *Path of Life*. A collection of spiritual quotations designed to enrich an individual's spiritual life every day, *Path of Life* includes quotations from countless religions as well as from spiritual, non-religious thinkers; Christianity and Islam coexisted with works by ancient philosophers.

As a result of his extensive spiritual journeys and spiritual writings, in time, Tolstoy grew into a moral figure in the eyes of the Russian public—he became the sage of Yasnaya Polyana, just as venerated for his spiritual beliefs as for his writing. His beliefs led him to renounce war and violence as well as anything else that proved violent, like hunting or eating meat. Indeed, Tolstoy's pacifism is one of the better-known manifestations of the beliefs of his later years. His pacifism guaranteed Tolstoy's afterlife as religious thinker, inspiring individuals as diverse as Mohandas Gandhi. During Tolstoy's lifetime, his pacifism led him to assume a proactive stance and support many individuals who refused to participate in the Russian army, like the Russian sect of Dukhobors. Unwilling to serve in the military, the Dukhobors were persecuted by the Tsarist regime. Prompted by their story, in 1899, Tolstoy wrote his first novel in decades, *Resurrection* [*Воскресение, Voskresenije*] and used the proceeds to fund the immigration of the Dukhobors to Canada.

As Tolstoy flung himself full-force into his search for meaning, his literary output greatly diminished. *The Death of Ivan Ilych* [*Смерть Ивана Ильича, Smert' Ivana Il'icha,* 1886] was the first work Tolstoy wrote after his so-called religious conversion. Like many of Tolstoy's post-conversion writings, despite its artistry, it served as a vessel for his ideological beliefs. Many later works like *Resurrection* served a similar function. While in earlier works, like *War and Peace* and *Anna Karenina*, Tolstoy had concealed his own desperate search for meaning under layers of fictional poetics, in *Resurrection* and *The Kreutzer Sonata* [*Крейцерова соната, Krejtserova sonata*, 1889], he bared the search, using fiction to articulate his religious beliefs. Even though Tolstoy's fiction grew scarce and seemingly bound to his religious beliefs, it still continued. As late as his eighties, Tolstoy kept making plans for new fictions, some as large in scope as *War and Peace*. His last work of fiction, *Hadji Murat* took as long as eight years (1896–1904) and exhibited incredible artistry. Though Tolstoy invested in writing simple works for the people, he could not rid himself of his writing talent or of its role in his life. Literature retained its importance for the author, shaping every stage of his journey toward truth.

***

For a man as fortunate and as venerated as he was, Tolstoy remained a seeker to the end. "Reading the aged Tolstoy stirs the heart," writes Irving Howe, partly in response to Gorky's view of Tolstoy as a perpetual seeker. "He will not yield to time, sloth, or nature. He clings to the waist of the life force. Deep into old age, he battles with the world, more often with himself, returning in his diaries, fictions, and tracts to the unanswerable questions that torment him. Blessed old magician, he is free of literary posture and the sins of eloquence."[22] Tolstoy persists in being raw and striving, never simplistically or artificially collected. In this sense, the messier and more energetic of his characters are the closest to his heart, for they bear pieces of his perpetual angst. Even in his death, though an old man, Tolstoy did not die in his quiet bed at home. He was running away from home, running toward some new ideal, toward some new freedom. When we think about it, Tolstoy's death at the stationmaster's quarters at Astapovo was terribly undignified. But Tolstoy never put much stock in being dignified; he preferred truth and authenticity to venerable old age. Tolstoy died, as he had lived, striving.

Notes

1. Turgenev, Ivan Sergeevich. *Essential Turgenev*. Ed. Elizabeth Cheresh Allen. Evanston, IL: Northwestern UP, 1994.

2. Gorky, Maksim. *Tolstoy and Other Reminiscences*. New Haven, CT: Yale UP, 2008. 65.

3. Troyat, Henri. *Tolstoy*. New York: Grove Press, 1967. 14.

4. Ibid.

5. Tolstoy, Leo. *Resident and Stranger*. Princeton, NJ: Princeton UP, 1989. 14.

6. Ibid.

7. Bartlett, Rosamund. *Tolstoy: A Russian Life.* New York: Houghton Mifflin Harcourt, 2011. 52–53.

8. Ibid. 413.

9. Wilson, A.N. *Tolstoy*. New York: W. W. Norton & Company, 2001. 101.

10. Maude, Aylmer. *The Life of Tolstoy: First Fifty Years.* London: Archibald Constable Co. Ltd., 1908. 57.

11. Wilson 97.

12. Gifford, Henry. *Tolstoy*. New York: Oxford UP, 1982. 19–20.

13. Eikhenbaum, Boris. *Tolstoy in the Sixties.* Ann Arbor: Ardis, 1982. 137–171.

14. Lukács, György. "Tolstoy and the Attempts To Go Beyond the Social." *Leo Tolstoy*. Ed. Harold Bloom. New Haven, CT: Chelsea House Publishers, 1986. 9.

15. Shklovsky, Viktor Borisovich. *Tolstoy*. Moscow: Progress Publishers, 1978. 28.

16. Popoff, Alexandra. *Sophia Tolstoy—A Biography*. New York: Simon and Schuster, 2010. 1–8.

17. Berlin, Isaiah. *The Hedgehog and the Fox*. New York: Simon and Schuster, 1970. 37.

18. Ibid.

19. All references pertain to Tolstoy's works and to the full edition of his writings: Polnoe sobranie sochinenii, v 90 tomakh, akademicheskoe iubileinoe izdanie. Vol. 48. Moskva: Gosudarstvennoe Izdatel'stvo Khudozhestvennoi Literatury, 1929–64. 187.

20. Ibid. Vol. 23. 60.

21. Ibid. Vol. 35. 190.

22. Howe, Irving. "The Old Magician—A Defense of the Late, Scolding Tolstoy." *The New Republic* 27 (April 1992): 30.

America Reacts to Dostoevsky and Tolstoy: Early Archival Evidence _____

Robert C. Evans
and Matthew Shoemaker

How did people in the United States react to the personalities and writings of Fyodor Dostoevsky and Leo Tolstoy in the second half of the nineteenth century? This question is difficult to answer, but it is difficult for contrasting reasons in each case. In the case of Dostoevsky, relatively little evidence of initial American reactions survives. In Tolstoy's case, however, so much information is available that examining and digesting it all proves a major challenge.

Several facts will suggest the nature and extent of the contrast. For instance, a search of the electronic *19th Century U. S. Newspapers* database elicited no "hits" for the names Dostoevsky or Dostoevskii, while a search of the same database for the name "Tolstoy" produced six hits (one of them not relevant to the author). A similar search of the *Proquest Historical Newspapers* database turned up only six "hits" for Dostoevsky before 1900, the first dating to 1895, and most of those items merely mention the author rather than making him their major focus. In contrast, the relevant number of returns for Tolstoy is 220, and many of the items deal with the author explicitly and at length. Comparable searches of other standard databases—especially newspaper databases—reveal comparable disproportions. There seems no point in listing them all.

Clearly, then, much work remains to be done in charting the American reception of these two writers. In Dostoevsky's case, the work will involve ferreting out articles or essays that may be hidden away in sources not easily accessible or searchable; in Tolstoy's case, the work will involve trying to make coherent sense of all the thousands of data that are very readily available. Research into this relatively unexplored topic promises to prove highly illuminating.[1]

Dostoevsky

One of the earliest available references to Dostoevsky in an American newspaper appeared on page ten of *The New York Herald* on July 24, 1879. This brief notice is part of a slightly longer piece arguing that "Russian literary news is meagre, and what there is of it is not encouraging." After reporting that Turgenev and Tolstoy have, for the time, ceased writing (the former because of political oppression), the unnamed author then asserts that "Dostoevsky and Vsevolod Krestovsky, relinquishing literature, have become government hirelings," while two other writers (Markoff and Aksakoff) have been forced into silence. "Native talent," the writer concludes, "is feeling the full force of aristocratic oppression, and while the blighting *régime* of terror holds sway in the imperial administration, no productions may be expected worthy of being added to the classical literature of Russia." Dostoevsky here, then, is somewhat surprisingly depicted as a sell-out and a traitor to the cause of freedom in Russia. Such a depiction, however, seems rare in the surviving record of American newspaper discussions of Dostoevsky.

If the majority of other early references to Dostoevsky in the Library of Congress's *Chronicling America* newspaper database is any indication, the Russian writer seems to have been presented mainly as a *victim* of oppressive conditions. An article titled "Russian Newspaper Men" and subtitled "A Thankless, Dangerous, and Poverty-Stricken Profession" was printed in a number of different American newspapers (probably as the result of syndication) and listed Dostoevsky as one of several figures who had been "sentenced to hard labor in the Siberian mines" (see, for instance, the Little Falls, Minnesota *Transcript* for October 9, 1879, p. 2—just one of three times this widely reprinted article appears in the *Chronicling America* database and surely not the most prominent venue).

By far the lengthiest and most interesting of the early newspaper pieces on Dostoevsky was published, however, on page two of the March 11, 1881 edition of *The New York Sun* under the headline "A Memorable Russian Funeral." The same article, under the same headline, appeared in such other papers as Canton, Ohio's *The Stark County Democrat* (March 31, 1881, p. 2). The publication of this piece in both a prominent big-city newspaper and in a relatively obscure small-town paper suggests that the article may have been even more widely available. In any case, this piece is especially valuable and seems worth reprinting in full:

MEMORABLE RUSSIAN FUNERAL.

Over Fifty Thousand Persons Following a Siberian

Exile to the Grave.

In 1849, a conspirator against the Czar's autocracy was sentenced to death in St. Petersburg. Czar Nicholas commuted his sentence to imprisonment in the Siberian mines for life. On March 11th that very conspirator was solemnly buried at the Czar's capital. Fifty thousand men, women and children followed the body to the grave. Czar Alexander has granted a pension of 2,000 roubles [sic] to the widow. The Grand Duchess Alexandra Josephovna sent her a letter of condolence, and her children placed a floral cross on the dead exile's coffin. Her imperial Highness, the Duchess Eugenia Maximilianovna also contributed a beautiful bouquet. His Eminence Metropolitan Isador donated a lot in the cemetery of Alexandro-Nevsky Laura, for the interment. The cities of Moscow and St. Petersburg sent their Mayors and delegations of Aldermen to attend the funeral. All the Russian universities were represented in the obsequies.

The dead man is Fedor Michaelovitch Dostoevsky. Nicholas loaded him with chains as a punishment for his love of liberty and hatred of despotism. Through his genius, his long suffering, and his devotion to the advancement of the people, he won the love of the nation, and has been accorded a niche among the immortal Russian writers and thinkers. He found God's spark among the most degraded human beings. Fitly was he termed "the anatomist of the soul," and "the poet of sorrows."

The Russians call all criminals "the dear unhappy ones," regarding them as the victims of fatal circumstances. They dearly loved Dostoevsky, who devoted his energies to the relief of the "unhappy ones," and who ably elucidated the fatal circumstances which annually send thousands to the dreary wastes of Siberia. He had shed his tears in a band of the unfortunates; he had trodden the long road beyond the Ural Mountains; his limbs had also been eaten by rusty irons; his own groans had been mingled with the groans of his unhappy comrades in prisons and mines, in the Siberian hell he had seen the tears of repentance, and heard the blasphemy of rage, the sighs of the innocents, prayers and curses, and weeping and singing. With the loving hand of a great artist he portrayed all these horrors. The Russian people have crowned him with a wreath of laurel. It will remain green forever.

Dostoevsky was born in 1821. He studied military engineering, but did not adopt it as a profession. He had a literary turn of mind. In 1846 he published "The Poor People," his first novel. It gave him a national reputation. In 1849 he was sent to Siberia with a band of political criminals. He found God's spark in the breast of every one of the miserable beings shut out from light of day in the mines. The discovery saved him. He probed the Russian character, and unearthed an all-forgiving love and mercy. His intellectual horizon was widened, and he saw a bright future for the nation.

Meantime Nicholas died. His son pardoned Dostoevsky. The novelist reappeared in St. Petersburg, and quickly published his great work, "Notes from the Dead House." In it he depicts all the horrors of Siberian prisons. It enshrined him in the affections of the Russian people. A year afterward he wrote another remarkable work, "The Miserable and Oppressed People." It was followed by the novel "Crime and Punishment," containing more profound psychological analysis of the motives that induce crime. This work softened the treatment of criminals in Russian courts. Since then Dostoevsky has written many novels, but none so strikingly effective. For the last two years he published an original periodical called the *Writer's Diary*. Although very popular, he died in poverty.

Epilepsy and a pulmonary complaint were the result of his confinement in the Siberian mines. They caused his death. Throngs surrounded the corpse for days, including the Grand Dukes and men and women of all classes. All who read, think, and study, bade him a final farewell. Children stood near his coffin and distributed flowers to visitors. Before the burial an envelope containing two roubles and the following note was found in the coffin:

For the Benefit of a Famine-Stricken Population
In Honor of God's Servant, Fedor Dostoevskfi,
who Upheld His Poor and Oppressed.

From a Poor Man.

Yesterday the remains were removed to the Church of Alexandro Nevskv Laura, and to-day they were buried. Over 50,000 persons were in the funeral procession. There were thirty groups, representing the male and female gymnasiums, male and female medical schools, universities, military, industrial and art schools, the musical conservatory, the stage, bar, press, Board of Trade, Church and municipal corporations. Each group carried wreaths of flowers and laurel leaves, with different mottoes. The wreath from Moscow bore this motto:

FROM THE HEART OF RUSSIA TO THE GREAT TEACHER.

No General, no statesman, no member of the imperial family has ever been so honored. Not the least notable feature of the procession was the absence of the police. The people themselves kept a perfect order. The procession was three hours in marching a mile and a half. The coffin was borne on the shoulders of friends, literary people, and students. On the way the choirs and the people sang, "Vechnaia Pamiat" (eternal memory). I never heard anything so solemn, grand and mournful, as that Russian funeral song.

To-day, at noon, Bishop- Nestor, assisted by a dozen priests, performed the solemn requiem. The Minister of Public Instruction and the Chief Censor of the Press were present. When the coffin was lowered into the grave sobbings were heard on all sides, and I did not see a face not bedewed with tears. The people were greatly moved by the pathetic voice of the daughter of the deceased, ten years old, "Good-bye, my dear, good, kind papa. Good-bye!" Speeches were made and verses read. The grave was covered with wreaths and bouquets and till nightfall was surrounded by people.

A subscription is opened for a monument in memory of the deceased, with the inscription, "He found God's spark."

Although this report is presented as an eyewitness account of the funeral, no author is mentioned in either appearance of the piece in the *Chronicling America* database. Anonymous publication was very typical in newspapers of this era. It is also possible that the author was not even American. The important thing, however, is what the article says and who could read it, not who wrote it.[2] This piece gives us insight into how Dostoevsky could have been understood by the relatively few Americans from this period who even knew of his existence. Dostoevsky is here presented not simply as a talented, insightful author, but as a victim of Imperial oppression and, above all, as an exemplar of spiritual and moral ideals. This view of him was common in late nineteenth-century America, at least if the scattered surviving evidence is any indication.

Thus, an article published on page five of the March 15, 1881 edition of *Chicago Inter-Ocean* shares a great deal of identical phrasing with the article just quoted, especially in commenting on *Notes from the House of the Dead* and also on *Crime and Punishment*. The article notes that, although Dostoevsky was "very popular, he died in poverty," and it then discusses his funeral by offering a condensed version of the account that appeared in *The New York Sun*.

Other references to Dostoevsky in the American press in the final decades of the nineteenth century—references that are usually very brief—almost always mention his imprisonment. This is how he appears, for instance, in articles in a variety of rather small newspapers over an extended period of years. The fact that such small newspapers and their readers showed any interest at all in a relatively unfamiliar Russian writer is itself impressive, but their interest typically had more to do with Dostoevsky the man than with Dostoevsky the author. References to his experiences as a prisoner appeared, for instance, in North Dakota's *The Bismarck Tribune* (October 17, 1879, p. 2); in Fowler, Indiana's *Benton*

Review (March 6, 1884, p. 7); in Indiana's *Albion New Era* (March 27, 1884, p. 3); in Iowa's *Malvern Leader* (April 3, 1884, p. 2); in Wisconsin's *Waunakee News* (July 20, 1899, p. 2); in Laurens, Iowa's *Pocahontas County Sun* (September 7, 1899, p. 7); and in Indiana's *Upland Monitor* (October 5, 1899, p. 4). Often these are reprints, but that fact in itself is significant, showing that syndication services believed that articles about Russian prisons would interest American readers. In such articles, Dostoevsky is mentioned more for his personal experiences as a victim of tsarist oppression than for his skill as a writer or his personal beliefs.

This fact makes an article on page five of the July 19, 1885 edition of *The New York Sun* relatively unusual. Dostoevsky is there described as a representative of a new turn to religion among Russian intellectuals. The article called him "the first educated Russian who was bold enough to declare in public that he believed in God and Christianity." It identified him as a "writer of genius who served his term in Siberia and who found God's spark in the hearts of men who were buried alive in the Siberian mines." The article credited Dostoevsky with having made "a series of brilliant sermons on that spark of his, denouncing the stone-hearted and infidel Russian public, Ivan Tourgeneff included." Yet although the article suggested that Dostoevsky's "voice seemed to be that of a man in a desert," it also claimed that his "preaching was not in vain" because of his influence on others. Here again, then, as in the account of Dostoevsky's funeral, the emphasis is on the author as a worthy spiritual and religious model.

Other early references to Dostoevsky in the American press, however, dealt with various other matters. One of these was his complicated romantic involvement with the talented Krukovsky sisters—one of whom is better known as Sonya Kovalevsky. This relationship was the topic of a number of newspaper pieces (see, for example, an article in *The San Francisco Call* for July 21, 1895, p. 21). Additionally, a very brief reference to Dostoevsky compared his work to that of the American writer Mary Wilkins (or, rather, compared hers to his; see *The New York Sun* for December 28, 1898, p. 6). But this glancing reference occurs in the last of the articles on Dostoevsky published in the nineteenth century and reprinted in the *Chronicling America* database. Other articles definitely exist and are cited or reproduced in other databases, but the articles discussed so far give a representative sense of the kind of information about Dostoevsky available to American newspaper readers before the turn of the century.

Perhaps the most significant publication about Dostoevsky in an American book printed before 1900 is his appearance in volume twelve of the forty-six-volume *Library of the World's Best Literature, Ancient and Modern* of 1896. This set, clearly designed to appeal to a large and educated readership, contains a lengthy introductory essay on Dostoevsky by Isabel F. Hapgood (1851–1928), a major scholar of Russian literature, who was also interested in relations between Russia and the West. Hapgood's essay is important because it suggests how an intelligent, highly-informed American could respond to Dostoevsky as the nineteenth century came to an end.

Hapgood begins by asserting that, in "certain respects Dostoevsky is the most characteristically national of Russian writers. Precisely for that reason, his work does not appeal to so wide a circle outside of his own country as does the work of Turgenieff and Count L. N. Tolstoy" (4779). Hapgood argues that Dostoevsky's highly unusual life had made him very distinctive as a writer, but she also asserts that his "special domain was the one which Turgenieff and Tolstoy did not understand, and have touched not at all, or only incidentally—the great middle class of society, or what corresponds thereto in Russia" (4779). She then discusses details of Dostoevsky's life—details so generally known today that they are not worth recounting here. One of the most interesting passages of her lengthy introduction to Dostoevsky, however, seems worth quoting at length. Most of his later novels, she writes,

> are of great length . . . [and] are full of digressions from the point, and there is often a lack of finish about them which extends not only to the minor characters but to the style in general. In fact, his style is neither jewel-like in its brilliancy, as is Turgenieff's, nor has it the elegance, broken by carelessness, of Tolstoy's. But it was popular, remarkably

well adapted to the class of society which it was his province to depict, and though diffuse, it is not possible to omit any of the long psychological analyses, or dreams, or series of ratiocinations, without injuring the web of the story and the moral, as chain armor is spoiled by the rupture of a link. This indeed is one of the great difficulties which the foreigner encounters in an attempt to study Dostoevsky: the translators have been daunted by his prolixity, and have often cut his works down to a mere skeleton of the original. Moreover, he deals with a sort of Russian society which it is hard for nonRussians to grasp, and he has no skill whatever in presenting aristocratic people or society, to which foreigners have become accustomed in the works of his great contemporaries Turgenieff and Tolstoy; while he never, despite all his genuine admiration for the peasants and keen sympathy with them, attempts any purely peasant tales like Turgenieff's 'Notes of a Sportsman' or Tolstoy's 'Tales for the People.' Naturally, this is but one reason the more why he should be studied. His types of hero, and of feminine character, are peculiar to himself. Perhaps the best way to arrive at his ideal — and at his own character, *plus* a certain irritability and tendency to suspicion of which his friends speak — is to scrutinize the pictures of Prince Myshkin ('The Idiot'), Ivan ('Humbled and Insulted'), and Alyosha ('The Karamazoff Brothers'). Pure, delicate both physically and morally, as Dostoevsky himself is described by those who knew him best; devout, gentle, intensely sympathetic, strongly masculine yet with a large admixture of the feminine element — such are these three; such is also, in his way, Raskolnikoff ('Crime and Punishment'). His feminine characters are the precise counterparts of these in many respects, but are often also quixotic even to boldness and wrongheadedness, like Aglaya ('The Idiot'), or to shame, like Sonia ('Crime and Punishment'), and the heroine of 'Humbled and Insulted.' But Dostoevsky could not sympathize with and consequently could not draw an aristocrat; his frequently recurring type of the dissolute petty noble or rich merchant is frequently brutal; and his unclassed women, though possibly quite as true to life as these men, are painful in their callousness and recklessness. (4784–85)

Unlike most previous American commentary on Dostoevsky, this is rich literary criticism rather than biography, with a few scattered critical comments. As Hapgood's essay—and its appearance in a major "set" of books—suggests, by the very end of the nineteenth century, Dostoevsky had begun to attain the kind of recognition and stature among American readers that has only grown exponentially in the years and decades since then.

Tolstoy

One especially interesting early reference to Tolstoy in an American newspaper appeared on page two of the July 19, 1978 edition of the *New York Herald*. It began by asserting that at:

> one time, and that not very long ago, the average American had a very vague idea of Russia as being a country governed by a Czar, where the people ate caviare [sic] and drank vodka and from where the leather was imported to make our travelling bags and pocket books. But times have changed, and at present there is no foreign country in which we take a greater interest and few that we know more about.

Reviewing Eugene Schuyler's newly published translation of Tolstoy's novel *The Cossacks*, the anonymous writer reports that Tolstoy, even more than Turgenev, "enjoys the widest reputation" as a novelist "in his own country." Yet the reviewer suggests that there is little point in comparing novelists who are so different in their styles, topics, and themes. The reviewer notes that:

> Tolstoy, though the nobleman, draws his subjects from among the common people, and lays his colors on with a sympathetic, but often rude hand, while Turguenieff writes of the upper and middle classes, and draws and moulds his characters . . . carefully . . . . Tolstoy suggests Walt Whitman to us more than any other English speaking writer. He has that same love for the simple and natural, and often, we must say it, the coarse.

An article likewise contrasting Tolstoy and Turgenev appeared in *Scribner's Monthly* for September 1878. The *Scribner's* piece explicitly offers itself as a kind of introduction of this new writer to American readers. It cites Schuyler, "recently prominent as a diplomat at St. Petersburg and Constantinople," as introducing

Tolstoy to the magazine by saying that he is "now the most popular novelist in Russia, and, after Tourgueneff [sic], incontestably the best" (753). But the magazine compares Turgenev to Tolstoy to the latter's disadvantage, finding:

> the gap between Tourgueneff and Tolstoy very great. Tolstoy may have more original force than the other, but Tourgueneff is a far more subtle artist. There are strong points of resemblance between the two styles. There is the same minute, apparently over minute, description of the sayings and doings of each character. Many phrases, many passages do not affect the story in one way or another, although they may have some good effect in a general way; they may add to the vividness of the impression by teaching the unimportant, as well as the important things which go to make up a character. The aimlessness of much of the talk, much of the description, is greater in [Tolstoy's] "The Cossacks" than in Tourgueneff's novels. A passage occurs which seems to be leading up to some action, some character sketch, some point of importance; we read on and find that nothing comes of it. Perhaps this is part of the comedy. Perhaps Tolstoy is satirising, more clumsily than Tourgueneff, a national Russian characteristic: that of always intending, or seeming to be about to do something, without summoning the energy to do it. (753)

The review then summarizes the plot of the novel, comments (unfavorably) on Cossacks in real life, and suggests that part of the problems with Russians is that they pay too much attention to Germans. Finally, however, the reviewer contends that as a novel, "'The Cossacks' cannot be classed among the exciting or the sensational; it has superior attractions. As an introduction to a strange people, it is of philosophical value; as a study of a mind that works out the problem of what people are put into the world for, it has higher qualifications yet." Ultimately, the review pronounces the book "remarkable" (754). Most of the earliest references to Tolstoy in American newspapers are reviews of, or brief references to, *The Cossacks*. It was by reading a translation of this novel that much of the English-speaking American public first became familiar with Tolstoy.

An article published on May 17, 1879 in an American magazine called *Littell's Living Age* (but actually reprinted from an English periodical) moves beyond such reviews and notices of a single book and begins charting Tolstoy's rise as an important Russian novelist, who was now becoming better-known in the English-speaking world, including the United States. At the same time, the article (by W. R. S. Ralston) explains why Tolstoy was not even better known by that point: "with Count Tolstoy's more recent and more ambitious novels"—including *War and Peace* and *Anna Karenina* —"it is difficult . . . to become acquainted, for they have not been translated into any familiar tongue" (409). Moreover, Ralston even predicts that "[n]either of these works seems likely to be translated into English. Among other deterrent causes may be mentioned their length. *War and Peace*, for instance, contains more than eighteen hundred large pages!" (409). Nevertheless, on the principle that a skeleton is better than nothing, Ralston then proceeds to summarize the plot of *War and Peace* at enormous length, while also briefly mentioning the recently published *Anna Karenina* (410–20).

Ralston, of course, was wrong in his prediction that Tolstoy's masterpieces would never be translated into English, and in the final two decades of the nineteenth century, American commentary on Tolstoy grew so rapidly and enormously that it is difficult to track and make sense of it all. Perhaps the best way, then, to indicate the nature of Tolstoy's American reputation at the end of the century is to quote from the same set of books—the *Library of the World's Best Literature*—cited earlier when trying to suggest how Dostoevsky was presented to a mass audience of American readers at the end of the 1800s.

The introductory essay included on Tolstoy in the *Library* was written, significantly, by one of the most prominent of all American literary intellectuals of the time—William Dean Howells. Howells begins by claiming that the normal way we build our understanding of other men does not apply to Tolstoy, stating that "such truth as related to dates and places ... is with him hardly at all structural: we do not try to build his moral or intellectual figure upon it or about it" (14985). Howells then tells the familiar story of Tolstoy's deliberate choice of a difficult life over a life of comfort and prosperity.

Howells does note some nineteenth-century criticisms of Tolstoy's choice of a hard life, but he defends Tolstoy against them. For example, he states that since Tolstoy had previously followed a more decadent lifestyle, some people thought "he naturally wished to atone for it by making everyone also lead a poor, dull, and ugly life" (14987). He also claims that Tolstoy tried to exceed Christ in following scripture. Howells, however, reminds the reader that Tolstoy "compels no man's conscience . . . [and] shapes no man's conduct" (14987). Another common criticism of Tolstoy was that he didn't truly live the life of poverty which, he claimed, would lead to happiness. Howells notes that Tolstoy's wife does not live in poverty with him and is thus able to promote her husband's survival. Howells believes, however, that these facts reflect Tolstoy's free choice of a lifestyle he would never force on others. As Howells states, Tolstoy believes that "self-renunciation must not accomplish itself at the cost of others' free choice" (14988). Responding to Tolstoy's detractors, Howells says that the author "has not differed from most other Christians except in the attempt literally to do the will of Christ" (14988), and that Tolstoy may be attempting to show that the religious should focus on the world of the present.

Howells then shifts to talking about Tolstoy's literary works, beginning by discussing the literary environment in contemporary Russia. He cites the Russian writers Gogol and Turgenev as having established a tradition of realism in Russian literature, a tradition thoroughly developed by Tolstoy's time. The difference between Tolstoy and previous writers, according to Howells, is that Tolstoy "replaced the artistic conscience" with "the human conscience" (14989).

To Howells, Tolstoy's ethics, which guided his life, are crucial to understanding his work. Throughout his writing, Tolstoy's ideals are relevant to all of society, from the poor to the prince, and Tolstoy deals with topics so sincerely that they appear new to the reader, as if they were being written about for the first time. In particular, the goodness of Tolstoy's characters stands out to Howells, and he gives several specific examples of their morality:

Until we read *The Cossacks* and witness the impulses of kindness in Olenin, we do not realize how much love has been despised by fiction, and neglected for passion. It is with a sort of fear and trembling that we find ourselves in the presence of this wish to do good to others, as if it might be some sort of mawkish sentimentality. But it appears again and again in the cycle of Tolstoy's work: in the vague aspirations recorded in *Childhood, Boyhood, and Youth;* in the abnegation and shame of the husband in *Anna Karenina,* when he wishes to forgive his wife's paramour; in the goodness of the *muzhik* to the loathsome sick man in *The Death of Ivan Ilyitch*; in the pitying patience of Prince Andrei Bolkonsky with Anatol Kuragin in *War and Peace,* where amidst his own anguish he realizes that the man next him under the surgeon's knife is the wretch who robbed him of the innocent love of his betrothed. (14990-91)

Howells also notes that the love and goodness of Tolstoy's characters are often contrasted with passion. He asserts that Tolstoy's treatment of passion helps separate him from his contemporaries, saying that "In most other novelists, passion is treated as if it were something important in itself ... But in Tolstoy, almost for the first time, we are shown that passion is merely a condition; and that it has almost nothing to do with happiness" (14991). Howells says that Tolstoy shows that selfish passion produces no true joy, and that giving into passion only leaves one bound by it. Howells also notes that Tolstoy generally links passion to death, to the point that they seem identical, and also that Tolstoy typically depicts passion and sin in males, which Howells believes may contribute to the distaste he provokes in a patriarchal society. Tolstoy's negative depictions of passion reflect his ethics, in which self-indulgent pleasures alone provide no true happiness, so that only in unselfish acts is real joy found. However, Howells asserts that Tolstoy is not specifically condemning passion and other ugly aspects of human nature; instead, he simply shows life as frankly and honestly as he can, accepting that shortcomings are parts of human life, and displaying the results, which may be moving or even humorous.

In his final paragraph, Howells comments on Tolstoy's techniques:

Of methods in Tolstoy, then, there can scarcely be any talk. He has apparently no method: he has no purpose but to get what he thinks, simply and clearly before us. Of style there seems as little to say; though here, since I know him only in translation, I cannot speak confidently. He may have a very marked style in Russian; but if this was so, I do not see how it could be kept out of the versions. In any case, it is only when you come to ask yourself what it is, that you realize its absence. His books are full of Tolstoy,—his conviction, his experience,—and yet he does not impart his personal quality to the diction as other masters do. It would indeed be as hard to imitate the literature as the life of Tolstoy . . . . (14994)

Howells' reaction to the Russian writer, both in defending how Tolstoy lived and in commenting on the writings themselves, shows the impact that Tolstoy's ideas had around the civilized world. His ability to present the human condition freshly and movingly, and the connection of his work to the peculiar and humble way he chose to live, both made Tolstoy (in Howells' opinion) not only a Russian cultural icon, but also a literary figure of continuing importance to readers around the globe.

Note
1. Helpful resources include the works by Leatherbarrow, Egan and Egan, and Wreath and Wreath.

Works Cited
Chronicling America. Library of Congress. n.d. Web. 11 Nov. 2013. <http://chroniclingamerica.loc.gov/>.

Egan, David R. and Melinda A. Egan. *Leo Tolstoy: An Annotated Bibliography of English Language Sources to 1978.* Metuchen, NJ: Scarecrow, 1978.

_____. *Leo Tolstoy: An Annotated Bibliography of English Language Sources from 1978 to 2003.* Lanham, MD: Scarecrow, 2005.

Hapgood, Isabel F. "Feodor Mikhailovitch Dostoévsky (1821–1881)." *Library of the World's Best Literature, Ancient and Modern.* Ed. Charles Dudley Warner, et al. 46 vols. New York: International Society, 1896. 8: 4779–4786.

Howells, William Dean. "Lyof Tolstoy (1828–)." *Library of the World's Best Literature, Ancient and Modern*. Ed. Charles Dudley Warner, et al. 46 vols. New York: International Society, 1897. 31: 14985-14994.

Leatherbarrow, W. J. *Fedor Dostoevsky: A Reference Guide*. Boston: Hall, 1990.

19th Century U. S. Newspapers. Gale Digital Collections. n.d. Web. 19 Nov. 2013. <http://gdc.gale.com/products/19th-century-u.s.-newspapers/>

Proquest Historical Newspapers. ProQuest. n.d. Web. 19 Nov. 2013. <http://www.proquest.com/en-US/catalogs/databases/detail/pq-hist-news.shtml>.

Wreath, P. J. and A. I. "Leo Tolstoy: A Bibliography of Criticism in English, from the Late Nineteenth Century Through 1979." *Canadian-American Slavic Studies* 14 (1980): 466–512.

"There is a way out:" *The Cherry Orchard* in the Twenty-First Century

Galina Rylkova

> "Since the appearance of Chekhov's early stories, criticism has been preoccupied with the question: Where is Chekhov in his works? What is his point of view and how does he stand in relation to his heroes, their moods and ideas?"
> —Robert Louis Jackson, *Chekhov: A Collection of Critical Essays*

Anton Chekhov (1860–1904) represents a unique author between the Golden and Silver Ages of Russian literature, a transition from bold realist strokes to impressionistic blurriness and momentous sensations. Chekhov was equally admired by realists, such as Leo Tolstoy and Ivan Bunin, and modernists, such as Vladimir Nabokov. Unlike Pushkin, Dostoevsky, and Tolstoy, Chekhov did not live to see any major political or cultural upheavals. He was born one year prior to the abolition of serfdom, which occurred in 1861, and died one year prior to the first Russian revolution of 1905. Unlike his esteemed predecessors and contemporaries, Chekhov was a professional doctor, and medicine, as he used to say, continued to be his loyal wife, while literature was his mistress. Although he responded to many dominant themes of the nineteenth-century literature (such as life, death, fate, crime and castigation, and the disintegration of the institution of marriage, to name only a few), he did this in a distinctly minor key. Chekhov is primarily famous for his short stories, which he started to write in his youth in order to support his parents and siblings, and for his plays, most notably, *The Seagull, Uncle Vanya, Three Sisters*, and *The Cherry Orchard*. Chekhov was also a prolific letter-writer, who succeeded in refining and perfecting this genre. As a pragmatist, Chekhov was not interested in dramatic solutions that, on Russian soil, tend to become final or apocalyptic. His manner of writing is often compared to impressionistic paintings. One of his most-quoted sayings is: "People dine, merely dine, but at that moment their happiness is being made or their life is being smashed." One reads Chekhov not only to learn what he chose to say in his writings, but also to grasp what he intentionally left unsaid. The latter makes Chekhov a particular favorite with literary scholars, students of narratology, and theater directors, since Chekhov appears to be boundless and open to continuous interpretation and re-interpretation.

The Cherry Orchard [*Вишневый сад, Vishnyovyj sad,* 1903] happened to be Chekhov's last work. This has prompted students of Chekhov to treat it as his final testament and to look for some eternal truths hidden between its lines. Those steeped in Russian literature naturally assume that, in his last year(s), the dying Chekhov was concerned more about the future of the Russian society than his thinning hair and the misbehavior of his intestines, which he described meticulously to his more intimate correspondents. *The Cherry Orchard* is also notable for Chekhov's painful attempts to make the Russian public accept his play as a comedy in contrast to the dramatic (merging upon tragic) interpretation suggested by Konstantin Stanislavsky and the Moscow Art Theater in 1904.[1] The standard definition of comedy as something that starts poorly, but has a splendid finale—unlike in tragedy where things start well, but end poorly—fails to convince many students of Chekhov. What is there to celebrate when the old orchard—the epitome of beauty—is being chopped down in Act IV?

The Cherry Orchard, nevertheless, does fit the bill of a comedy. In Act I, Lopakhin explains the gravity of the situation to everyone concerned:

As you already know, the cherry orchard will be sold to pay your debts, the auction is set for August twenty second, but don't worry, dear lady, don't lose any sleep, there's a way out... [...] Your estate lies only thirteen miles from town, the railroad runs past it, and if the cherry orchard and the land along the river were subdivided into building lots and then leased out for summer cottages, you'd have an income of at the very least twenty-five thousand a year. [...] The location is wonderful, the river's deep. Only, of course, it'll have to be spruced up, cleared out... for example, tear down all the old sheds, and this house, say, which is absolutely worthless, chop down the old cherry orchard… (991)[2]

Lyubov Andreevna Ranevskaya, the owner, is devastated and unreservedly rejects Lopakhin's plan. Her beloved orchard and the estate, in her view, cannot be wiped out, no matter what. "I love this house, without the cherry orchard I couldn't make sense of my life, and if it really has to be sold, then sell me along with the orchard," she moans in Act III (1022). However, in Act IV Ranevskaya talks about losing the estate as a foregone conclusion: "Good-bye, dear old house, old grandfather. Winter will pass, spring will come again, but you won't be here any more, they'll tear you down" (1036). The situation is resolved of its own accord, with the friend of the family, Lopakhin, buying the estate and beginning the cutting down of the orchard even before the estate's owners move out. Even as the orchard is being cut down, all the characters are beginning to feel much better, they sleep better, and some of them are downright happy. Even Lopakhin, whom Chekhov entrusts with cutting down the orchard, continues to be everyone's dear friend. How do the characters achieve this sense of inner equilibrium? What exactly makes Ranevskaya and the others resign themselves to the situation and calm down?

Of course, one can see the cherry orchard as the embodiment of the outdated pre-revolutionary way of life or—nowadays— of everything (such as education and culture, children's creative development, libraries, museums, provincial theatres, nature preserves, recreational parks and many other things) that does not bring easily calculable annual profits. But one also needs to examine the play from a perspective that presumably Chekhov himself might have had in the period between 1902 and 1904, when the play was written and staged. Chekhov was a professional doctor. "When someone has been sick for a long time, everybody in his household, deep inside, wishes him to be dead," Chekhov recorded in one of his last notebooks.[3] This raises two questions: at what point is it possible and reasonable to accept the inevitability of someone's death and to stop providing medical treatment to a terminally sick person, and how can this be done with the least possible suffering both on the part of the sick person and his or her close circle?

Chekhov's short life span coincided with what Philippe Aries describes as a transition from one cultural view of death to another.[4] Chekhov died at a time when death was becoming increasingly clinical through relocation of the ill from private homes to hospitals and various hospices, thus allowing death to be treated as invisible and facilitating its denial. This concept of death (as something that "turns [one's] stomach [...] like the biological acts of man" and has accordingly to be postponed at all cost) has been prevalent ever since the end of the nineteenth century and contributes to our definition of death today.[5] Aries's analysis can be used to explain the allegedly ruthless scene from *The Cherry Orchard*, when the owners hear their beloved orchard being destroyed, thus becoming aware of its imminent end. Why didn't the new owner, Lopakhin, have enough tact to wait until they were all gone? Because being tactful was not an issue: the resolution of the play was not as cruel as many critics seem to imply today. The orchard, like a typical nineteenth-century man, was dying in a familiar setting, surrounded by friends and family. That is also why all attempts to send the old servant Firs to the hospital fail: he is left to die in his masters' house, in full view of the sympathetic theatregoers, who have come to know and love him in the course of a three-hour-long performance.

In the twenty-first century, when medical science and technology have developed to such an unprecedented extent that they can sustain a sick person's life for incredibly long periods of time, the question of when one needs such interventions and when they should stop has arisen in all of its uncomfortable starkness. And the problem is not so much the amount of money that prolonging somebody's life requires, or the fact that oftentimes the person in question is in a coma and, for all intents and purposes, is dead to the outside world; the problem is also in the fact that prolonging a sick person's life often requires all the physical and mental resources of both the patient and his or her family members, who cannot resign themselves to the idea that curing the patient is impossible and that many of the medical procedures not only fail to alleviate the state of the patient but, in fact, may cause the patient unfathomable suffering. Is it better to prolong a permanent state of suffering or to accept the inevitable and devote the remaining time to easing the person's suffering, to interacting with the sick person, and to achieving mutual forgiveness? How can one relinquish what is immeasurably dear, but what can no longer be preserved?[6]

The Cherry Orchard is a poignant metaphor epitomizing many situations in the new twenty-first century. When writing the play, Chekhov was already a very sick person. He could not think about how different people would react to his death. In Act I, Gaev (Ranevskaya's brother) sums up the situation: "If a large number of cures is suggested for a particular disease, it means the disease is incurable" (998). That is the news that one has to come to terms with. It takes time. From my perspective, *The Cherry Orchard* is, first and foremost, a story about how a group of people collectively resigns itself to the death of the dearly loved *old grandfather* [старый дедушка, *staryj dedushka*, Act IV]. That is precisely how Ranevskaya refers to the old house with the orchard. This essay offers a new look at the structure of *The Cherry Orchard*. How, for example, is one to explain the seemingly nonsensical ball in act three? It begins to make perfect sense once one realizes that some people can only come to terms with certain information and internalize certain knowledge if they are in motion. Ranevskaya is such a person. Viewed from the perspective of some people's need to be in motion in order to process important information, the structure and plot of the play become clearer and more logical. In fact, Chekhov takes his heroes and his audience through four stages of coming to terms with the terrible news that the orchard and the house are doomed. In Ranevskaya's case, he helps her deal with shock and overcome her refusal to accept the inevitable. She leaves quite content.

So how is this achieved from act to act? In the first act, the news of the grave condition of the orchard is introduced in the context of the company's very early/late arrival, great confusion, and general tiredness. The thought that the orchard will soon be lost does not sink in. In the second act, everyone is sitting motionlessly in the vicinity of a cemetery, listening to one another talk, and finally, tacitly arriving at the decision to do nothing. It should be noted that making a decision and learning to live with it are two separate matters. In the third act, the same decision is further internalized through motion. Ranevskaya announces that she wishes to return to Paris and admits that she is still in love with the person who was partially responsible for everybody's financial ruin and, consequently, for the ruin of the cherry orchard. All this happens while she dances with Petya Trofimov, talks with him, then quarrels and makes up with him, and finally dances with him again. Her urging Petya to find himself a mistress, that is, "to fall," suddenly materializes in Petya's literally taking a tumble down the staircase. The fourth act is devoted to the general exodus. Everybody has to vacate the premises physically, that is, to walk or ride away. What I suggest is considering each act on the basis of the predominant type of absorbing and internalizing new/unexpected information in it: act one is visual, act two is audial/auditory/aural, act three is kinesthetic/kinetic, and act four is also kinesthetic but in a different way: the characters' bodily movements are employed not to absorb new information but to reinforce/consolidate certain newly acquired skills. Let us take a closer look at each act and its characters.

Act I

Act I portrays a predominantly visual perception of the external world. It is emphasized that it is May, the orchard is in bloom, there are many lengthy descriptive passages (Dunyasha describes Yepikhodov; Ranevskaya is described by Lopakhin; Anya describes Ranevskaya's life in Paris, and she also describes her drowned brother Grisha; Lopakhin describes himself, etc.). The characters are invited to recognize/recall something by seeing. "Will [Ranevskaya] recognize me?" Lopakhin worries (983). Anya: "Mama, do you remember what room this is?" (984) Varya: "Your rooms, the white and the violet, are still the same as ever, Mama dear" (984). Gaev to Ranevskaya: "The orchard's all white. You haven't forgotten, Lyuba? There's that long pathway leading straight on, straight on, like a stretched ribbon, it glistens on moonlit nights. You remember?

You haven't forgotten?" (995). Gaev suddenly has a revelatory moment (almost an epiphany):

> Lyuba, do you know how old this cupboard is? [...] This cupboard was built exactly one hundred years ago. [...] (*Stroking the cupboard.*) Dear, venerated cupboard! I salute your existence, which for over a century has been dedicated to enlightened ideas of virtue and justice; your unspoken appeal to constructive endeavor has not faltered in the course of a century, sustaining (*through tears*) in generations of our line, courage, faith in a better future and nurturing within us ideals of decency and social consciousness (993).

Ranevskaya starts hallucinating: "Look, our poor Mama is walking through the orchard ... in a white dress! (*Laughs with joy.*) There she is" (996). The verbs of seeing/looking and their derivatives abound in act one. Varya, after Lopakhin fails to propose to her, states: "It's hard for me even to look at him."[7] Here is how Ranevskaya describes her return home from France: "God knows, I love my country, love it dearly. I couldn't look at it from the train, couldn't stop crying" (990). The characters repeatedly compare each other's looks. Gaev tells Anya that she looks exactly like her mother when she was Anya's age (989). Ranevskaya tells Varya that she "looks the same as ever, like a nun" (984).

By the end of act one, however, Ranevskaya starts noticing that everyone has changed and grown old, as if she is finally exhausted by her sight-seeing activity: "Well now, Petya? Why have you become so homely? Why have you got old? [...] You got old too, Leonid" (997). Ranevskaya clearly experiences everything through her body, and sheer contemplation or prolonged periods of listening to other people make her uncomfortable and less prone to understand them. Anya describes her mother's reaction to the deaths of her husband and a son: "Six years ago father died, a month later our brother Grisha drowned in the river, a sweet little boy, seven years old. Mama couldn't stand it, she went away, went away without looking back... (*Shivers.*) How well I understand her if only she knew" (987-88). In act three, Ranevskaya describes the same situation in her own words: "I went abroad, went for good, never to return, never to see that river again… I shut my eyes, ran away, out of my mind […]" (1007). To move literally away, to perform a physical action—that is how kinesthetic people react to a new environment/situation. That is how they tend to process any new information. Anya understands Ranevskaya completely because she is similarly kinesthetic. If Anya welcomes the new life, then she literally has to be moving forward and she complements this act kinesthetically by throwing the keys to her mother's estate into a deep well (act two). Ranevskaya incessantly displays the urge to move, to touch, to hug and to kiss. When she receives the telegrams from her estranged lover, she first tears them to pieces without reading, later she reads them and only then does she tear them to pieces, as if she needs this procedure to engrain in her mind the irrevocability of her decision to stop living with the man who does not respect her and in part is responsible for squandering the family fortune.

Young children are naturally kinesthetic. They need to touch, to smell, to put new things in their mouths, and to crawl on different types of surfaces in order to learn how to interact with the world. Act one abounds in the words "nursery," "childhood," "child/children." In fact, some characters are emotionally transported to their childhood experiences. Ranevskaya says: "The nursery, my darling, beautiful room… I slept here when I was a little girl… (*Weeps.*) And now I feel like a little girl… (*She kisses her brother and Varya and then her brother again.*)" (984). Gaev (Ranevskaya's next of kin) also reacts to everything kinesthetically. Throughout the play, he utters interjections and makes bodily movements with his imaginary cue, as if he is involved in a continual game of billiards. He irritatingly sucks some hard candies and has a heightened sense of smell ("it smells of chicken/herring/patchoulis"), which is typical of people with a kinesthetic learning ability. It is not surprising, therefore, that Gaev and Ranevskaya fail to understand Lopakhin, who has a very logical and visual state of mind. He can easily visualize what he is talking about, while Ranevskaya needs an object, something that she can touch and feel: "Can I really be sitting here? (*Laughs.*) I feel like jumping up and down and swinging my arms. (*Covers her face with her arms.*)" (990). Lopakhin invites her to listen to him and to contemplate a wonderful future that he envisions for her and her estate. But Ranevskaya literally cannot sit still.

> LOPAKHIN. [...] The only thing I want is for you to believe in me as you once did, for your wonderful, heartbreaking eyes to look at me as they once did. [...]
> RANEVSKAYA. I can't sit still, I just can't... (*Leaps up and walks about in great excitement.*) I won't survive this joy... Laugh at me, I am silly .... My dear little cupboard. (*Kisses the cupboard.*) My little table. (990)

Lopakhin continues to paint his attainable and prosperous future, while both Gaev and Ranevskaya are incapable of following his train of thought. Ranevskaya: "I don't quite follow you, Yermolai Alekseich. [...] Chop it down? My dear, forgive me, but you don't understand at all" (991). "What drivel!" Gaev echoes with indignation (992).

Act II

Much has been written about the use of space in Chekhov's plays. However, in the case of *The Cherry Orchard* it is not only important to appreciate where the action takes place, but also where it does not: it never takes place in the orchard.[8] The whole of act two takes place beside the road near the cemetery. The orchard can be seen at a distance behind the "towering poplars" and is visually fused together with the decrepit tombstones (1001). In this act, the characters tacitly agree to do nothing about the orchard. Acoustically, this state of dreadful inertia is punctuated by "the sound of a breaking string, dying away mournfully" (1012). Act two is predominantly aural: Yepikhodov plays his guitar, he wants to have a heart-to-heart conversation with Dunyasha. But Dunyasha is smitten with Ranevskaya's valet Yasha, his Parisian sophistication and ability to "discuss anything" (1004). Sharlotta pours out her feelings, but no one is interested. Most of the time, the characters are sitting static, obligated to listen to one another. Ranevskaya talks at length about her sins. Petya delivers his famous monologues about "human pride" (1010) and about "all Russia [being] our orchard" (1015).

Lopakhin unsuccessfully attempts to make Ranevskaya say something in response to his proposition to rent the orchard and the adjacent land to the growing population of summer folk: "Give me a one-word answer: yes or no? Just one word!" (1004). Ranevskaya characteristically conveys her disgust at making such irreversible decisions by complaining about the smell and invoking a succession of unpleasant sensations that she has recently experienced at a railroad restaurant: "Who's been smoking those revolting cigars around here... [...] And why did I go out to lunch... That nasty restaurant of yours with its music, the tablecloths smelt of soap... Why drink so much, Lyonya? Why eat so much?" (1004-5). Gaev also feels out of sorts and itches to break away from this awkward situation: "You ride to town and have lunch... yellow to the center! I should go home first, play one game..." (1004). Finally both Ranevskaya and Gaev decide that Lopakhin's plan is "vulgar," which makes him lose his patience: "I'll burst into tears or scream or fall down in a faint. It's too much for me! You are torturing me to death!" (1006). Lopakhin's words would have been infinitely more understandable to Ranevskaya had he indeed implemented his threats. Later she remarks to Lopakhin: "You all live such gray lives, you talk such nonsense" (1007).

At the end of act two, Petya (an eternal student) and Anya, Ranveskaya's seventeen-year-old daughter, are left alone. Petya is in love with Anya and he chooses his words carefully so that they will appeal to her kinesthetic way of processing his novel ideas:

Varya's afraid we'll suddenly fall in love, so she hangs around us all day. Her narrow mind can't comprehend that we're above love. Avoiding the petty and specious that keeps us from being free and happy, that's the goal and meaning of our life. Forward! We march irresistibly toward the shining star, glowing there in the distance! Forward! No dropping behind, friends! (1014)

Not surprisingly, Anya finds Petya's utterances irresistible: "Anya (*stretching up her arms*). You speak so well! [...] The house we live in hasn't been our house for a long time, and I'll go away, I give you my word" (1014). In his final crescendo, Petya employs all available means of communicating his enthusiasm—visual, aural, and kinesthetic as if Chekhov wanted his monologue to reverberate with every listener: "I foresee happiness, Anya, I can see it already… […] Here is happiness, here it comes, drawing closer and closer, I can already hear its footsteps. And if we don't see it, can't recognize it, what's wrong with that? Others will see it" (1015-6). To avoid Varya, Petya and Anya decide to go to the river. Act two ends with an empty stage and with Varya's voice yelling: "Anya! Anya!" (1016).

Act III

In act three, Ranevskaya throws a party for the locals and invites a renowned Jewish orchestra. The fête is made to coincide with the day of the auction. Everyone has to dance and when "the Station Master stops in the middle of the ballroom [to] recite Aleksey Tolstoy's 'The Sinful Woman'," the guests barely listen to him "and the recitation breaks off" (1024). Characters continually rush in, then hurriedly leave the scene. They stumble. They whirl. Even those who do not dance perform various tricks of magic (like Sharlotta) or play billiards and break cues (like Yepikhodov). Keeping up the appearance of a debonair hostess might have provided someone with an excuse to suppress his or her fears at least for the duration of the party. Ranevskaya, however, drops her pretenses and openly acknowledges her worst anxieties and a hidden desire to reunite with her Parisian lover. She does this while dancing with Petya, while being literally in his arms, challenging him, and allowing herself to be confronted by him. The evening is interrupted by the arrival of Gaev and Lopakhin, who has succeeded in acquiring the cherry orchard for himself. Varya first mistakenly hits him with a stick (an inversion of intimacy) and when she learns that he is the new owner, "removes [her household] keys from the belt, throws them on the floor in the middle of the drawing room and exits" (1029).

Lopakhin's concluding remarks deploy a series of verbs that denote physical action. His stumbling movements accentuate them, it is only logical that Ranevskaya was finally able to hear him.

LOPAKHIN. (*Reproachfully.*) Why, oh, why, didn't you listen to me? My poor, dear lady, you can't undo it now. (*Tearfully.*) Oh, if only this were all over quickly, if somehow our ungainly, unhappy life could be changed quickly. [...] So what? Music, play in tune! Let everything be the way I want it! (*Ironically.*) Here comes the new landlord, the owner of the cherry orchard! (*He accidentally bumps into a small table and almost knocks over the candelabrum.*) I can pay for everything! (1030)

Meanwhile, Anya rushes to console Ranevskaya by suggesting a set of physical actions that she can perform in response to her loss of the beloved estate: "Come with me, come, dearest mother, let's go away from here, let's go!...We'll plant a new orchard, more splendid than this one, you'll see it, you'll understand, and joy, peaceful, profound joy will sink into your heart, like the sun when night falls, and you'll smile, Mama! Let's go, dearest! Let's go!..." (1030).

Act IV

In act four, Chekhov leads all characters through a series of kinesthetic exercises and rituals. They are made aware of their bodies, the ways they move and gesticulate. Petya instructs Lopakhin to "break [himself] of that habit—arm waving. [...] You've got delicate, gentle fingers, like an artist, you've got a delicate, gentle heart..." (1033), and pompous Yasha tells the heartbroken Dunyasha that if she "behaves respectably, then [she] won't have to cry" (1035). Sharlotta is singing for the first time, which Gaev interprets as a sign of her being happy. Earlier he observes that everyone looks healthier and even sleeps better after they have lost their family estate.

RANEVSKAYA. [...] (*Kissing her daughter ardently.*) My precious, you are radiant, your eyes are sparkling like two diamonds. Are you happy? Very?
ANYA. Very! A new life is beginning, Mama!
GAEV (*gaily*). As a matter of fact, everything's fine now. Before the sale of the cherry orchard, we were all upset, distressed, but then, once the matter was settled finally, irrevocably, everyone calmed down, even cheered up... I'm a bank employee now, I 'm a financier...

yellow to the center, and you, Lyuba, anyway, you're looking better, that's for sure.
RANEVSKAYA. Yes. My nerves are better, that's true. [...] I sleep well. (1036)

It is difficult to say good-bye to many happy memories, but no one is going to suffer for long. "In twenty minutes we start for the station," Lopakhin announces at the beginning of this Act. Absolutely everyone has to leave the house at exactly the same time.

RANEVSKAYA. We are going—and there won't be a soul left here.
LOPAKHIN. Not until spring. (1041)

"Outside it's October, but sunny and mild," Lopakhin says a few minutes earlier. Then why is there such a rush to start cutting down the orchard on the day of everyone's departure, especially if tomorrow, we are told, there will be no one to continue with the job? The only explanation is that they start to cut down the trees so that every character can start internalizing the finality of this moment, absorbing its irrevocability through every pore of their skin, hearing the sound of wood being chopped while they are leaving their beloved house forever. The characters keep repeating, as if hypnotized, that they are leaving: Varya is leaving , I have to leave, now I can leave/ go; we have to leave; Let's go! Time to leave! Let's go! Let's go! We are leaving/going; we are leaving, we are leaving ("Варя уходит." «Надо уходить.» «Теперь можно и ехать.» «Надо ехать.» «В дорогу!» «Господа, пора ехать!» «Идем, господа!» «Идем!» «Идем!» «Мы идем.»).There will be no return. It is as if Chekhov wanted to teach his characters (all of them without exception) how to depart, how to leave, how to bid farewell. The main function of the eighty-seven-year old Firs is to witness this exodus, to confirm that, indeed, everyone has left. Although the lonely and sick Firs may seem a tragic figure before the final curtain, his imminent death should not be seen as a tragedy. Arthur Schopenhauer (1788–1860), a philosopher who had a huge impact on Chekhov, might suggest that Firs is at the age when people die naturally, slowly and blissfully, almost without noticing that they are dying.[9] "My mistress has come home! I've been waiting! Now I can die..." Firs declares joyfully in Act I (988). Nobody takes his words seriously, but perhaps they should have.

In *The Enigma of Health*, the philosopher Hans-Georg Gadamer (1900–2002) talks about the turning point in a doctor's relationship with his dying patients:

> Although there is a great deal that we can hide and repress, fabricate and replace, even a doctor who is able to help patients survive critical phases of their organic life through the extraordinary means of automated and mechanical substitutes for functioning organs is still, eventually, forced to recognize the patient as an individual human being. This takes place when, finally, the doctor is confronted with the momentous decision as to when the instrumental preservation of the patient's merely vegetative existence can, or ought to be, withdrawn.[10]

In Chekhov's play, the cherry orchard epitomizes this "merely vegetative existence" and Chekhov, along with his characters, assumes the responsibility for bringing this existence to an end. Chekhov's contemporaries and subsequent generations of critics tend to identify Chekhov with the dying orchard. But this is only one aspect of this relationship. In his play, Chekhov acts both as the patient and the physician (significantly, *The Cherry Orchard* is Chekhov's only play that lacks a doctor among its characters). The patient, his relatives and we (readers and theater-goers) are given time to accept the idea that death is imminent, to prepare for this misfortune and to spend some meaningful time together.

The Cherry Orchard is the last play in Chekhov's famous quartet that includes *The Seagull* [*Чайка, Chaika*, 1896], *Uncle Vanya* [*Дядя Ваня, Djadja Vanja*, 1897], *Three Sisters* [*Три сестры, Tri sestry*, 1900], and *The Cherry Orchard*. Even a cursory look at the first three plays reveals one overarching theme: characters' continual inability to break away from what is dear to them, but which turns their existence into a perpetual hell. In *The Seagull*, Konstantin Treplyov wants to distinguish himself and to break away from his mother and the art and the lifestyle that she has come to embody. He succeeds in leaving her only by committing suicide. In *Three Sisters*, the title characters' problem is not that they cannot go to their beloved Moscow, but that they cannot discard this useless dream and start living in the present, making the most of what is available to them at the moment. In *Uncle Vanya*, Voynitsky complains that he could have been another Schopenhauer, or a Dostoevsky or Nietzsche, had he had the strength and willpower to leave his mother and his sister's family. *Uncle Vanya* has recently received a lot of attention as the first play devoted to ecological issues. Indeed, one of the play's characters, Astrov, argues for the preservation of forests, and he starts planting trees to avert the looming ecological catastrophe. But while Astrov talks a lot about the need to preserve natural resources, he forgets that people are just as important as any animals and trees. By the end of the play, Astrov goes back to his nursery while the rest of the characters find themselves in total disarray. As Gadamer reminds us about the initial meaning of the word ecology:

> The Greek word *oikos* meant the domestic house and in this connection we also speak of the 'household'. One learns to keep house with the means, energy and time that are available. The Greek word, however, means something more than this. For it includes not only the ability to manage by one's self, but also the ability to manage along with other people. One form of help which each of us can provide for ourselves, it seems to me, is to learn properly how to integrate this reliance on one another into our own lived existence.[11]

In *The Cherry Orchard* the trees are being chopped down while the characters survive. The characters learn how to negotiate and endure together under the most stressful of circumstances. And this might be one of the enduring lessons of this boundless play.

Notes

1. Stanislavsky wrote to Chekhov in 1903: "This is not a comedy, not a farce as you have written, this is a tragedy, whatever escape toward a better life you open up in the last act… I wept like a woman. I wanted to control myself

---

but I couldn't. I hear what you say: 'Look you must realize it is a farce'...
no, for simple men this is a tragedy. I feel a special tenderness and love
for this play." Quoted in Loehlin, James N. *Chekhov: The Cherry Orchard.*
Cambridge: Cambridge University Press, 2006. 4. Plays in Production Ser.

2. All quotations from *The Cherry Orchard* are from Chekhov, Anton. *The Complete Plays.* Trans. Laurence Senelick. New York/London: W.W. Norton & Company, 2006. Figures in parentheses correspond to page numbers in this edition.

3. P. Chekhov, *Polnoe sobranie sochinenii i pisem v tridtsati tomakh*, Sochineniia, Vol. 17. Moscow: Nauka, 1983. 38.

4. Aries distinguishes between five cultural views of death that were typical of different historical periods: "the tame death," "the death of the self," "remote and imminent death," "the death of the other," and "the invisible death." See Aries, Philippe. *The Hour of Our Death.* New York: Alfred A. Knopf, 1981.

5. Ibid. 563, 569.

6. See the growing literature devoted to these issues: Byock, Ira. *Dying Well: The Prospect of Growth at the End of Life.* New York: Riverhead Books, 1997; Dowbiggin, Ian. *A Merciful End: The Euthanasia Movement in Modern America.* Oxford, UK: Oxford UP, 2003; Gilbert, Sandra M. *Death's Door: Modern Dying and the Ways We Grieve.* New York: W.W. Norton, 2006; Orfali, Robert. *Death with Dignity: The Case for Legalizing Physician-Assisted Dying and Euthanasia.* Minneapolis: Mill City Press, 2011, to name but a few.

7. Here I am using Michael Heim's translation, which is closer to the original Russian "tiazhelo mne ego videt'." Chekhov, Anton. *The Essential Plays.* Trans. Michael Henry Heim. New York: The Modern Library, 2003. 200.

8. This is remarkable, since in Chekhov's earlier plays, *Platonov* and *Ivanov*, whole Acts take place in the orchards/gardens.

9. Cf. "Little by little in old age, the passions and desires, with the susceptibility for their objects, are extinguished; the emotions no longer find anything to excite them; for the power of presenting ideas to the mind always becomes weaker, its images fainter; the impressions no longer cleave to us, but pass over without leaving a trace, the days roll ever faster, events lose their significance, everything grows pale. The old man stricken in years totters about or rests in a corner now only a shadow, a ghost of his former self. What remains there for death to destroy? One day a sleep is his last, and his dreams are." Arthur Schopenhauer, *The World as Will and Representation/ Supplements to the Fourth Book.* <http://en.wikisource.org/wiki/The_World_as_Will_and_Representation/Supplements_to_the_Fourth_Book>.

10. Gadamer, Hans-Georg. *The Enigma of Health: The Art of Healing in a Scientific Age.* Stanford, CA: Stanford UP, 1996. 79.

11. Ibid.

Russia 'Musically' in the Nineteenth Century: Questions of East and West _____

Anna G. Piotrowska

The idea of ballet—combining music, dance, and design—as a uniquely Russian artistic expression, independent from Western patterns, not only encouraged the presentation of exclusively Russian themes, but also captured 'genuine' Russian taste, or at least the Western imagination of what 'Russian' meant. When the notable Russian art critic and music patron, Serge Diaghilev (1872–1929) presented his famous productions of *Ballets Russes* in Paris, he, a clever impresario, deliberately portrayed Russia on stage during the first *saison* (1909–1910) as an exotic *milieu*, including in the program, among others, Arabian and Polovtsian dances and Persian motifs (Maes 9). However, Diaghilev was walking on very thin ice, as he wanted to please and perhaps astonish the choosy Parisian audience, while simultaneously trying to promote his own vision of modern art. Consequently, Diaghilev referred to an old and well-established tradition of perceiving Russia—not only musically—in the light of its acclaimed exoticism. This exoticism was already attributed to music cultivated and composed in Russia throughout the entire nineteenth century, as one of the most dominant art forms in the cultural life of the Golden Age. Among the various reasons why Russia was musically perceived as exotic, one of the most obvious seems to be from the influence of French encyclopaedists' writings. Moreover, the image of musical Russia in the accounts of eighteenth- and nineteenth-century foreign travelers and music critics alike is described as unique, with elements of exoticism (e.g. César Cui). Such an attitude towards Russia resulted in the production of many instrumental miniatures by non-Russian composers, who willingly titled works with references to Russian exoticism, without depicting any distinctive musical features.

Accordingly, Russia was associated with musical exoticism, including:

1. Highlighting Byzantine roots of Russian culture. This tendency was observed in the realm of academic studies of music. References to the traditions of old Rus' as an emanation of exoticism were frequent in works of prominent Russian Romantic composers, for example Alexander Borodin (1833–1887) or Nikolai *Rimsky-Korsakov* (1844–1908).

2. Establishing a symbolic function of a Russian singing peasant—the primitiveness of the Russian countryside was supposedly expressed by means of music, especially in *a cappella* singing practices. Russian nineteenth-century composers themselves, while contributing to the creation of a Russian national identity in music, relied on the late eighteenth-century legacy, established under the rule of Catherine II, which similarly and deliberately emphasized the role of a singing Russian peasant.

3. Perceiving the music of Russia as closely connected with that of Caucasian, Siberian, and other so-called 'uncivilized' or 'barbarian' peoples and their musical traditions. Stressing the links with remote, non-European, and therefore 'exotic' places was especially seen in operatic works, like *Demon* by Anton Rubinstein (1829 –1894). Composers willingly depicted the fringes of society, such as gypsies or Cossacks and also often set entire operas in previous epochs, in order to depict traditions of a more archaic and more severe Russia. Those who resisted this general tendency, for example Pyotr Tchaikovsky (1840—1893), were not treated as 'truly Russian' composers.

Although it is said that "The East is the East only to the West" (Taruskin 153), it can be claimed that indeed, the first type of Russian exoticism in music referred to the perception of Russia as exotic by the rest of Europe. The second, or internal type, focused on musical practices considered exotic even within Russia itself. It seems that these two tendencies influenced each other, leaving a strong impact on the formation of Russian national music. It can be further suggested that nineteenth-century Russian exoticism in music served as both an internal and an external tool for defining the country itself.

Russia and a 'near exoticism'

In the nineteenth century, destinations that were considered distant in relation to the West, like the Iberian Peninsula or Eastern Europe, were perceived as exotic and, therefore, fascinating. Countries on the geographic fringes of Europe, especially Russia and Spain, were treated as representatives of, to use Gilbert Chase's term, "semi-oriental exoticism" (291). Viewing certain European countries—such as Russia—in terms of exoticism falls under the category, which can be tagged as a 'near exoticism' (Piotrowska 91). Two of these exoticized countries of the Romantic epoch, i.e. Spain and Russia, shared a bond as Russian composers (often being gentlemen of leisure) willingly travelled to Spain in order to avoid Russia's harsh winters. Once in Spain, they quickly seized the opportunity to compose pieces alluding to local traditions. For example, the great Russian composer Mikhail Glinka (1804 –1857), often considered the father of national Russian music, resided in Spain from 1845 to 1847, visiting Madrid, Granada, and Seville. He felt inspired by the country to the extent that he composed works that drew heavily from Spanish sources he had encountered there *(Cañibano)*. When, in the early twentieth century, native Spanish composers embarked on a mission to create truly national Spanish musical forms, they were confused to learn that most Europeans already knew some Spanish music as presented to them in the nineteenth century by Russian composers, such as Mikhail Glinka and Mily Balakirev. Edgar Istel (1880–948) noted, "strange to say, the Russian composers were the first to have success in written Spanish symphonic music so conceived that on a first hearing it was thought that we had copied the Russians" (501).

Richard Taruskin, a contemporary American musicologist researching traditions of Russian professional music, claims that for Russian composers like Glinka, the appeal of Spanish tunes could have been comparable to the attractiveness of Russian ones in the sense that the composers were more interested in the sounds and musical effects they evoked, rather than in the actual meanings or possible interpretations elicited through the incorporation of these tunes in their compositions. For them, the source of the melodies

was of secondary importance, because what really mattered was achieving the desired color of the orchestration. In that respect, Taruskin argues that Glinka was a typical representative of the eighteenth-century tradition of turning to exoticism as a picturesque embellishment of music, regardless of the country of origin (116). However, the inspirational role played by Russian folkloric music for Glinka was evidenced in observations of him at the piano playing folk songs. The composer exploited some of them in his works. Yet as confirmed by his own enthusiasm towards Spanish folk material, we may suspect that even Russian composers considered Russian musical traditions, including peasant and religious sources, as creative inspiration for their works, often viewing them as exotic in their non-Westernness.

To support this idea we turn to distinguished twentieth-century German musicologist Carl Dahlhaus, who claimed that referring to a 'near exoticism' was closely connected to the notion of folklorism. He wrote about "stylistic quotations interpolated into a polyphonic setting governed by the principles of art music," and, in his opinion, "exoticism and folklorism, then, have analogous aesthetic functions, manifested musically in the notably stereotype devices they use to represent both local and alien milieu" (Dahlhaus 305). Dahlhaus illustrates how significantly the differences between 'exoticism' and 'folklorism' are blurred by recalling stereotypical musical elements, such as empty fifths or fourths or chromaticism, which are widely used to evoke both exotic and folkloric associations. On one hand, these devices can be observed in works with non-Western themes (e.g. in the opera *Djamileh* by Georges Bizet), but also in Western works with titles that explicitly refer to folklore (e.g. *Twenty-five Norwegian Folk Songs and Dances*, Op.17 by Edvard Grieg).

Why then, was Eastern European music, including Russian music, considered exotic in the nineteenth century? According to an early twentieth-century German writer, Oscar Bie, musical cultures of Central and Eastern Europe engaged the European arts too late to be incorporated into a more Western style, sustaining in return their "wisdom, songs and dances as an exotic collection, valuable ethnologically" (Bie 345). This statement from the 1920s is clearly

embedded in the Germanocentric musicology, which declares the German/Austrian musical legacy as 'mainstream' and subsequently reflects a general nineteenth-century attitude towards Eastern Europe as endowed with music full of "sinful exotic allure" (346). Eastern Europe was treated as a place not devoid of undiscovered exotic beauty, and thus, was often chosen as a destination by travelers seeking excitement and adventures, for whom more exotic locations, such as Africa or Asia, were prohibitively expensive.

As Larry Wolff convincingly argued in his 1994 book *Inventing Eastern Europe: The Map of Civilization on the Mind of Enlightenment,* the distinction between industrialized Western Europe and largely agrarian Eastern Europe was already beginning to take shape in the era of the Enlightenment. This distinction was supported by the intellectual agendas of the elites and later was developed and deepened, owing to the emergence and popularity of the concept of 'civilization'. Wolff shows that it was, among others, Voltaire's writings on Russia (as well as Jean-Jacques Rousseau's on brave Poles, etc.), which helped to create a new image of Eastern Europe in the West. Christian Friedrich Daniel Schubart mentions music, among other Russian artistic genres, in his 1785 work, *Ideen zu einer Ästhetik der Tonkust,* published posthumously in 1806. Schubart described it as savage and primitive, comparing Russian folk songs to the sound of birds (especially wild ducks). He underlined the close proximity of Russians to their cattle and to nature in general, claiming that people there must have been tempted towards imitating sounds of animals. Similarly, an Englishman, William Coxe, the author of *Account of the Russian Discoveries Between Asia and America* of 1780 and *Travels into Poland, Russia, Sweden and Denmark* of 1784, traveled to Russia in 1778 and 1779 and described the singing of peasants he encountered there to be like hooting and whistle-like cat calls.

Exoticism from Within

Another factor that enabled the perception of Russia as culturally exotic in comparison to Western Europe was the tendency to underline its Byzantine roots (Sabaneev 178–180). The Romantic elevation

of medieval and neoclassical traditions in Russia took the form of religious rituals with uniquely Russian elements. In musical culture, the primeval Russian traditions were revived in the nineteenth century, during which the Russian state was more firmly politically established (particularly following the defeat of Napoleon). This became the pretext for compositions with great volume (e.g. *1000 Years* [1000 лет] by Mily Balakirev (1837–1910); this *Second Overture on Russian Themes* for orchestra was later renamed by the composer as *Rus'* [Русь]). Nineteenth-century musical practices of the Russian Orthodox Church were willingly performed in their archaic forms (e.g. in Old Church Slavonic and usually performed *a capella*), despite the fact that they had evolved from older traditions as well. Also in the nineteenth century, Russia's researching of the musical past involved studying sacred music of the Russian Church (Velimirovic). Following Byzantine tradition, after the 988 conversion to Christianity in Kievan Rus', the monastic chant was cultivated, since instrumental accompaniment was forbidden (Frolova 923). However, the so-called *znamennyi* chant (знаменное пение, знаменный распев), which involved all-male, melismatic, unified singing, had disappeared by the nineteenth century. This was facilitated by the fact that, as Marina Ritzarev claims in *Russian Music Before Glinka*, the Russian Orthodox Church, already in the early phase of its functioning, adopted an isolationist policy against Latin, Jewish, and Islamic heresies. Therefore, as a dominating force, it quickly succeeded in establishing strong national tendencies. As a result, something genuinely *Russian* also was *sacred*, whereas anything *Western* was more *secular*. In the nineteenth century, traditional religious practice—including ritual music—began to be interpreted through the prism of national tendencies, notwithstanding their sometimes quite vague meaning for the nineteenth-century Russians, who no longer were exposed to the *znamennyi* chant on a daily basis. The focus on the triad, that is, the *religious–national– old* (i.e. *traditional*) as opposed to the *profane–extraneous–new (*i.e. *modern)* seems to have been one of the most powerful "factors that prevented Russia from completely joining the Western European entity" (Ritzarev, *Russian Music Before Glinka*). The Russian intelligentsia seemed to favor domestic traditions unknown in the West. The religious music of old Russia might have been interpreted by Western Europeans as strange and—considering the tendency of the epoch—even exotic.

It is highly possible that Russians promoted their Russianness as a reaction to tendencies observed in the eighteenth century. By that time, Russian cultural trends were oriented towards secularization and Westernization. Contacts with Western musical traditions were more consistent beginning with the rule of Ivan the Terrible (1530–1584) and flourished as a result of Peter the Great's founding of Saint Petersburg in 1703, an act which opened his so-called 'window to Europe.' Radical changes were made, which greatly affected musical composition through the invitation of foreign musicians to Saint Petersburg. Even the great Baroque composer Johann Sebastian Bach (1685–1750) supposedly inquired about a position at the court of Empress Catherine I, Peter the Great's widow (Ritzarev). Among the musicians working in Russia in the eighteenth century are internationally renowned figures, such as Giovanni Paisiello (1740–1816), who arrived in 1776 in Petersburg on invitation from Catherine II. Domenico Cimarosa (1749–1801) visited in 1787. In the eighteenth century, owing to, among others, the rule of Catherine II, who was originally from Germany, there were also many German émigré musicians *(Schwab 30–50)*. As a consequence, in Russia, the term 'German music' meant 'foreign music' to such an extent that these notions essentially became synonymous (Sabaneev 17). Also in the nineteenth century, a considerable number of internationally renowned virtuosos either stayed in Russia or visited, most notably John Field (1802–21), Johann Nepomuk Hummel (1822), Karol Lipiński (in 1820s and 1830s), Henri Vieuxtemps (1835, 1845–52), Franz Liszt (1842, 1843), and Hector Berlioz (1847) as well as singers, including Henrietta Sontag (1830) and Paulina Viardot (1843–6, 1853) (Frolova, 925). Musical institutions in operation in St. Petersburg, like the Philharmonic Society, performed a primarily Western repertoire. The newly established Russian music conservatory followed the Western model of education criticized by ardent supporters of national values, which were supposed to be expressed also in music composed and performed in Russia. Anton Rubinstein was condemned for his views on the development of Russian music by the means of its professionalization via Western models. The Italian opera company that performed opera for the very first time in Russia in 1731 enjoyed significant popularity too, and it was as late as 1885 when it was eventually closed (Frolova 928). By that time, the eighteenth-century trend towards Westernization in Russia had expanded significantly. Even native Russian composers preferred non-Russian genres in order to prove their skills and musicianship. In other words, Western models of composition were still viewed as the mainstream methods of creation. However, new tendencies in the nineteenth century led to a struggle between various trends and orientations. This subsequently built up the image of Russian national music. Russian composers approached Western musical forms critically for a change (Roeder 292). The source of inspiration for Russian composers aspiring to create a national musical tradition was still the complex and multi-genre peasant music independent of Western influences.

The Singing Peasant
Research in folklore intensified worldwide in the second half of the nineteenth century, but this became especially true in Russia. In the 1880s, the national instrument, the *balalaika*, was implemented in orchestras. Folk choirs were established, including the creation of the famous and still active Pyatnitsky Russian Folk Chorus in 1910. One of the most nationalistic Russian composers, Mily Balakirev (1837–1910), was very interested in the folk tunes he intended to use in his compositions, carefully choosing them from existing anthologies (Frolova 928). However, even in his case, as Taruskin asserts, "the national character remained a purely stylistic phenomenon," yet the efforts of the composer "to purify the national character of his style" are to be underlined (Taruskin, *Defining Russia* 131–132). Moreover, already Balakirev's contemporaries believed that "Russian music might have taken another direction had it not been for Balakirev's influence" (Stasov 96). Indeed the composer, admired by *Rimsky-Korsakov,* is considered—next to Glinka—as a

pivotal figure in developing the fusion of traditional Russian music with Western classical patterns. The figure of the simple Russian peasant as an embodiment of the Russian soul through traditional folk music emerged in Russia in the eighteenth century. In 1751, the first collection of Russian songs, *Idle Hours Away from Work, or A Collection of Various Songs with Assigned Tones for Three Voices* (*Между делом безделье, или Собрание разных песен с приложенными тонами на три голоса*) by politician and amateur musician Grigory Teplov (1717–1779) was published. The surging interest in folklore in the nineteenth century melded perfectly in musical form with this earlier interest in Russian folk music from a century earlier.

Glinka is credited with establishing national tendencies in Russian music, although some evidence suggests that he was a musical hero, a stature created by his peers and posterity (Maes 11). Sometimes, Glinka is even classified as a populist. According to his contemporaries, including his apologist Vladimir Stasov (1824–1906), Glinka was truly interested in creating a distinctive Russian style of musical composition. Certainly as a very young boy staying with his grandmother in the village of Novospasskoye (Новоспаіcское) in Smolensk Governorate, the composer must have heard peasant choirs performing *podgolosnaya* (underneath the voice), a technique in which improvised dissonant harmonies accompany the melodic lines. However, as Taruskin argues, Glinka "cared little for the *style russe per se*," and in his private correspondence, he expressed his views quite openly, stating that he was "finished with Russian music" or that he "decided to shut down the Russian song factory" (Taruskin, *Defining Russia* 113–114). Nevertheless, it was Glinka's 1836 opera *A Life for the Tsar* (*Жизнь за царя*), originally entitled *Ivan Susanin* (*Иван Сусанин*) that originated the new tradition of composing 'national' operas in Russian, which became more common by the mid-eighteenth century. *The Miller Who Was a Wizard, a Cheat and a Matchmaker* (*Мельник—колдун, обманщик и сват*), a musical comedy with spoken dialogues featuring popular Russian tunes by Mikhail Sokolovsky, is widely acknowledged as the first opera in Russian (Olin 148). Based on authentic historical events, *A Life for the Tsar* is set in 1612, a period known as the 'Time of Troubles,' which was fraught with uncertain leadership and political discord. The tragic opera features the heroic Ivan, who sacrifices his life for the tsar. The tsar is endangered by the Poles, who symbolically represent Western influence. Conversely, the theme of defeating westernization appears in Russian opera as well, including the wildly famous *Boris Godunov* (1868–1873) by Modest Mussorgsky (1839–1881). Glinka proved his position as a composer of national operas, later presenting *Ruslan and Lyudmila* (*Руслан и Людмила*)—after Alexander Pushkin's 1820 poem of the same title—set in the time of Kievan Rus' (composed between 1837 and 1842).

The Five

The amalgam of folklore, allusions to peasant culture through folk songs, the elevation of peasant heroes in opera librettos, and references to religious roots established what became known as *Russian musical nationalism.* The mingling of the sacred and the secular was continued by the most radical and most distinctively Russian group of composers known as The Five, or the Mighty Handful [Могучая кучка, *Moguchaya kuchka*]. The Five—comprised of Balakirev, Rimsky-Korsakov, Cui, Mussorgsky, and Borodin—is sometimes even considered to be the "cradle of Russian national music" (Seroff). The main ideologist of The Five became Stasov—a Slavophile who sharply criticized any composition that he considered to be insufficiently or not uniquely Russian. Fearing that westernization of Russian music presented a threat and could "undermine the indigenous development of a Russian national music" (Frolova 927), he felt responsible for shepherding Russian music in the right direction, which he believed to be the popularization of Russian national music. The Five were, in his opinion, the only true representatives of Russian music. In his writings, other progressive attempts at musical creation were considered anti-Russian and, therefore, unworthy of mention or attention. Stasov radically adhered to the idea of using folk songs in professional compositions (Ridenour 79). As Marina Frolova claims, his way of reasoning was widespread, not only in Russia but also in the West, and thus contributed to the perception of Russia as eccentric, exotic, and most importantly, closed off toward external influence. The country was seen instead as concentrating on its own, internal sources (Frolova 928). Stasov's propaganda helped to establish the position of Balakirev, the leader of The Five, as an emblematic national composer, a future prophet supposedly blessed by Glinka for embarking on the mission of creating Russian music and, in an almost xenophobic way, rejecting Western influences. Taruskin suggests that other members of The Five, namely Mussorgsky, "was Stasov's creation — in more ways than one. He manufactured not only Mussorgsky's historiographical image but also, to a considerable extent and for a considerable time, the actual historical person" (Taruskin, *Musorgsky* 7).

The Five can only be described as a nationalist phenomenon with the clear aim of promoting Russian music—not only in opposition to musical German influences, but also searching internally, so to speak, for the understanding and definition of what Russian artistic music should be. For example, Balakirev's harmonization (often in the Dorian mode, avoiding dominant relations, which were believed to be characteristic for German music) was adopted by his peers and soon became one of the most recognizable features of Russian national music. Balakirev himself praised what he labelled as the 'Slav quality' of other composers, too: he was mainly responsible for sustaining, in Russia, the image of ethnically Polish Frederic Chopin as a Slavic composer (Samson 9).

Barbarian Associations

An important factor of exoticizing Russian music in the eyes of the West was portraying Russia as a wild and barbaric, even savage, country, in which gypsies and Cossacks thrived. The Slavophile glorification of the Russian past mythologized the Cossacks as important players. Their international fame added to the perception of Russia as a wild and barbaric country. In reality, the Cossacks were a rather loose band of vigilantes on the margins of society, who usually sought refuge from "the political, military, economic, and penal systems of Polish, Ukraine, or Muscovy to live on what they hoped would be the freer frontier" (Kornblatt 7). Cossack culture was based on overtly male-oriented activities with a clear sense of duty (e.g. embarking on raids, engaging in skirmishes, consequential or not). Hence in European culture, the Cossacks were perceived as wild, masculine heroes on horseback, capable of fierce violence and aggression on the battlefield but idealized as free and fearless warriors. In the eyes of Europeans, the Cossack culture presented an ambiguous mixture associated both with positive and negative traits. It is suggested that this larger-than-life image of the Cossacks was frozen in time and mythologized through the nineteenth and twentieth centuries in Europe, since no one else but the Cossacks ideally embodied the image of Russia as a wild and untamed frontier. The Cossack musical repertoire, which includes dancing and folk songs traditionally performed by all male groups, contributed to their mythologization and advanced the portrayal of Russia as a stern and exotic land (Ulrich 9).

In the West, Russia was also loosely connected with other European nomads: gypsies. The fame of the Russian gypsy choirs that reached Western Europe can be regarded as a repercussion of exotic sentiments towards Russia in general. In 1887, the French music critic Camille Bellaigue (1858–1930) included in his *Un Siècle de Musique Française* [*A Century of French Music*] a report from a trip to Moscow that not only described the traditions and costumes of Russian gypsies, but also their music. The author drew attention to the technical side of Russian gypsy performance, in which women dominate singing to the accompaniment of the guitar (Bellaigue, 262–263). Russian gypsy music conveys sentiments of prevailing melancholy and sentimentality: "Gypsy songs reflect only one feeling: melancholy. Sadness comes straight from their hearts" (Bellaigue 264). Bellaigue emphasized the relatively insignificant interest in the West of studying Russian gypsies and their music: "Gypsies, Russians hold the secret of their songs. Science also does not penetrate the mystery of divine ignorance. Indeed, it is necessary to undertake research together with attempts to understand" (Bellaigue 267). Bellaigue was not, however, completely right, since some information on Russian gypsies circulated in nineteenth century Europe, appearing either in the form of travel journals—like that of British author George Borrow—or transmitted through literary works, such as Alexander Pushkin's poem *Gypsies* [*Цыганы, Tsygany*], which was translated into French by Prosper Mérimée. Popularized in nineteenth-century Europe, piano miniatures quite often had titles highlighting alleged associations of gypsies with Russia. For instance, dating from 1861, *Les Bohemiens, Chansons populaires Russes,* [*The Gypsies, Popular Russian Songs*] Op. 57 for solo piano by Jacques Blumenthal shows that composers quite often confuse details with facts. On the title page of the composition, there is an annotation informing readers that the piece is, in fact, a transcript of a popular song from 'petite Russie' (little Russia), which was a name reserved for Ukraine. The so-called 'characteristique morceau' (characteristic music) in *Air Bohemien Russe* (*Tziganes*) (*Russian Gypsy Melody* [*Gypsies*]) Op. 30 by N. de Wolkoff for piano from 1882, despite its title suggestion, simply resembles a typical *czardas* cultivated by Hungarian gypsies. In the piano accompaniment, the sound of the violin is imitated, as the violin is an instrument stereotypically associated with Hungarian, but not with Russian gypsies.

Not only are associations with gypsies prevalent, but also featured is the Tatars' impact on the creation of Russian music (Sabaneev 29). Similarly, Georgian and Armenian motifs infiltrated Russian musical culture not only as a consequence of the political situation of the empire, but also in the light of their commonly acknowledged linkages to the traditions of Byzantium. For example, Balakirev's symphonic poem *Tamara* (1867–82) is considered an example of such a composition, employing Caucasian exoticism (Campbell 514). For Western European intellectuals, as discussed earlier, faraway places were exotic. Their appearance in Russian compositions enabled them to explore the unique geography of Russia, between East and West, making it more feasible to incorporate non-Western or Asian elements. In other words, such musical works as *Borodin's In the Steppes of Central Asia* [*В средней Азии, V srednej Asii*] constituted a sort of mental bridge for understanding the Russian tendency to incorporate elements of Asian origin. Exotic even for Russians themselves, these references are easily traced in the titles of several musical works (e.g. Balakirev's 1869 *Oriental Fantasy* Op. 18, otherwise known as *Islamey* [Исламей]). The above mentioned 1880 symphonic poem, *In the Steppes of Central Asia*, overtly combines East and West with the Asiatic, as represented by sustained wind instruments (specifically, the English horn) playing over a *pizzicato* of strings. These strings represent musical Russia, described sometimes as a musical "*style russe* cliché" (Taruskin, *Defining Russia...* 149).

Russian 'exoticism' of the nineteenth century is a sophisticated phenomenon that is situated at the crossroads of European imagination, pertaining to musical Russia and Russia's own search into its musical traditions from previous epochs and different regions. The unique geographic position of Russia and its influence on politics and culture has continued to contribute a multitude of possible explanations for creating such an image. It also allows for various assumptions concerning the mechanisms of actual application, dissemination, and interpretations of this vision of Russian musical culture. The complexity of motifs and topics that need to be considered and even the sheer number of them (e.g. the non-West in Russian music, correlations with Georgian, Armenian, and neighboring non-Russian art, music, and folk music of various peoples) is beyond the scope of this chapter. It seems, however, that musical 'exoticism' of Russia as embodied in the nineteenth-century Russian and European imagination is worth further investigation and critical insight and may, in the future, lead to new and interesting observations.

Works Cited

Abraham, Gerald. *On Russian Music.* New York: Books for Libraries Press, 1970.

Asafyev, Boris. "The Great Russian Composer." Ed. Dmitri Shostakovich. *Russian Symphony: Thoughts About Tchaikovsky.* New York: Philosophical Library, 1947. 6–15.

Bellaigue, Camille. *Un Siècle de Musique Francaise*, Paris: Libraire Ch. Delagrave, 1887.

Bie, Oskar. *Die Oper.* Berlin: S. Fischer Verlag, 1920.

Brown, David. *The New Grove Russian Masters.* New York: W.W. Norton, 1986.

Brown, Malcolm Hamrick. "Native Song and National Consciousness in Nineteenth-Century Russian Music." *Art and Culture in Nineteenth-Century Russia.*Ed.Theofanis George Stavrou. 7th ed. Bloomington, IN: Indiana UP, 1983. 57–84.

Campbell, Stuart. "Balakirev, Mily Alekseyevich". *The New Grove Dictionary of Music and Musicians.* Ed. Stanley Sadie. Vol. 2. London: MacMillan Publishers, 2001. 510–521.

Cañibano, Antonio Álvarez, ed. *Los papeles españoles de Glinka 1845–1847,* Madrid: *Centro de Documentación Musical,* 1996.

Chase, Gilbert. *The Music of Spain.* New York: Dover Publications, Inc., 1959.

Coxe, William. *Account of the Russian Discoveries between Asia and America.* London: Cadell, 1780.

_____. *Travels into Poland, Russia, Sweden and Denmark.* London: Cadell, 1784.

Cui, César. *La Musique en Russie.* Paris: Fischbacher, 1880.

Dahlhaus, Carl. *Nineteenth–Century Music.* Berkeley, CA: U of California P, 1989.

Figes, Orlando. *Natasha's Dance: A Cultural History of Russia.* New York: Metropolitan Books, 2002.

Frolova, Marina. "Russian Federation. Art Music." *The New Grove Dictionary of Music and Musicians.* Ed. Stanley Sadie. Vol. 2. London: MacMillan Publishers, 2001. 923–928.

Istel, Edgar. "Manuel de Falla: A Study." *The Musical Quarterly* 12 (4): 497–525.

Kearney, Leslie, ed. *Tchaikovsky and His World.* Princeton, NJ: Princeton UP, 1998.

Keldysh, Georgiy V., ed. *Istoria russkoi muzyki (History of Russian Music).* Moscow: Muzyka, 1983.

Kornblatt, Judith Deutsch. *The Cossack Hero in Russian Literature.* Madison WI: U of Wisconsin P, 1992.

Leonard, Richard Anthony. *A History of Russian Music.* London: Macmillan, 1968.

Maes, Francis. *A History of Russian Music: From Kamarinskaya to Babi Yar.* Los Angeles: UCLA Press, 2002.

Olin, Emily. *Singing in Russian: A Guide to Language and Performance.* Lanham: Scarecrow Press, 2012.

Piotrowska, Anna G. *Gypsy Music in European Culture.* Boston: Northeastern UP, 2013.

Ridenour, Robert C. *Nationalism, Modernism and Personal Rivalry in Nineteenth-Century Russian Music*. Ann Arbor: UMI Research Press, 1981.

Ritzarev, Marina. *Eighteenth-Century Russian Music*. Aldershot: Ahsgate, 2006.

_____. *Russian Music before Glinka: A Look from the Beginning of the Third Millennium*. n.d. Web. 9 Mar. 2011. <http://www.biu.ac.il/hu/mu/min-ad02/ritzarev.html>.

Roeder, Thomas Michael. *A History of the Concerto*. Portland, OR: Amadeus Press, 1994.

Sabaneev, Leonid Leonidovič. *Geschichte Der Russischen Musik*. Trans. Oskar von Riesemann. Leipzig: Breitkopf und Härtel, 1926.

Samson, Jim. "Chopin's Reception: Theory, History, Analysis." *Chopin Studies 2*. Eds. John Rink, Jim Samson, Cambridge, UK: Cambridge UP, 1994. 1–17.

Schubart, Christian Friedrich Daniel. *Ideen zu einer Ästhetik der Tonkust*. Wien: bey J. V. Degen, 1806.

Schwab, Alexander. *"Migration deutscher Komponisten* und *Musiker zwischen* dem *südlichen Ostseeraum* und Russland im 18. Jahrhundert." *Musik und Migration in Ostmitteleuropa*. Ed. Heike Müns. Oldenbourg: Wissenschaftsverlag, 2005: 33–50.

Seroff, Victor Ilyitch. *The Mighty Five: The Cradle of Russian national music*. New York: Allen, Towne & Heath, 1948.

Stasov, Vladimir. *Selected Essays on Music*. London: Barrie and Rockliff, 1968.

Taruskin, Richard. *Defining Russia Musically*. Princeton, NJ: Princeton UP, 1997.

_____. *Musorgsky: Eight Essays and an Epilogue*. Princeton, NJ: Princeton UP, 1993.

_____. *On Russian Music*. Los Angeles: UCLA Press, 2009.

Ulrich, Rachel. *Power and Pride: The Mythologization of the Cossack Figure in Russian History and Its Impact on Modern Russian National Identity*. n.d. Web. 15 Apr. 2011. < http://russianfolklorefriends.org/images/Kaleidoscope_final_submission.pdf>.

Velimirovic, Miloš. "The Present Status of Research in Slavic Chant." *Acta Musicologica* 44.2 (1972): 235–265.

Vodarsky-Shiraeff, Alexandra. *Russian Composers and Musicians: A Biographical Dictionary*. New York: The H.W. Wilson Company, 1983.

Wolff, Larry. *Inventing Eastern Europe. The Map of Civilization on the Mind of Enlightenment*. Stanford, CA: Stanford UP, 1994.

Zetlin, Mikhail. *The Five*. Trans. George Panin. Westport, CT: Greenwood Press, 1975.

RESOURCES

Additional Works of Russia's Golden Age _____

Long Fiction

Chernyshevsky, Nikolai. *What Is To Be Done?* Trans. Michael R. Katz. Ithaca, NY: Cornell UP, 1989.

Dostoevsky, Fyodor. *Notes from Underground.* Trans. Michael R. Katz. Norton Critical Editions Series. 2nd ed. New York: W.W. Norton & Company, 2000.

Dostoevsky, Fyodor. *Crime and Punishment.* Trans. Constance Garnett. Dover Thrift Editions. Mineola, NY: Dover Publications, 2001.

Dostoevsky, Fyodor. *The Brothers Karamazov.* Trans. Richard Pevear and Larissa Volokhonsky. New York: Farrar, Straus, and Giroux, 2002.

Gogol, Nikolai. *Dead Souls.* Trans. Richard Pevear and Larissa Volokhonsky. New York: Viking, 1996.

Goncharov, Ivan. *Oblomov.* Transl. David Magarshack. London: Penguin, 1954.

Lermontov, Mikhail. *Hero of Our Time.* Trans. Paul Foote. London: Penguin, 1966.

Pavlova, Karolina. *A Double Life.* Trans. Barbara Heldt. Oakland, CA: Barbary Coast Books, 1978.

Pushkin, Alexander. *Eugene Onegin: A Novel in Verse.* Trans. Vladimir Nabokov. Princeton: Princeton UP, 1975.

Pushkin, Alexander. *Tales of Belkin and Other Prose Writings.* Trans. John Bayley. London: Penguin, 1998.

Tolstoy, Leo. *Anna Karenina.* Trans. Constance Garnett. New York: Random House, 1965.

Turgenev, Ivan. *Fathers and Sons.* Trans. Richard Freeborn. Oxford: Oxford UP, 1991.

Short Fiction

Chekhov, Anton. *Anton Chekhov's Short Stories.* Trans. Ralph Matlaw. Norton Critical Editions Series. New York: W.W. Norton & Company, 1979.

Gogol, Nikolai. *The Collected Tales of Nikolai Gogol.* Trans. Richard Pevear and Larissa Volokhonsky. New York: Viking, 1998.

Leskov, Nikolai. *The Enchanted Wanderer and Other Stories*. Trans. Richard Pevear and Larissa Volokhonsky. New York: Knopf, 2013.

Tolstoy, Leo. *Tolstoy's Short Fiction*. Trans. Michael Katz. 2nd ed. New York: W.W. Norton, 2008. Norton Critical Editions Ser.

Turgenev, Ivan. *Hunter's Sketches*. Trans. Richard Freeborn. London: Penguin, 1967.

Poetry

Obolensky, Dmitrii, ed. *The Heritage of Russian Verse*. Bloomington, IN: Indiana UP, 1976.

Pushkin, Alexander. *Eugene Onegin: A Novel in Verse*. Trans. Vladimir Nabokov. Princeton, NJ: Princeton UP, 1975.

Boyd, Brian and Stanislav Shvabrin, eds. *Verses and Versions: Three Centuries of Russian Poetry*. Trans. Vladimir Nabokov. New York: Harcourt, 2008.

Theater

Chekhov, Anton. *Chekhov: The Four Major Plays: Seagull, Uncle Vanya, Three Sisters, Cherry Orchard*. Trans. Curt Columbus. Chicago: Ivan R. Dee, 2005.

Gogol, Nikolai. *The Government Inspector*. In *The Diary of a Madman, The Government Inspector, and Selected Stories*. Trans. Ronald Wilks. New York: Penguin, 2006.

Bibliography

[English or translated sources only]

Bagby, Lewis, ed. *Lermontov's A Hero of Our Time: A Critical Companion.* Evanston, IL: Northwestern UP, 2002.

Bely, Andrei. *Gogol's Artistry.* Trans. Christopher Colbath. Evanston, IL: Northwestern UP, 2009.

Berlin, Isaiah. *Russian Thinkers.* London: Viking, 1978.

Bethea, David. *The Pushkin Handbook.* Madison, WI: U of Wisconsin P, 2006.

Brown, William Edward. *A History of Russian Literature of the Romantic Period.* Ann Arbor, MI: Ardis, 1986.

Chances, Ellen B. *Conformity's Children: An Approach to the Superfluous Man in Russian Literature.* Columbus, OH: Slavica Publishers, 1978.

Chizhevsky, Dmitry. *History of Nineteenth-Century Russian Literature.* Trans. R. N. Parker. 2 vols. Nashville, TN: Vanderbilt UP, 1974.

Cornwell, Neil, ed. *The Routledge Companion to Russian Literature.* London: Routledge, 2002.

Dinega, Alyssa W. *Russian Literature in the Age of Realism. Dictionary of Literary Biography*, Vol. 277. Detroit, MI: Gale, 2003.

Emerson, Caryl. *The Cambridge Introduction to Russian Literature.* Cambridge, UK: Cambridge UP, 2008.

Fanger, Donald. *Dostoevsky and Romantic Realism.* Evanston, IL: Northwestern UP, 1998.

Frank, Joseph. *Between Religion and Rationality: Essays in Russian Literature and Culture.* Princeton, NJ: Princeton UP, 2010.

Greenleaf, Monika and Stephen Moeller-Sally, eds. *Russian Subjects: Empire, Nation, and the Culture of the Golden Age.* Evanston, IL: Northwestern UP, 1998.

Jones, Malcolm V. and Robin Feuer Miller, eds. *The Cambridge Companion to the Classic Russian Novel.* Cambridge, UK: Cambridge UP, 1998.

Kahn, Andrew, ed. *The Cambridge Companion to Pushkin.* Cambridge, UK: Cambridge UP, 2006.

Kelly, Catriona. *A History of Russian Women's Writing: 1820–1992.* New York: Clarendon Press, 1994.

_____. *Russian Literature: A Very Short Introduction.* Oxford, UK: Oxford UP, 2001.

Leatherbarrow, W.J., ed. *The Cambridge Companion to Dostoevsky*. Cambridge, UK: Cambridge UP, 2002.

_____ and Derek Offord, eds. *A History of Russian Thought*. Cambridge, UK: Cambridge UP, 2010.

Leighton, Lauren G. *Russian Romantic Criticism: An Anthology*. Westport, CT: Greenwood Press, 1987.

Massie, Suzanne. *Land of the Firebird*. Blue Hill, ME: Hearttree Press, 1998.

Moser, Charles, ed. *The Cambridge History of Russian Literature*. Cambridge, UK: Cambridge UP, 1992.

Nabokov, Vladimir. *Lectures on Russian Literature*. New York: Houghton Mifflin Harcourt, 1981.

Offord, Derek, ed. *The Golden Age of Russian Literature and Thought: Selected Papers from the Fourth World Conference for Soviet and East European Studies, Harrogate, 1990*. New York: St. Martin's Press, 1990.

Orwin, Donna Tussing. *Tolstoy's Art and Thought: 1847–1880*. Princeton, NJ: Princeton UP, 1993.

Rydel, Christine A., ed. *Russian Literature in the Age of Pushkin and Gogol: Prose. Dictionary of Literary Biography*. Vol. 198. Detroit, MI: Gale, 1999. 375 vols.

Stone, Jonathan. *Historical Dictionary of Russian Literature*. Plymouth, UK: Scarecrow Press, 2013.

Terras, Victor, ed. *Handbook of Russian Literature*. New Haven, CT: Yale UP, 1985.

_____. *A History of Russian Literature*. New Haven, CT: Yale UP, 1991.

Wachtel, Andrew and Ilya Vinitsky. *Russian Literature*. Cambridge, UK: Polity Press, 2009.

Walicki, Andrzej. *A History of Russian Thought: From the Enlightenment to Marxism*. Redwood City, CA: Stanford UP, 1979.

Wesling, Molly. *Napoleon in Russian Cultural Mythology*. New York: Peter Lang, 2001.

About the Editor

Rachel Stauffer is Assistant Professor of Russian and Program Coordinator of Russian at Ferrum College in rural Southwestern Virginia. She obtained a BA in Russian Studies and Spanish at Randolph-Macon Woman's College (now Randolph College) and an MA and PhD in Slavic Languages and Literatures from the University of Virginia. At Ferrum, she is a one-person department, teaching all levels of Russian language and courses in Russian and Soviet cinema, literature, and culture and contributing to the establishment and development of globally-oriented programs at the college. A linguist by training, her research focuses on problems in the acquisition of Russian phonetics among speakers of American regional dialects. She also has interests in tracing non-Western influences on Russian culture.

This volume on Russia's Golden Age unites her teaching interests in Russian literature and her love of writing and collaborative scholarship. In 1994, she checked out *Anna Karenina* from her high school library and never returned it, definitively deciding to major in Russian because of that one, very long novel. Studying Russian led to moving to Moscow, where she studied Russian and Georgian, while also working as a civilian security guard in the consular and residential sections of the U.S. Embassy in the late 1990s. As a graduate student, she studied in Irkutsk and Siberia, and her job at the University of Virginia provided opportunities to travel to China and Korea. She takes any opportunity to visit Russia when possible.

Contributors

Kathleen Conti, an internationally awarded photographer, received her undergraduate degree in history and Soviet studies at Randolph College, formerly Randolph-Macon Woman's College. She studied the controversies surrounding the National D-Day Memorial following the installation of a bust of Josef Stalin as part of the Memorial's allied leaders exhibit. She received her Masters in Russian and East European studies from the University of North Carolina at Chapel Hill, where she conducted a comparative study of the funeral trains of Abraham Lincoln and Tsar Alexander III. Currently pursuing her doctoral degree in European history at the University of Wisconsin–Madison, Kathleen focuses her research on the intersections of history, memory, and politics in the Soviet Union's public sphere.

Robert C. Evans is I. B. Young Professor of English at Auburn University at Montgomery, where he has taught since 1982. In 1984, he received his PhD from Princeton University, where he held Weaver and Whiting fellowships as well as a University fellowship. In later years, his research was supported by fellowships from the Newberry Library, the American Council of Learned Societies, the Folger Shakespeare Library, The Mellon Foundation, The Huntington Library, the National Endowment for the Humanities, the American Philosophical Society, and the UCLA Center for Medieval and Renaissance Studies. He is the author or editor of nearly thirty books on such topics as Ben Jonson, Martha Moulsworth, Kate Chopin, John Donne, Frank O'Connor, Brian Friel, Ambrose Bierce, Amy Tan, early modern women writers, pluralist literary theory, literary criticism, twentieth-century American writers, American novelists, Shakespeare, seventeenth-century English literature, and the poetry of World War I.

Frank Jacob is assistant professor for modern history at the Universität Würzburg in Würzburg, Germany. He studied modern history, ancient history, and Japanese Studies and received his MA in 2010 from Universität Würzburg. In 2012, he received his PhD from the Universität Erlangen–Nürnberg. He is the editor of the serial *Comparative Studies from a Global Perspective*, some edited volumes, and the author of several books treating the subject of German and Japanese history. His research fields are the First World War from a global perspective, Holocaust Studies, Japanese food history, media studies, and the

Russo-Japanese War. He is a member of the Society for Military History, the Historical Society, and the International Association for Comparative Studies of China and the West.

Katya Jordan is Instructor of Russian in the Foreign Languages and Literatures Department at Virginia Tech. Her research interests include nineteenth- and twentieth-century Russian literature, representation of visual art in literature, and Russian cultural and national identity. SheZ has taught a number of courses and presented several papers at Slavic Studies conferences on Russian language and literature.

Mary Helen Kashuba, SSJ, DML, is currently Professor of French and Russian and Department Chair at Chestnut Hill College in Philadelphia, where she has taught since 1963. She received her AB from Chestnut Hill College, her MA in Russian from Fordham University, and her Doctorate in French and Russian from Middlebury College, Vermont. She is the author of over forty scholarly articles printed in the US and abroad, including the Modern Language Association and *L'Amitié Charles Péguy.* She is also the author of a history of Chestnut Hill College, *Tradition and Risk* (1999), and a number of publications dealing with the history of the Sisters of Saint Joseph. She has received numerous awards and honors, including a Fulbright Grant to France, two study grants to Russia, the Dorothy S. Ludwig Excellence in Teaching Award, the PSMLA Educator of the Year Award, the Frank Mulhern Leadership Award for Pennsylvania, and the Lindback Award for Distinguished Teaching. In 2011, she was promoted to *officier* in the *Palmes Académiques,* an honor conveyed by the French Government. She has served on many Boards, including PSMLA, the Northeast Conference for the Teaching of Foreign Languages, and the American Council on the Teaching of Foreign Languages. She was Region IV Representative and Vice-President of the American Association of Teachers of French and has served as National French Contest Administrator for the Philadelphia Chapter since 1978. She is currently President of the American Association of Teachers of French. She served as chief evaluator for the Pennsylvania Governor's Institute in World Languages from 2001–2008, as evaluator for the Foreign Language Assistance Program, and has been an Advanced Placement reader in French for several terms since 1990. She regularly gives presentations and workshops at local, national, and international meetings and professional associations.

Ani Kokobobo is assistant professor of Russian literature in the Slavic Department at the University of Kansas. She received her PhD from Columbia University in 2011 and specializes in nineteenth-century Russian literature and culture. She is currently at work on two book projects: a monograph on the emergence of the grotesque in Russian literature as a response to Alexander II's Great Reforms (*Freakish Others and Monsters Within: Russian Literature and the Grotesque, 1869–1899*), and an edited volume on the evolution of Russian literature at the end of the nineteenth century (*Russian Literature at the Fin de Siècle: Twilight of Realism,* under contract with Cambridge University Press). Her articles have appeared in *Slavic Review*, *The Russian Review*, and *Tolstoy Studies Journal*.

Tatyana Kovalevskaya (Buzina) received her BA from Lomonosov Moscow State University and her PhD from Yale University. She has authored over forty articles, published in Russia and the United States, and three books: *Dostoevsky and Social and Metaphysical Freedom*, Edwin Mellen Press, 2003; *Self-Deification in the European Culture*, St. Petersburg, 2011 (in Russian); and *Homo heroicus in English Literature*, St. Petersburg, 2012 (in Russian). Her academic interests include philosophical and religious anthropology and comparative studies, nineteenth-century Russian literature, and early modern English literature. Currently, she is full professor at the English language department of the Russian State University for the Humanities in Moscow.

Michael Marsh-Soloway is a PhD Candidate in the Department of Slavic Languages and Literatures at the University of Virginia. In January 2014, he will be embarking on a six-month expedition to St. Petersburg to conduct research for his dissertation, titled *Mapping the Mathematical and Scientific Consciousness of F.M. Dostoevsky: An Investigation into the Author's Education and Development of Thought at the Nikolaev Military Engineering Institute*. In 2011, Michael participated in the U.S. Department of State Critical Language Scholarship program and studied at Bashkir State Pedagogical University in Ufa in the Republic of Bashkortostan in the southwestern Urals. His research interests include the Russian novel, Golden Age Russian poetry, linguistics, and film.

Anna G. Piotrowska is mainly interested in sociological and cultural aspects of musical life. She has authored three books in Polish as well as published numerous articles (in Polish, English, German, Slovak, Georgian). In 2011, her book *Topos muzyki cygańskiej w kulturze europejskiej* won the honorary W. Felczak and H.

Wereszycki Award from the Polish Historical Association, and in 2013, its English version was published. Piotrowska was a Fulbright Fellow at Boston University, and in 2009, she was awarded the Moritz Csaky Preis at The Austrian Academy of Sciences. She was also the recipient of a Mellon Fellowship in Edinburgh University, UK. Currently, Piotrowska is associated with the Department of Theory and Anthropology of Music at the Institute of Musicology, Jagiellonian University in Kraków, Poland.

Galina Rylkova is Associate Professor of Russian Studies at the University of Florida, Gainesville. She received her PhD from the University of Toronto in Slavic Languages and Literatures. She has published articles on a wide range of topics, including cultural memory about the Russian Silver Age and the writings of Chekhov, Tolstoy, Dostoevsky, Nabokov, Akhmatova, and Pasternak. She is the author of *The Archaeology of Anxiety: The Russian Silver Age and Its Legacy*, published by the University of Pittsburgh Press in 2007. Her research interests include the psychology of creative personalities, Chekhov, cultural memory, biography, and Russian theater. She is currently working on her second book, *Creative Lives: The Art of Being a Successful Russian Writer*.

Matthew Shoemaker is an advanced, non-traditional student at Auburn University at Montgomery and is preparing for graduate school and a career in research and teaching.

Index _____

Ural Mountains 121, 190
Uspensky, Nikolai 65

Varangian Rurikid xvii
Varangian Rus xvii
Varangians xv, xvii
Variegated Stories 29
Varnhagen, Karl August 142
Varya 208, 209, 210, 212, 213, 215
Vasilii III xx
*Vasilii Trediakovsky: The Fool of
    the 'New' Russian Literature*
    xxviii
Vasilyevich, Pyotr 149
Vdokhnovenie 39
Velimirovic 225, 235
Velimirovic, Miloš 235
Venevitinov, Dmitrii Vladimirovich
    45
*Verführerische Lektüren in der Prosa
    des russischen Realismus* 154
Verkhovensky, Stepan 164
Versilov 167
Viardot-Garcia, Pauline 143
Viardot, Paulina 226
Viardots 145, 151
Viazemsky 12, 37, 38, 39, 40, 41
Viazemsky, Petr Andreevich 39
Vickery, Walter N. 86
Victor Terras xxviii, 103, 104, 105,
    106, 107, 124, 127, 139
Vienna 40
Vieuxtemps, Henri 226
Vii 128, 129, 136
Vikings xv, xvii
Vinitsky, Ilya 19, 241
Visconti, Luchino 170
Vissarion Belinsky x, 5, 20, 84, 127,
    143, 152, 156
Vodarsky-Shiraeff, Alexandra 235
Vogt 62
Voinaimir 67
Volga River xiv

Voltaire xxvi, 45, 74, 85, 224
Voltairean 34
Voltairefrancophile 39
von Arnim, Bettina 142
von Benckendorff, Alexander 104
von Humboldt, Alexander 142
*Vorträge und Abhandlungen zur
    Slavistik* 154, 155
Voskresenie 67
vremia 51
*Vybrannye mesta izperepiski s
    druz'iami* 59

Wachtel, Andrew 19, 241
Waddington, Patrick 155
Walicki, Andrzej 69, 241
War and Peace x, 16, 27, 67, 82, 172,
    177, 178, 179, 180, 181, 182,
    184, 185, 198, 200
*War for the Public Mind: Political
    Censorship in Nineteenth-
    Century Europe* 104
War of 1812 5, 19
Waugh, Daniel xxviii
Waunakee News 193
Wellek, René 32
Western Georgia 115, 122
Westernizers 11, 57, 59, 60, 63, 142
What Is To Be Done? 16, 160, 177,
    238
Who is to blame? 52
*Wie aus Bauern Russen wurden. Die
    Konstruktion des Volkes in
    der Literatur des russischen
    Realismus 1860–1880* 155
Wilkinson, Myler 155
Wilson, A. N. 175, 176
Wilson, John 77
Winter Notes on Summer Impressions
    51
Wolff, Larry 224
Wolff, Tatiana 109
Woodward, James B. 155